RICK BARRY'S
Super
SPORTS TRIVIA GAME

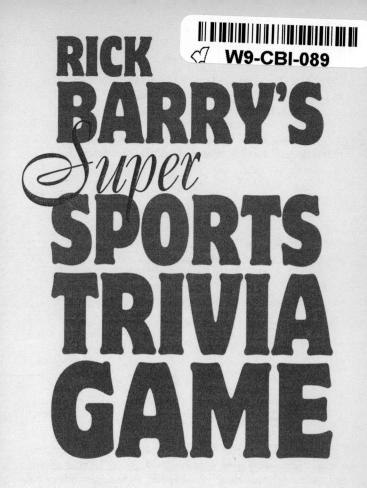

SQUAREONE
PUBLISHERS

COVER DESIGNERS: Phaedra Mastrocola and Jacqueline Michelus
COVER PHOTOS: Getty Images, Inc.
RESEARCH ASSISTANTS: Dave Frattini, Dennis Golin,
and Gene Friedman
EDITORS: Marie Caratozzolo and Joanne Abrams
TYPESETTERS: Gary A. Rosenberg and Theresa Wiscovitch

Square One Publishers
115 Herricks Road
Garden City Park, New York 11040
www.squareonepublishers.com
(516) 535-2010 • (866) 900-BOOK

CONTENTS

*This is for all of those sports trivia buffs
who remember more about my career than I do,
and for my son Canyon,
whose accomplishments I hope to be reading about
in a sports trivia book some day.*

ACKNOWLEDGMENTS

Wow, what an adventure!

Many thanks to Dave Frattini, Dennis Golin, and Dr. Gene Friedman. Without their tremendous sports knowledge, trivia expertise, and hours of research, this book wouldn't exist.

My appreciation also goes to Mark Stewart and Mike Kennedy of JockBio.com for their willingness to prepare my bio for the book.

Special thanks to my publisher, Rudy Shur, and editor, Marie Caratozzolo, of Square One Publishers for believing in the concept of this book and overseeing its completion.

Appreciation goes out to David Stern and the NBA, Bob Wussler, Tony Salvadore, and Bob Agnew for providing me with the opportunities that have made my life so enjoyable.

I also want to take this opportunity to thank my brother, Dennis, as well as my friends Allen Bernstein, Bob and Barbara Murray, Jim Schmit, Tom Fields, Clifford Ray, Marc and Karlyn Sachs, Dr. Fernando and Chris Borges, and Stew and Jane Marcus for being there for me regardless of the circumstances.

Heartfelt thanks are extended to my children: Scooter, Jon, Brent, Drew, Shannon, and Canyon for bringing so much joy to my life.

Finally, loving thanks to my wonderful wife, Lynn, for her ideas, encouragement, and countless hours spent on the overall project. Now that it's done, maybe I'll get some hot food for dinner.

How to Play the Games

Welcome, sports fans. Are you ready to put your knowledge of athletic facts and details to the test? My trivia book is guaranteed to offer the challenge, while providing endless hours of fun and enjoyment. The games in this book have been designed in a way that allows you, the reader, to play either alone or with others. In most trivia books, when looking up the answer to a question, the reader is able to see the answers to other questions at the same time. This book doesn't allow that to happen, but you must first understand how to play the games. Ready?

THE BASICS

There are eighty games in this book, and each game has twelve questions. Every game is also numbered and has been given a title that reflects the basic category of its questions, such as "Memorable Performances," "Remarkable Rookies," "Lovable Losers," and "Fabulous Firsts." Throughout, you'll also find a number of games titled "Grab Bag," which include a potpourri of questions from various sports.

THE PAGE SETUP

Each page holds four frames that are situated from the top of the page to the bottom (as seen in the example on the next page). Each frame is divided in half. The left half contains a question. The right half contains the answer to the question from a previous page. (Seem a little confusing? Not to worry—it actually sounds more complicated than it really is.) Stay with me . . .

Questions
are always on the
left side of each frame.

Answers
(to questions from previous
pages) are always on the
right side of each frame.

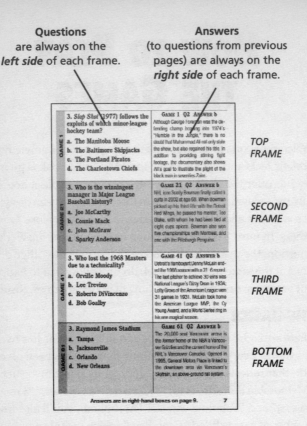

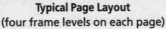

Typical Page Layout
(four frame levels on each page)

PLAYING THE GAME

The most important point to keep in mind is that the twelve questions for each game are not read from the top of the page to the bottom. Rather, they are found on the same frame level on succeeding pages. Let me help make this clearer with an example and some accompanying graphics.

Let's start with Game #1, which begins in the *top frame* of page 1—a *right-hand* page. Here, you will find the name and number of the game you are about to play.

Turn the page and look at the next *right-hand* page (page 3) for the game's first question, which is located on the left side of the *top frame* (see graphic below).

So where's the answer to this question? Turn the page again and continue to look at the *top frame* of the next *right-hand* page (page 5). As shown below, the answer is located on the right side of the frame. On the left side of this frame, you'll find the second question of Game #1.

**Question #1 is on
left side of top frame.**

**Answer to Question #1 is
on next right-hand page—
right side of top frame.**

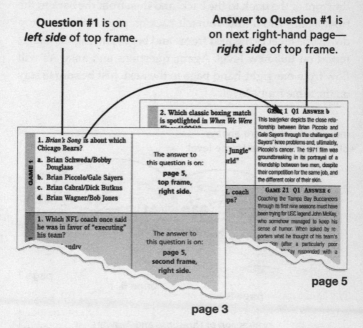

2. Which classic boxing match is spotlighted in *When We Were Kings* (1996)?

1. *Brian's Song* is about which Chicago Bears?
a. Brian Schweda/Bobby Douglass
b. Brian Piccolo/Gale Sayers
c. Brian Cabral/Dick Butkus
d. Brian Wagner/Bob Jones

The answer to this question is on:
page 5, top frame, right side.

1. Which NFL coach once said he was in favor of "executing" his team?

The answer to this question is on:
page 5, second frame, right side.

GAME 1 Q1 ANSWER b
This tearjerker depicts the close relationship between Brian Piccolo and Gale Sayers through the challenges of Sayers' knee problems and, ultimately, Piccolo's cancer. The 1971 film was groundbreaking in its portrayal of a friendship between two men, despite their competition for the same job, and the different color of their skin.

GAME 21 Q1 ANSWER c
Coaching the Tampa Bay Buccaneers through its first nine years must have been trying for USC legend John McKay, who somehow managed to keep his sense of humor. When asked by reporters what he thought of his team's execution (after a particularly poor performance), McKay responded with a

page 5

page 3

The answer to the first question of Game #1 is on the following
right-hand page—and appears on the right side of the top frame.
The left side of the top frame has the game's next question.

And that's how you continue—turning the page for each new question (Q), and finding its answer (A) on the following *right-hand* page (see graphic below).

Beginning with the top frame (*and staying in that top frame*), play the games, which flow from one *right-hand* page to the next until you have reached the last page. Then simply make a U-turn and continue playing the games—still in the top frame—from the back of the book to the front. While going in this direction, however, the answers to the questions will be found on consecutive *left-hand* pages.

Once you've completed the games in the top frame from the front of the book to the back, and then from the back to the front again, you'll find yourself back on page 1. Simply drop down one level to the next frame and begin playing the games found on this new level. Again, questions and answers will flow from one right-hand page to the next. Just be sure to stay on the same frame level.

Individual games are always
played on the same frame level.

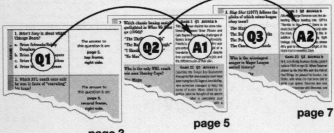

Progression of Questions and Answers

THERE'S HELP ON EVERY PAGE . . .

To be absolutely sure there's no confusion while playing the games, helpful instructions are provided on each and every page. I promise you, once you get the hang of it, you're going to love it. So kick back and get ready to be entertained, amused, and enlightened by challenging questions and their fascinating fact-filled answers.

LET THE GAMES BEGIN . . .

GAME 1

"Sports on the Silver Screen"

Do You Remember These Sports-Themed Flicks?

Turn to page 3 for the first question of Game 1.

GAME 21

"Coaching Legends"

Remember These Famous Field Marshals?

Turn to page 3 for the first question of Game 21.

GAME 41

"The 1960s"

Peace, Love, and Some Great Sports Stories

Turn to page 3 for the first question of Game 41.

GAME 61

"Sports Arenas"

Location . . . Location . . . Location

Turn to page 3 for the first question of Game 61.

Game 21 begins on page 1, second frame from the top.	**GAME 20 Q12 ANSWER a** A college All-American at the University of Illinois, as well as a pro football Hall of Famer, Grange was also nicknamed "The Great Galloping Ghost" for his impressive ability to elude tacklers.
Game 41 begins on page 1, third frame from the top.	**GAME 40 Q12 ANSWER a** Pitching for nine different teams in his twenty-year career, Newsom amassed a record of 211 wins and 222 losses for a .487 winning percentage. He is the only 200-game winner with a losing lifetime record.
Game 61 begins on page 1, bottom frame.	**GAME 60 Q12 ANSWER b** On March 29, 1999, then-Ranger Wayne Gretzky scored his final NHL goal against the NY Islanders. A few weeks later, he hung up his skates for good after an emotional 2–1 loss to the Pittsburgh Penguins in Madison Square Garden. Wayne finished his career with 894 goals, 1,962 assists, and 2,857 points—all NHL records.
The End.	**GAME 80 Q12 ANSWER b** No words can truly describe the 222–0 beating that Georgia Tech inflicted on Cumberland in 1916. Already up by over 100 points at halftime, Tech coach John Heisman went along with the officials' suggestion to shorten the quarters to more quickly expedite the ending of the game.

GAME 1	**1.** *Brian's Song* is about which Chicago Bears? **a.** Brian Schweda/Bobby Douglass **b.** Brian Piccolo/Gale Sayers **c.** Brian Cabral/Dick Butkus **d.** Brian Wagner/Bob Jones	The answer to this question is on: **page 5,** **top frame,** **right side.**
GAME 21	**1.** Which NFL coach once said he was in favor of "executing" his team? **a.** Tom Landry **b.** Hank Stram **c.** John McKay **d.** Weeb Ewbank	The answer to this question is on: **page 5,** **second frame,** **right side.**
GAME 41	**1.** Which famous NFL star abruptly called it quits after the 1965 season? **a.** Paul Hornung **b.** Gale Sayers **c.** Jim Brown **d.** Sonny Jurgensen	The answer to this question is on: **page 5,** **third frame,** **right side.**
GAME 61	**1.** The Pyramid **a.** Charlotte **b.** Memphis **c.** Atlanta **d.** Nashville	The answer to this question is on: **page 5,** **bottom frame,** **right side.**

12. Red Grange

a. Harold
b. Martin
c. John
d. William

The son of German immigrants, Gehrig was born Heinrich Ludwig Gehrig. Later, his name was Americanized to Henry Louis.

---

12. Of all the 200+ game-winning pitchers, who has the lowest win/loss percentage?

a. Bobo Newsom
b. Robin Roberts
c. Joe Niekro
d. Nolan Ryan

By winning gold in the 100-meter dash, 200-meter dash, long jump, and 4x100 meter relay, "The Fastest Man in the World" truly upset the apple cart. Adolph Hitler had not counted on an American black man stealing the show in Berlin, and abruptly left the stadium after Owens' second medal.

---

12. Against which goalie did Gretzky score his last NHL goal in 1999?

a. Brian Boucher
b. Wade Flaherty
c. Trevor Kidd
d. Damian Rhodes

In 1983, after thrashing the Devils 13–4, the usually reserved Gretzky had some harsh words about the league's East Rutherford occupants. "It's disappointing. These guys had better get their act together, like putting better personnel on the ice. It's ruining hockey. They're putting a Mickey Mouse organization on the ice."

---

12. Which NCAA football team once lost by a score of 222–0?

a. Prairie View A&M University
b. Cumberland College
c. Rensselaer Polytechnic Institute
d. Columbia University

Beginning with the last game of the 1956 season and ending in December of 1960, Hall of Famer Johnny Unitas threw touchdown passes in a record 47 straight games. He won an MVP Award and two championships during the streak. No other signal caller has come closer than 30 consecutive games.

GAME 1

2. Which classic boxing match is spotlighted in *When We Were Kings* (1996)?

a. "The Thrilla in Manila"

b. "The Rumble in the Jungle"

c. "I Shook Up the World"

d. "No Mas"

GAME 1 Q1 ANSWER b
This tearjerker depicts the close relationship between Brian Piccolo and Gale Sayers through the challenges of Sayers' knee problems and, ultimately, Piccolo's cancer. The 1971 film was groundbreaking in its portrayal of a friendship between two men, despite their competition for the same job, and the different color of their skin.

GAME 21

2. Who is the only NHL coach to win nine Stanley Cups?

a. Toe Blake

b. Scotty Bowman

c. Dick Irvin

d. Al Arbour

GAME 21 Q1 ANSWER c
Coaching the Tampa Bay Buccaneers through its first nine seasons must have been trying for USC legend John McKay, who somehow managed to keep his sense of humor. When asked by reporters what he thought of his team's execution (after a particularly poor showing), McKay responded with a deadpan, "I'm in favor of it."

GAME 41

2. Who was the last Major League hurler to win 30 games in a season?

a. Bob Gibson

b. Denny McLain

c. Dave McNally

d. Tom Seaver

GAME 41 Q1 ANSWER c
At the peak of his career, Cleveland Browns' fullback Jim Brown left the NFL at age 30 to pursue an acting career. Before leaving the game, Brown had accumulated 12,312 ground yards and 126 total touchdowns in nine seasons.

GAME 61

2. General Motors Place

a. Seattle

b. Vancouver

c. Portland

d. Sacramento

GAME 61 Q1 ANSWER b
A true sight to behold, the 21,000-seat pyramid-shaped arena is located in Memphis, Tennessee. Home to the NBA's Memphis Grizzlies and the University of Memphis basketball teams, the thirty-two story structure ranks as the third-tallest pyramid in the world.

---

11. Lou Gehrig

a. Louis
b. Heinrich
c. Albert
d. Ludwig

The flamboyant golfer Juan Rodriguez was born in Puerto Rico. He took to the game at a very young age, and shot a 67 at the tender age of 12!

11. How many gold medals did Jesse Owens capture at the 1936 Summer Olympics?

a. Three
b. Four
c. Five
d. Six

Taking home three ABA MVP Awards from 1974 to 1976, and then winning the NBA MVP in 1981, Julius Erving is the only individual to capture both league's Player of the Year award. A member of first the Virginia Squires and then the New York Nets, Erving dazzled crowds with his flashy play, and continued the party in the NBA.

11. Which team did Gretzky once refer to as a "Mickey Mouse organization"?

a. Los Angeles Kings
b. Philadelphia Flyers
c. New Jersey Devils
d. Hartford Whalers

From 1980 to 1989, Gretzky earned league MVP every year except 1988, when it went to Mario Lemieux. Scoring 70 goals and 98 assists that season, Lemieux finally beat out "The Great One." The fact that Lemieux accomplished those stats while playing for the last-place Penguins makes it that much more impressive.

11. Which quarterback threw a touchdown pass in 47 consecutive NFL games?

a. Fran Tarkenton
b. Joe Montana
c. Dan Marino
d. Johnny Unitas

In 1979, the NHL made it mandatory for all incoming players to wear a helmet, but current players did not have to conform to the standard. The last player to play without a helmet was four-time Stanley Cup winner Craig MacTavish, who retired after going topless for the St. Louis Blues in the 1996-1997 season.

3. *Slap Shot* (1977) follows the exploits of which minor-league hockey team?

a. The Manitoba Moose
b. The Baltimore Skipjacks
c. The Portland Pirates
d. The Charlestown Chiefs

GAME 1 Q2 ANSWER b
Although George Foreman was the defending champ heading into 1974's "Rumble in the Jungle," there is no doubt that Muhammad Ali not only stole the show, but also regained his title. In addition to providing stirring fight footage, the documentary also shows Ali's goal to illustrate the plight of the black man in seventies Zaire.

3. Who is the winningest manager in Major League Baseball history?

a. Joe McCarthy
b. Connie Mack
c. John McGraw
d. Sparky Anderson

GAME 21 Q2 ANSWER b
NHL icon Scotty Bowman finally called it quits in 2002 at age 68. When Bowman picked up his third title with the Detroit Red Wings, he passed his mentor, Toe Blake, with whom he had been tied at eight cups apiece. Bowman also won five championships with Montreal, and one with the Pittsburgh Penguins.

3. Who lost the 1968 Masters due to a technicality?

a. Orville Moody
b. Lee Trevino
c. Roberto DiVincenzo
d. Bob Goalby

GAME 41 Q2 ANSWER b
Detroit's flamboyant Denny McLain ended the 1968 season with a 31–6 record. The last pitcher to achieve 30 wins was National League's Dizzy Dean in 1934; Lefty Grove of the American League won 31 games in 1931. McLain took home the American League MVP, the Cy Young Award, and a World Series ring in his one magical season.

3. Raymond James Stadium

a. Tampa
b. Jacksonville
c. Orlando
d. New Orleans

GAME 61 Q2 ANSWER b
The 20,000-seat Vancouver arena is the *former* home of the NBA's Vancouver Grizzlies and the current home of the NHL's Vancouver Canucks. Opened in 1995, General Motors Place is linked to the downtown area via Vancouver's Skytrain, an above-ground rail system.

GAME 20

10. Chi Chi Rodriguez

a. Miguel

b. Wilson

c. Juan

d. Carlos

GAME 20 Q9 ANSWER c
Born in Baltimore, Maryland, Ruth was named after his father, George Herman Ruth, Sr. When Baltimore Orioles (then a Red Sox farm team) owner Jack Dunn signed Ruth at the age of 19, he was referred to as "Jack's newest babe," and the nickname stuck.

GAME 40

10. Who is the only player to win an MVP Award in both the NBA and the ABA?

a. Dave DeBusschere

b. George Gervin

c. Julius Erving

d. Artis Gilmore

GAME 40 Q9 ANSWER b
One of the best post-scoring celebrations is credited to Atlanta Falcons' Jamal Anderson, who danced his team to Super Bowl XXXIII. Although the Falcons lost to Denver in the big game, the highlight of the 1998 NFL season was Atlanta coach Dan Reeves' attempt to do the dance after beating the Vikings in the NFC Championship Game.

GAME 60

10. During the 1980s, who was the only player besides Gretzky to win a Hart Trophy?

a. Mario Lemieux

b. Brett Hull

c. Steve Yzerman

d. Marcel Dionne

GAME 60 Q9 ANSWER d
By scoring his 1,851st career point on October 15, 1989, Wayne Gretzky surpassed Gordie Howe to become the NHL's all-time leading scorer. The fact that it was a game-tying goal against his former team, the Edmonton Oilers, made it that much sweeter. Gretzky's point number 1,852 was the game-*winning* goal in overtime of the same contest.

GAME 80

10. Who was the last NHL player to play without a helmet?

a. Rod Langway

b. Craig MacTavish

c. Al Iafrate

d. Clark Gillies

GAME 80 Q9 ANSWER a
The vociferous media giant skippered the yacht *Courageous*, which captured the America's Cup in 1977. The one-game manager of the Atlanta Braves brought his 24-hour Cable News Network to prominence in the 1980s.

GAME 1

4. In *Bull Durham* (1988), Kevin Costner's character is named:

a. Crash Davis
b. Roy Hobbs
c. Rick Vaughn
d. Jake Taylor

GAME 1 Q3 ANSWER d
While Paul Newman called his work in *Slap Shot* "the most fun I have ever had making a movie," most people remember the wacky Hanson brothers in those gaudy Charlestown Chiefs jerseys. Ironically, this fictional hockey team has garnered more recognition than any real minor-league franchise.

GAME 21

4. Who was the first coach to lose four Super Bowls?

a. Dan Reeves
b. Don Shula
c. Marv Levy
d. Bud Grant

GAME 21 Q3 ANSWER b
With 3,731 regular season victories, and another 24 in World Series play, Connie Mack leads the pack. Mack spent the first three seasons of his managerial career with the Pittsburgh Pirates from 1894 to 1896, and then re-emerged in 1901 to spend the next *fifty* seasons guiding the AL's Philadelphia Athletics.

GAME 41

4. Where was the first Super Bowl held?

a. Houston
b. Miami
c. New Orleans
d. Los Angeles

GAME 41 Q3 ANSWER c
Golf's biggest gaffe occurred during the 1968 Masters, which ended in a tie between Roberto DiVincenzo and Bob Goalby. There was no playoff, however, because DiVincenzo had signed an incorrect scorecard showing he had a 4 on the seventeenth hole instead of the 3 he actually scored. Because of this error, the title went to Goalby.

GAME 61

4. Minute Maid Park

a. Oklahoma City
b. Houston
c. Arlington
d. San Antonio

GAME 61 Q3 ANSWER a
Home of the NFL's Tampa Bay Buccaneers since 1998, this venue replaced the antiquated Tampa Stadium as the area's largest outdoor arena. With a seating capacity of 75,000, the "Ray Jay" played host to Super Bowl XXV in 2001. The arena also holds college football's annual Outback Bowl.

9. Babe Ruth

a. John
b. Herman
c. George
d. Wilbur

GAME 20 Q8 ANSWER d
An All-American at the University of Minnesota and a Chicago Bears football Hall of Famer, Nagurski went on to become a world wrestling champion after retiring in 1938.

9. Which NFL running back did a dance called "The Dirty Bird"?

a. Ickey Woods
b. Jamal Anderson
c. Ricky Watters
d. Rodney Hampton

GAME 40 Q8 ANSWER d
Just months before the end of his final term, President Regan made his way up to the broadcast booth to call just over an inning of a September 1988 contest between the Cubs and Pirates at Wrigley Field. The brief performance made Reagan the first sitting President to call a game. Many felt he should have stuck to his day job.

9. Against which team did Gretzky break Gordie Howe's NHL career-scoring record?

a. Vancouver Canucks
b. Winnipeg Jets
c. Calgary Flames
d. Edmonton Oilers

GAME 60 Q8 ANSWER b
The darkest day in Edmonton sports history was August 9, 1988, when Oilers owner Peter Pocklington shipped "The Great One" to LA along with Mike Krushelnyski and Marty McSorley for Jimmy Carson, Martin Gelinas, three first-round draft picks, and $15 million.

9. In which sport did media mogul Ted Turner capture a championship?

a. Yachting
b. Archery
c. Polo
d. Badminton

GAME 80 Q8 ANSWER c
With 81 career victories on the PGA Tour, "Slammin" Sam Snead stands atop the win list. The winner of seven majors, Snead's best season came in 1951, when he captured eleven tournaments, including the PGA Championship. Jack Nicklaus ranks second, with 70 career wins on the Tour.

5. Which former hoops star plays a gun-toting psycho in *White Men Can't Jump* (1992)?

a. Kareem Abdul-Jabbar
b. Wilt Chamberlain
c. Marques Johnson
d. Robert Parish

GAME 1 Q4 ANSWER a
Although Crash's main job in the film is to tutor boisterous rookie Nuke Lalouche (Tim Robbins), it is the angst and eventual peace of Costner's character that is the focal point of this ballpark classic. Costner also starred in baseball-related films *Field of Dreams* (1988) and *For the Love of the Game* (1999).

5. With which team did Joe Torre post his first winning season as a manager?

a. New York Mets
b. New York Yankees
c. St. Louis Cardinals
d. Atlanta Braves

GAME 21 Q4 ANSWER d
Any coach would be happy just to make it to four Super Bowls. Bud Grant did so and then proceeded to lose them all. With defeats for his Minnesota Vikings in Super Bowls IV, VIII, IX and XI, Grant became the first coach to accomplish the feat, but was soon joined by Don Shula, Marv Levy, and Dan Reeves.

5. Who swept tennis's Grand Slam twice in the 1960s?

a. Rod Laver
b. John Newcombe
c. Roy Emerson
d. Fred Stolle

GAME 41 Q4 ANSWER d
Super Bowl I took place on January 15, 1967 at the Memorial Coliseum in Los Angeles, featuring the Green Bay Packers and the Kansas City Chiefs. Led by the passing of Bart Starr and the receiving of Max McGee, who caught seven passes on two touchdowns, the Packers trounced their AFL opponents 35–10.

5. Thomas and Mack Center

a. San Francisco
b. Oakland
c. Las Vegas
d. Fresno

GAME 61 Q4 ANSWER b
Minute Maid Park had been called Enron Field until 2002, when the sponsorship changed. Opened in 2001, this home to the Houston Astros boasts a retractable roof, and a nineteenth-century locomotive above the outfield wall, which makes a celebratory ride after a Houston home run.

8. Bronko Nagurski

a. Bruno
b. Bernard
c. Barnabus
d. Bronislaw

GAME 20 Q7 ANSWER c
Hall of Famer catcher Lawrence Berra became Yogi because of the way he used to sit on the ground with his legs folded under like a Hindu holy man.

8. Who was the first President to deliver the play-by-play of a Major League baseball game?

a. Richard Nixon
b. Gerald Ford
c. Jimmy Carter
d. Ronald Reagan

GAME 40 Q7 ANSWER c
Inducted in the Builders category of the Hockey Hall of Fame in 1989, the first director of the NHL Players Association resigned in shame nine years later, after he was found to have defrauded hockey players out of millions of dollars. Several players threatened to remove their plaques unless Eagleson's plaque was eliminated.

8. Along with getting players, how much money did Edmonton get in the Gretzky trade?

a. $10 million
b. $15 million
c. $25 million
d. $30 million

GAME 60 Q7 ANSWER c
When playing for LA, Gretzky was the center on a line with Bernie Nicholls. The year before Wayne arrived, Nicholls had scored 32 goals. When Wayne joined the team, Nicholls scored an amazing 70 times with 80 assists—an indication of how much Wayne improved the play of those around him.

8. Which golfer has won the most career PGA Tour events?

a. Ben Hogan
b. Jack Nicklaus
c. Sam Snead
d. Arnold Palmer

GAME 80 Q7 ANSWER d
One of the biggest farces in NFL history occurred during the Giants' last game of the 2001 season. Brett Favre basically laid down so buddy Michael Strahan could break the NFL's single-season sack record. Because the obviously staged "sack" cheapened such a significant record, it was blasted from coast to coast.

6. Rocky Balboa overcomes what personal hurdle in *Rocky II* (1979)?

a. Dyslexia
b. Illiteracy
c. Impotence
d. Shyness

GAME 1 Q5 ANSWER c
When an injury prematurely ended his basketball career in the mid-'80s, Marques Johnson looked to Hollywood. In addition to his cameo in *White Men Can't Jump,* Johnson also appeared in hoops-themed flicks *Blue Chips* (1994) and *Forget Paris* (1995). He also guest starred on several network television shows, such as *L.A. Law.*

6. Who is the only baseball manager to guide four different teams to division titles?

a. Billy Martin
b. Joe Torre
c. Lou Piniella
d. Sparky Anderson

GAME 21 Q5 ANSWER d
After five miserable seasons at the helm of the hapless Mets, Joe Torre moved to Atlanta in 1982, and led the Braves to their first division title in thirteen years, with an 89-73 record. Atlanta got bounced in the NL Championship Series by Torre's future employer, the St. Louis Cardinals.

6. How many teams did the NHL add in its 1967 expansion?

a. Two
b. Four
c. Six
d. Eight

GAME 41 Q5 ANSWER a
Rod Laver is also the only man to accomplish this difficult feat twice—first in 1962, and then again in 1969, one year after the Open Era began.

6. MCI Center

a. Charlotte
b. Philadelphia
c. Raleigh
d. Washington DC

GAME 61 Q5 ANSWER c
Opening its doors in the mid-1980s, Las Vegas's Thomas and Mack Center has played host to the basketball team of the University of Nevada-Las Vegas, several boxing matches and concerts, and the Las Vegas Gladiators arena football team. In the past, the arena was also home to the IHL's Las Vegas Thunder hockey team.

7. Yogi Berra

a. Peter
b. Paul
c. Lawrence
d. Michael

After winning the Heisman Trophy in 1985, Vincent Edwards Jackson was one of the few athletes to participate in two different professional sports at the same time—baseball and football. Bo got his nickname from his brother, who shortened the original nickname: "Wild Boar."

---

7. Who is the only person to resign from the Hockey Hall of Fame?

a. John Ziegler
b. Harold Ballard
c. Alan Eagleson
d. Angus Campbell

A brilliant soccer star, Diego Maradona will always be remembered as captain of the 1986 World Cup champion team from Argentina. Maradona also won the MVP of the tournament that year, and was named the Player of the '80s. Later, he flourished in Italy, leading Napoli to league titles in 1987 and 1990.

---

7. Which player scored 70 goals on a line with Gretzky in 1988-1989?

a. Luc Robitaille
b. Mike Krushelnyski
c. Bernie Nicholls
d. Marty McSorley

In 1978, Indianapolis Racers new owner, Nelson Skalbania, signed junior sensation Wayne Gretzky to fill the seats. After scoring only 3 goals in 8 games for the club, Gretzky was sold to a fellow WHA club, the Edmonton Oilers, for $800,000. A few months later, the Racers ceased operation and folded the franchise in December of 1978.

---

7. Which quarterback did Michael Strahan "sack" to break the NFL single-season record?

a. Drew Bledsoe
b. Jay Fiedler
c. Jeff Garcia
d. Brett Favre

Going 27–6 for the AL Champion Oakland A's in 1990, Bob Welch not only won the Cy Young Award that year, he also remains the last pitcher to win 27 games in a season. In the early 1980s, Welch went public with his drinking problem in a book entitled *Five O'Clock Comes Early: A Young Man's Battle with Alcoholism.*

---

7. Which of the following actors did *not* portray a New York Yankee?

a. Gary Cooper

b. Tommy Lee Jones

c. William Bendix

d. John Goodman

7. Who is the only NCAA coach to take six different college teams to bowl games?

a. Pop Warner

b. Amos Alonzo Stagg

c. Bear Bryant

d. Lou Holtz

7. Which golfer blew a 7-stroke lead with nine holes left in the 1966 US Open?

a. Billy Casper

b. Ken Venturi

c. Tommy Jacobs

d. Arnold Palmer

7. Pimlico Race Course

a. Philadelphia

b. New York

c. Baltimore

d. Lexington

GAME 1 Q6 ANSWER b
After a director tears Rocky (Sylvester Stallone) apart for being unable to read the cue cards on the set of an after-shave commercial, the Italian Stallion decides to join the ranks of the literate.

GAME 21 Q6 ANSWER a
Best known for his love-hate relationship with Yankee owner George Steinbrenner, Billy Martin did find success outside the Bronx. In addition to two divisional crowns with the Yankees (1976, 1977), the man responsible for "Billy Ball" also won divisions with the Minnesota Twins (1969), Detroit Tigers (1972), and Oakland A's (1981).

GAME 41 Q6 ANSWER c
After many years with only six teams in the league, the NHL expanded to twelve for the 1967-1968 season. It brought pro hockey to the West Coast, placing teams in Los Angeles (Kings) and the Bay Area (Seals). Other cities that benefited were Philadelphia (Flyers), Pittsburgh (Penguins), and Minneapolis (North Stars).

GAME 61 Q6 ANSWER d
Situated in the nation's capital, the MCI Center's tenants include the Washington Wizards of the NBA, Washington Capitals of the NHL, Washington Mystics of the WNBA, and the Georgetown Hoyas basketball squad. The state-of-the-art 20,000-seat arena opened in 1997.

6. Bo Jackson

a. Robert
b. Vincent
c. Boris
d. Anthony

Born in Los Angeles, Edwin Donald Snider migrated east, where he endeared himself to Brooklyn Dodgers fans as "The Duke of Flatbush." Snider is still the only player to hit 4 home runs in two different World Series (1952 and 1955).

6. Former soccer sensation Diego Maradona came from which country?

a. Argentina
b. Uruguay
c. Bolivia
d. Peru

One of the most recognized NASCAR drivers, due to his Pepsi commercials and a 2003 appearance on *Saturday Night Live*, Jeff Gordon can be identified on track by his number 24 and his rainbow-colored Chevy, which bears the insignia of longtime sponsor, DuPont.

6. Before Edmonton, for which pro team did Wayne play?

a. Indianapolis Racers
b. Cincinnati Stingers
c. Chicago Cougars
d. Calgary Cowboys

Brent Gretzky made his NHL debut in 1993 with Tampa, getting a goal and an assist in 10 games. The next season, Brent was again called up and had 1 assist in 3 contests. It was, however, the last time he made it to the big show, and as of 2003, Wayne's younger brother was still in the minors.

6. Who was the last Major League pitcher to win 27 games in a season?

a. Steve Carlton
b. Bob Welch
c. Pedro Martinez
d. Sandy Koufax

Taking his passion for golf to the executive level, former President Eisenhower had a putting green installed on the White House lawn so he could work on his short game. When he noticed that squirrels were ruining the green, the Commander in Chief had the rodents eradicated from the grounds.

Answers are in right-hand boxes on page 14.

8. Which NFL star appears in *Something About Mary* (1998)?

a. Brett Favre

b. Marcus Allen

c. Emmitt Smith

d. Troy Aikman

GAME 1 Q7 ANSWER b
Cobb (1994) stars Tommy Lee Jones as the legendary Ty Cobb, whose career was with the Detroit Tigers and Philadelphia Athletics. William Bendix played Yankee great Babe Ruth in *The Babe Ruth Story* (1942), while John Goodman portrayed Ruth in *The Babe* (1992). *The Pride of the Yankees* (1942) starred Gary Cooper as Yankee Lou Gehrig.

8. Which coach has the most victories in the NBA playoffs?

a. Lenny Wilkens

b. Phil Jackson

c. Pat Riley

d. Red Auerbach

GAME 21 Q7 ANSWER d
Even more incredible is that Lou Holtz took the teams to bowl games during his second year at each school. The schools were William & Mary (1970), North Carolina State (1973), Arkansas (1978), Minnesota (1985), Notre Dame (1987), and South Carolina (2000). Holtz's only National Championship came in 1988 with Notre Dame.

8. Who won baseball's last hitting Triple Crown?

a. Frank Robinson

b. Mickey Mantle

c. Carl Yastrzemski

d. Brooks Robinson

GAME 41 Q7 ANSWER d
With a massive lead going into the final nine holes, fan favorite Arnold Palmer seemed poised to capture his second open of the decade; but a funny thing happened on the way to the trophy presentation as Billy Casper tied him at the eighteenth hole, and then took the title in a playoff.

8. Roland Garros Stadium

a. Paris

b. Athens

c. Rome

d. Milan

GAME 61 Q7 ANSWER c
Home to the middle leg of thoroughbred racing's Triple Crown, Baltimore's Pimlico Racecourse, which opened in 1870, is the second oldest racetrack in America (Saratoga in Upstate New York is the oldest). Nicknamed the "Old Hilltop," Pimlico has hosted the Preakness Stakes on the third Saturday of May since 1909.

5. Duke Snider

a. Edgar

b. Elvin

c. Edward

d. Edwin

Although only 5'9" and 175 pounds, the Brooklyn Dodger Hall of Fame shortstop got his famous nickname when he was younger due to his great prowess as a marbles player.

---

5. What is top NASCAR driver Jeff Gordon's number?

a. 14

b. 4

c. 34

d. 24

Teams from SIU suffered with the "Maroons" moniker for years, until campus officials decided that a more imaginative name was needed. After a 1951 school-wide vote, Salukis—a regal Egyptian hunting dog—was the overwhelming winner. The most famous Saluki athlete is NBA Hall of Famer Walt "Clyde" Frazier.

---

5. For which NIIL team did Wayne's brother Brent briefly play?

a. Edmonton Oilers

b. Tampa Bay Lightning

c. New Jersey Devils

d. Hartford Whalers

Right before the 1996 trading deadline, the LA Kings dealt Wayne to his wife's hometown St. Louis Blues for three minor leaguers and draft picks. Gretzky played the last eighteen regular season games with the Blues, scoring 21 points; then he competed in their thirteen playoff contests, contributing 2 goals and 14 assists.

---

5. Which American President had a putting green set up behind the White House?

a. Gerald Ford

b. John F. Kennedy

c. Dwight Eisenhower

d. Lyndon Johnson

Just one year after eliminating Cleveland from the playoffs with "The Shot," Jordan lit up the Cavaliers again on March 28, 1990 for his career-best output of 69 points in a 117–113 overtime Bulls victory. Craig Ehlo, who was better than average, had the unfortunate assignment of guarding Michael during both outings.

---

9. What does Woody Harrelson lose in *Kingpin* (1996)?

a. His mother's ring

b. His hand

c. His new car

d. His virginity

GAME 1 Q8 ANSWER a
Playing one of Cameron Diaz's many boyfriends, three-time MVP Brett Favre has a short cameo in the film. Already stamping himself as one of the all-time greats in football, Favre was actually drafted *behind* less-than-stellar quarterbacks Dan McGwire (Mark's brother), Todd Marinovich, and Browning Nagle in the 1991 NFL draft.

9. Who was the last NHL coach to win four consecutive Stanley Cups?

a. Glen Sather

b. Al Arbour

c. Toe Blake

d. Punch Imlach

GAME 21 Q8 ANSWER b
Posting 175 victories while coaching the Bulls and Lakers through 2004, the now-"retired" Phil Jackson stands atop the list. Passing Pat Riley's mark of 155 with the Lakers final victory over the Nets in the 2002 Finals, "The Zen Master" accomplished the feat in only eleven trips to the postseason.

9. After which event of the 1968 Summer Olympics did the famed medal ceremony protests take place?

a. 400-meter hurdles

b. 200-meter dash

c. Long jump

d. 800-meter dash

GAME 41 Q8 ANSWER c
In the late 1960s, there was much talk of Boston's Carl Yastrzemski as being the greatest ball player of all time. During his 1967 Triple Crown season, he batted .326 with 44 homers and 121 runs batted in. Yaz spent his entire twenty-three-year career with the Red Sox, and entered the Hall of Fame in 1989.

9. Target Center

a. Chicago

b. Minneapolis

c. Denver

d. Salt Lake City

GAME 61 Q8 ANSWER a
This annual home of tennis's French Open—the second major tournament of the year—received its name from Roland Garros, a French aviation expert. The Open has been held on the Roland Garros court every year since 1928, with the exception of five years in the early 1940s due to World War II.

4. Pee Wee Reese

a. Harry

b. Harmon

c. Harold

d. Harrison

GAME 20 Q3 ANSWER a
Undefeated Heavyweight Champion, Rocco Marchegiano made the obvious name change for the sake of brevity. The great Marciano actually lost one bout, but it was as an amateur to Coley Wallace.

---

4. What is the nickname of sports teams from Southern Illinois University?

a. Spartans

b. Salukis

c. Sidewinders

d. Saints

GAME 40 Q3 ANSWER c
Secretariat blazed his way to icon status during the 1973 Triple Crown, always being ridden by Ron Turcotte. The Canadian jockey learned about horses while helping his father in the lumberjack trade. Turcotte was permanently disabled in a riding accident five years after his famous journey.

---

4. For which NHL team did Gretzky play only 31 games in 1996?

a. Calgary Flames

b. Winnipeg Jets

c. St. Louis Blues

d. Dallas Stars

GAME 60 Q3 ANSWER c
Born and raised in Brantford, Ontario, Wayne, at age 6, was skilled enough to play with older kids. At age 10, he scored 378 goals and 120 assists in 85 games with a local youth team. In his one year of junior hockey with the Soo Greyhounds, Wayne scored 182 points and earned the Rookie of the Year Award from the Ontario Hockey League.

---

4. Which team did Michael Jordan torch in his career-high 69-point game?

a. New York Knicks

b. Cleveland Cavaliers

c. New Jersey Nets

d. Los Angeles Lakers

GAME 80 Q3 ANSWER c
By the end of his career in 1960, Ted Williams had amassed 521 home runs to go along with his .344 batting average—the highest of any 500 home run club member. "The Splendid Splinter" accomplished these feats while playing mostly in lefty-unfriendly Fenway Park, and while missing most of five seasons due to military service.

10. Which NFL player starred in the 1955 movie *Unchained*?

a. Frank Gifford
b. Elroy Hirsch
c. Steve Van Buren
d. Bob Waterfield

GAME 1 Q9 ANSWER b
Woody Harrelson comically portrays Roy Munson, a down-and-out former bowling legend who lost his hand in a ball return. Several prominent athletes have cameos in the film, notably pro bowler Mark Roth, announcers Chris Schenkel and Chris Berman, and famed pitcher Roger Clemens.

10. Which "legendary" coach had the worst winning percentage of any Cincinnati Bengals leader?

a. Dick LeBeau
b. Dave Shula
c. Bruce Coslet
d. Homer Rice

GAME 21 Q9 ANSWER b
By leading the New York Islanders to four victories in a row during the 1980s, Al Arbour is the last NHL coach to manage this feat. Glen Sather came close in the late '80s by guiding the Edmonton Oilers to four cups in five years. Before Arbour, the last coach to win four in a row was Montreal's Scotty Bowman in the late 1970s.

10. What was Bob Gibson's record-shattering ERA in 1968?

a. 1.04
b. 1.12
c. 1.19
d. 1.21

GAME 41 Q9 ANSWER b
During the medal presentation of the 200-meter run in Mexico City, American runners Tommie Smith (gold) and John Carlos (bronze) bowed their heads and raised their black-gloved fists skyward in a salute to Black Power and a protest against racism and oppression.

10. Ohio Stadium

a. Cleveland
b. Cincinnati
c. Columbus
d. Dayton

GAME 61 Q9 ANSWER b
Taking over two years to build, Minnesota's Target Center opened its doors in 1990, and has the distinction of being the first wholly nonsmoking venue in the United States. It also boasts a rising arena floor. The complex's main occupant is the NBA's Minnesota Timberwolves.

3. Rocky Marciano

a. Rocco

b. Raymond

c. Alphonse

d. Anthony

GAME 20 Q2 ANSWER b
Born Jerome Hanna Dean in Lucas, Arkansas, the All-Star pitcher was one of the key players in the St. Louis Cardinal's famous "Gas House Gang" that dominated baseball in the early 1930s.

3. Which jockey rode Secretariat for the 1973 Triple Crown races?

a. Angel Cordero, Jr.

b. Jorge Velasquez

c. Ron Turcotte

d. Eddie Maple

GAME 40 Q2 ANSWER b
In a seventeen-year career playing with six teams, Smith played in the Fall Classic five times. He was on the winning side with Philadelphia in 1980, St. Louis in 1982, and Kansas City in 1985. He came up short with Atlanta twice—in 1991 and 1992.

3. In which Ontario town was Gretzky raised?

a. St. Catharine's

b. Hamilton

c. Brantford

d. Sudbury

GAME 60 Q2 ANSWER b
Gretzky became a part-owner of the Phoenix Coyotes in March of 2000. Without him, the team would have almost certainly moved from Arizona (the previous owners had a tentative deal with Microsoft magnate Paul Allen to relocate to Portland). As managing partner, Gretzky is deeply involved in the day-to-day operations of the franchise.

3. Which player has the highest career batting average of any 500 home run hitter?

a. Jimmie Foxx

b. Barry Bonds

c. Ted Williams

d. Babe Ruth

GAME 80 Q2 ANSWER d
Panamanian sensation Laffit Pincay passed Bill Shoemaker's 8,833 career wins in 1999 to become thoroughbred racing's winningest jockey. In 2003, during the Santa Anita meet, a horse threw Picay to the ground, causing him to suffer a spinal cord injury, which forced his retirement. Pincay ended his career with 9,531 wins.

11. Which footballer *did not* appear in *The Longest Yard*?

a. Ray Nitschke
b. Sonny Sixkiller
c. Timmy Brown
d. Ernie Wheelwright

GAME 1 Q10 ANSWER b
Elroy "Crazylegs" Hirsch—star receiver for the Los Angeles Rams and longtime Athletic Director at the University of Wisconsin—turned in an inspired performance in this prison movie, whose theme song is "Unchained Melody."

11. Who is the only NBA coach to win three straight titles on three separate occasions?

a. Red Auerbach
b. John Kundla
c. K.C. Jones
d. Phil Jackson

GAME 21 Q10 ANSWER a
Dick LeBeau carved out his niche by leading the Bengals to a 12–33 record during his three seasons with the team. Fired after the 2002 season, LeBeau's win percentage was an embarrassing .267, worse than any of the team's other coaches.

11. Which player made the final out of the 1969 World Series?

a. Frank Robinson
b. Boog Powell
c. Davey Johnson
d. Brooks Robinson

GAME 41 Q10 ANSWER b
After an amazing season that prompted Major League Baseball to lower the pitching mound, Cardinals ace Bob Gibson compiled a mind-numbingly record-low earned run average of 1.12. The low ERA, coupled with Gibson's 22 wins and 268 strikeouts, made him that season's winner of both the National League MVP and Cy Young Award.

11. The Saddledome

a. Quebec City
b. Edmonton
c. Calgary
d. Toronto

GAME 61 Q10 ANSWER c
Home of the 2003 NCAA Champion Ohio State Buckeyes football team, Ohio Stadium proudly resides in the city of Columbus. Built in 1922, this grand arena has undergone several facelifts over the years. With seating capacity for over 100,000, the stadium swelled to a record 105,539 fans for a game against rival Michigan in November 2002.

2. Dizzy Dean

a. James

b. Jerome

c. Clyde

d. Andrew

GAME 20 Q1 ANSWER a
When just a tot, superstar golfer Woods was given the nickname "Tiger" after a Vietnamese soldier who was a close friend of his dad.

2. Who is the only player to appear in five World Series with four different teams?

a. Eddie Stanky

b. Lonnie Smith

c. Don Baylor

d. Dave Winfield

GAME 40 Q1 ANSWER d
While the feat of winning eleven consecutive tournaments in one year seems amazing, it isn't as impressive as you might think. Byron Nelson put the streak together in 1945, when most of the better golfers were serving in the military. Nelson was exempt from the draft due to a medical condition.

2. In which NHL franchise does Wayne Gretzky have an ownership stake?

a. Calgary Flames

b. Phoenix Coyotes

c. Toronto Maple Leafs

d. Los Angeles Kings

GAME 60 Q1 ANSWER c
When Gretzky and Jones were married in July of 1988 in Edmonton, the nuptials were broadcast all across Canada. Jones, who has appeared in such films as *Staying Alive* (1983) and *Police Academy 5* (1988), met Wayne in 1984 when he was a judge on *Dance Fever* and she was a dancer.

2. Which jockey has won the most career races?

a. Angel Cordero, Jr.

b. Bill Shoemaker

c. Eddie Arcaro

d. Laffit Pincay, Jr.

GAME 80 Q1 ANSWER a
In the late 1930s, Walker Smith, Jr. started boxing under the name of retired fighter Ray Robinson. The young boxer's trainer, George Gainford, commented that his style and fluid motions were "sweet as sugar." Others agreed, and the nickname stuck. Louis Barrow was the real name of boxer Joe Louis.

GAME 1

12. In *Major League* (1989), after stealing a base, Willie Mays Hays takes his gloves and:

a. Tosses them to a fan
b. Stacks them in his locker
c. Nails them on a wall
d. Sells them after the game

GAME 21

12. Who is the only manager to win a World Series in both the American and National Leagues?

a. Casey Stengel
b. Sparky Anderson
c. Yogi Berra
d. Whitey Herzog

GAME 41

12. Who scored the only Jets touchdown in Super Bowl III?

a. Emerson Boozer
b. Matt Snell
c. Don Maynard
d. George Sauer

GAME 61

12. Comerica Park

a. Detroit
b. Milwaukee
c. Indianapolis
d. Buffalo

GAME 1 Q11 ANSWER c
A number of pro athletes appear in this 1974 Burt Reynolds cult classic, which centers around a prison football game. Philadelphia Eagles running back Timmy Brown, however, wasn't one of them. Brown did appear in a number of other films, including *M*A*S*H* (1972), *Nashville* (1975), and *Frequency* (2000).

GAME 21 Q11 ANSWER d
Phil Jackson led the Bulls to three titles in a row beginning with the 1990-1991 season, and then again starting with the 1995-1996 season. Jackson's 1999-2000 season with the Lakers kicked off his third "three-peat" accomplishment. Red Auerbach is the consecutive title leader, winning eight in a row with the Celtics.

GAME 41 Q11 ANSWER c
The man who flied out to Cleon Jones, giving the Mets their first World Series title, was the same man who managed them to their second championship in 1976. A three-time All-Star second baseman with the Orioles from 1968 to 1970, Davey Johnson also turned heads when he belted 43 home runs in 1973 with the Atlanta Braves.

GAME 61 Q11 ANSWER c
Built in the early 1980s in anticipation of the 1988 Winter Olympics, Calgary's Saddledome boasts a unique saddle-shaped roof. Home to the NHL's Calgary Flames and the Western Hockey League's Calgary Hitmen, the arena is part of a complex that includes the Calgary Stampede and Stampede Park Racetrack.

1. Tiger Woods

a. Eldrick
b. Meldrick
c. Elvin
d. Melvin

The answer to
this question is on:

**page 24,
top frame,
right side.**

1. Which golfer holds the record for most consecutive PGA Tour wins?

a. Tiger Woods
b. Ben Hogan
c. Jack Nicklaus
d. Byron Nelson

The answer to
this question is on:

**page 24,
second frame,
right side.**

1. Which actress did Gretzky marry in 1989?

a. Vicki Moss
b. Kim Alexis
c. Janet Jones
d. Kelly McGillis

The answer to
this question is on:

**page 24,
third frame,
right side.**

1. What is boxing legend Sugar Ray Robinson's real name?

a. Walker Smith
b. Raymond Luten
c. Garfield Jennings
d. Louis Barrow

The answer to
this question is on:

**page 24,
bottom frame,
right side.**

GAME 2

"Amazing Announcers"

Do You Know the Guys Who Call the Action?

Turn to page 29 for the first question.

GAME 1 Q12 ANSWER c
The outfielder with blazing speed, Willie Mays Hays (Wesley Snipes) buys himself 100 pairs of batting gloves with the hope of retiring each set after a stolen base. While never stated in the film, it is implied that Hays reaches the mark, as throughout the picture his bedroom wall gets more and more cluttered with gloves.

GAME 22

"Father and Son"

Apples that Didn't Fall Far from the Tree

Turn to page 29 for the first question.

GAME 21 Q12 ANSWER b
Sparky Anderson captured back-to-back World Series titles with the National League Cincinnati Reds in 1975 and 1976. In 1984, he piloted the American League Detroit Tigers to win baseball's top prize. Anderson was inducted into Cooperstown with the Class of 2000.

GAME 42

"MVPs"

Tops in Their League for at Least One Season

Turn to page 29 for the first question.

GAME 41 Q12 ANSWER b
A game that will be forever remembered because of Joe Namath's guarantee of victory featured a single Jets touchdown—a 4-yard run by Matt Snell to open the game's scoring. Jim Turner added 3 field goals to put New York up 16–0. The 17-point-favored Baltimore Colts mustered only 1 touchdown late in the game.

GAME 62

"All-Star Games"

Gotta Love Those Special Competitions

Turn to page 29 for the first question.

GAME 61 Q12 ANSWER a
Built in 2000 to replace the dilapidated Tiger Stadium, Comerica Park is a full-featured attraction that includes a Ferris wheel, a carousel, a museum, beer halls, water fountains, and granite sculptures of tigers.

GAME 20

"Given First Names"

The Names Their Mamas Gave Them

Turn to page 26 for the first question.

GAME 19 Q12 ANSWER c
For nearly fifteen years, legendary Pete Rose steadfastly denied the allegation that he bet on Major League Baseball while managing the Cincinnati Reds. This quote, spoken during a 1990's press conference, was one of his more memorable denials. In 2003, he finally came clean and admitted that he had, in fact, bet on the games.

GAME 40

GRAB BAG

Turn to page 26 for the first question.

GAME 39 Q12 ANSWER c
In 1974, the NBA continued its rapid expansion by placing a franchise called the New Orleans Jazz in Louisiana. The Jazz moved to Utah in 1979, where it has lived happily ever after, but the NBA returned to Bourbon Street in 2002, when the Charlotte team moved and became the New Orleans Hornets.

GAME 60

"The Great One"

How Well Do You Know Wayne Gretzky?

Turn to page 26 for the first question.

GAME 59 Q12 ANSWER d
For a good part of his career, Andre Agassi sported long, flowing locks, but once his hair began thinning, he endorsed Schick Extreme for shaving his pate. In addition to plugging razors, this most recognized male tennis player has also endorsed Canon's "Rebel" camera and Nike products.

GAME 80

GRAB BAG

Turn to page 26 for the first question.

GAME 79 Q12 ANSWER b
During the 1969-1970 season, Bobby Orr's huge overtime goal brought Boston its first Stanley Cup in twenty-nine years. The Bruins legend also took home the Norris Trophy as top defenseman, the Art Ross Trophy for leading the league in scoring, the Hart Trophy for regular season MVP, and the Conn Smythe Award for the playoff MVP.

GAME 2	**1.** Which famed pigskin announcer's trademark line is "Whoa Nellie"? **a.** Dick Enberg **b.** Brent Musberger **c.** Keith Jackson **d.** John Madden	The answer to this question is on: **page 31,** **top frame,** **right side.**
GAME 22	**1.** Which Major League Baseball father-and-son hold the home-run record? **a.** The Griffeys **b.** The Alomars **c.** The Hundleys **d.** The Bonds	The answer to this question is on: **page 31,** **second frame,** **right side.**
GAME 42	**1.** Who is the only player to capture three Super Bowl MVP Awards? **a.** Joe Montana **b.** Terry Bradshaw **c.** Troy Aikman **d.** Roger Staubach	The answer to this question is on: **page 31,** **third frame,** **right side.**
GAME 62	**1.** Which team won the highest scoring NHL All-Star Game in history? **a.** East **b.** World **c.** West **d.** North America	The answer to this question is on: **page 31,** **bottom frame,** **right side.**

GAME 19

12. "No one will ever prove I did, and I can't prove I didn't because I can't prove a negative."

a. O.J. Simpson
b. Ray Lewis
c. Pete Rose
d. Allen Iverson

GAME 19 Q11 ANSWER b
In a comment regarding the abundance of NBA players with endorsements, Shaquille O'Neal offered this barb during the summer of 1996—just days after signing a multi-year deal with the Los Angeles Lakers for the "paltry" sum of $121 million.

GAME 39

12. In which city did the original New Orleans NBA franchise eventually settle?

a. Orlando
b. Minneapolis
c. Salt Lake City
d. Cleveland

GAME 39 Q11 ANSWER b
After relocating to Missouri for the 1995 season, long-time college headman Rich Brooks took the helm, and guided the Rams to a 13–19 record in 1995-1996. Brooks was replaced by Dick Vermeil, who, in his first two years as coach, went a combined 9–23 before leading the Rams to the Super Bowl following the 1999 season.

GAME 59

12. Which men's razor has tennis star Andre Agassi endorsed?

a. Gillette
b. Bic
c. Remington
d. Schick

GAME 59 Q11 ANSWER a
Advil recruited aging fireballer Nolan Ryan for a major ad campaign in the mid-'90s. "If it relieves his aching joints after throwing 90 mph fastballs, imagine what it can do for you." Ryan actually used the product, and professed, "I was popping Advils all day," before tossing his seventh and final no-hitter in 1991.

GAME 79

12. Who was the first NHL player to win four individual trophies in one season?

a. Gordie Howe
b. Bobby Orr
c. Stan Mikita
d. Maurice Richard

GAME 79 Q11 ANSWER a
After winning the first 3 games of the 1942 Finals, Detroit appeared ready to celebrate. Toronto, however, had other plans, and became the first team to rally from a 3–0 series deficit to take the Cup. The 1975 Islanders, who defeated Pittsburgh in a second-round matchup, is the only other team to emerge from a 3-game hole.

2. Who holds the record for the most consecutive NBA broadcasts?

a. Marty Glickman
b. Chick Hearn
c. Walt Frazier
d. Johnny Most

GAME 2 Q1 ANSWER c
College football icon Keith Jackson called his first game in 1952, a 14–13 Stanford win at Washington State. But it was in 1966, when ABC acquired broadcast rights to NCAA football, that Jackson began to carve out his legend. Along with college football, Jackson's announcing has covered sports from NASCAR racing to the Olympic games.

2. Who were the first father and son to each record 600 NHL goals?

a. The Howes
b. The Hulls
c. The Espositos
d. The Dionnes

GAME 22 Q1 ANSWER d
With father Bobby's 332 home runs, and son Barry's ever-growing total, the Bonds family currently holds the round-tripper record with more than 1,000. If Barry keeps up his current pace, he will both smash Hank Aaron's individual record, and make the father-son mark unattainable for generations to come.

2. Who is the last player to win back-to-back American League MVP trophies?

a. Juan Gonzalez
b. Roger Maris
c. Frank Thomas
d. Ken Griffey, Jr.

GAME 42 Q1 ANSWER a
Leading the San Francisco 49ers to victory in four Super Bowls (XVI, XIX, XXIII, and XIV), Joe Montana is the only man to win three big-game MVP trophies. He missed the award in XXIII, when, on the strength of his 11 receptions for 215 yards and a touchdown, the MVP went to Montana's favorite target, Jerry Rice.

2. What was the only year baseball didn't have an All-Star MVP?

a. 1994
b. 1980
c. 2002
d. 1981

GAME 62 Q1 ANSWER d
Paced by 3 goals and 2 assists from first-time All-Star Bill Guerin, the North American squad downed the World team 14–12 in the 2001 All-Star Game in Denver. After a five-year experiment of pitting North America's best against the stars of the rest of the World, the game returned to its traditional East versus West format in 2003.

11. "I'm tired of hearing about money. . . . I just wanna play the game, drink Pepsi, and wear Reebok."

a. Grant Hill

b. Shaquille O'Neal

c. Charles Barkley

d. Scottie Pippen

In 1946, while managing the Brooklyn Dodgers, a reporter approached Leo Durocher to pick the skipper's brain regarding his cross-town rival New York Giants, who were in seventh place in the National League. "Nice guys finish last," was the summation of his comments.

---

11. Who was the Rams first head coach after moving to St. Louis?

a. Chuck Knox

b. Rich Brooks

c. John Robinson

d. Dick Vermeil

The 1997-1998 season saw the first NHL team move into NASCAR country, when the Hartford Whalers relocated from Connecticut to Greensboro (eventually Raleigh), North Carolina, becoming the Carolina Hurricanes. After the novelty wore off, fan interest declined, but the 'Canes advance to the 2002 Stanley Cup Finals changed all that.

---

11. Which pain reliever was hawked by Hall of Fame flamethrower Nolan Ryan?

a. Advil

b. Ben Gay

c. Tylenol

d. Bufferin

Longtime NFL fullback Craig "Ironhead" Heyward appeared half-naked in several advertisements for Zest Bodywash. The former Colt projected an image of masculinity while using the seemingly feminine soap and a puffy washcloth, which he referred to as a "thingy."

---

11. Which team blew a 3 to 0 game lead in the 1942 Stanley Cup Finals?

a. Detroit Red Wings

b. Boston Bruins

c. Toronto Maple Leafs

d. Chicago Blackhawks

Swedish defenseman Börje Salming joined Toronto in 1973. He holds the Toronto record for assists (620), and his career points (768) rank high as well. After sixteen seasons with Toronto, Salming ended his NHL career in 1989 with Detroit. He returned home to play three final seasons in the Swedish Elite League.

3. About which announcer did *Sports Illustrated* say, "He is to tennis what pasta is to Italy"?

a. Bill Macatee

b. Ted Robinson

c. John McEnroe

d. Bud Collins

Sports broadcasting legend Chick Hearn died in 2002, but from opening day 1965 to December 2001, Hearn never missed a beat, calling an incredible 3,338 consecutive Los Angeles Lakers contests. Joining the Lakers in the 1960-1961 season, Hearn is as much a part of Lakers lore as Magic Johnson, Kobe Bryant, and Shaquille O'Neal.

3. In which sport did NBA star Grant Hills' father compete?

a. Baseball

b. Football

c. Track & Field

d. Golf

When he scored goal number 600 in 1999, Brett Hull joined father Bobby as the only father-son tandem to each register 600 goals. Bobby tallied 604 NHL lamplighters before moving to the WHA in 1971 where he added another 303 goals. When the WHA folded, Bobby returned to the NHL to score 6 more goals for an NHL career total of 610.

3. Which NBA player won consecutive MVP honors while playing with different teams?

a. Wilt Chamberlain

b. Charles Barkley

c. Kareem Abdul-Jabbar

d. Moses Malone

Frank Thomas received the awards after the White Sox' division-winning 1993 season, and then again in the strike-shortened 1994 campaign. "The Big Hurt" was on a torrid run when the season was halted in August of '94. He finished the abbreviated year hitting .353 with 34 homers and 101 runs batted in.

3. Who was the surprise winner of the 1986 NBA All-Star Game's Slam Dunk Contest?

a. Kenny Walker

b. Spud Webb

c. Dee Brown

d. Mugsy Bogues

The 2002 All-Star Game in Milwaukee ended in a 7–7 tie and became the first contest without an MVP since the award's inception in 1962. With depleted pitching rosters, managers Joe Torre (AL) and Bob Brenly (NL) confronted Commissioner Bud Selig, who called the game a draw.

10. "Nice guys finish last."

a. Tom Landry
b. Bear Bryant
c. Leo Durocher
d. Connie Mack

GAME 19 Q9 ANSWER a
In April of 1967, Cassius Clay's name was announced at a US military induction center in Houston, Texas. Clay, now known as Muhammad Ali, refused to accept his assignment to the Army. When journalists questioned his decision, he responded with this famous one-liner. He successfully appealed his criminal charges.

10. Which NHL team renamed its franchise after moving from Hartford?

a. Nashville Predators
b. Columbus Blue Jackets
c. Carolina Hurricanes
d. Phoenix Coyotes

GAME 39 Q9 ANSWER d
After years of losing in Washington, and with only one World Series to show for it (1925), Senators' owner Calvin Griffith took the bold step of moving the franchise to Minnesota in late 1960. He renamed the franchise the Twins in honor of the Twin Cities of Minneapolis and St. Paul.

10. Which NFL player appeared in ads for Zest in the 1990s?

a. Warren Sapp
b. Craig Heyward
c. Tim Brown
d. Dorsey Levens

GAME 59 Q9 ANSWER b
O.J. Simpson was once seen regularly in Hertz rental car ads, running through airports and hurdling over luggage. After O.J.'s famous trial, Hertz stopped using sports figures altogether. Interestingly, during their famous low-speed chase, Simpson and Al Cowlings were in a white Bronco that Hertz had given Simpson as a courtesy car.

10. Börje Salming spent virtually all of his Hall of Fame career with which team?

a. Montreal Canadiens
b. Detroit Red Wings
c. New York Rangers
d. Toronto Maple Leafs

GAME 79 Q9 ANSWER b
During the 1944-1945 season, Montreal's Maurice "Rocket" Richard became the first player to score 50 goals—a mark that was tied three times. Twenty-one years later, Chicago's Bobby Hull broke the record by scoring his 51st goal—a blistering 40-foot slapshot—against the Rangers.

4. Which NHL announcer goes by the nickname "Grapes"?

a. Mike Emrick

b. Barry Melrose

c. Don Cherry

d. Mike Lange

The year was 1963 when Bud Collins, an unknown journalist from the *Boston Globe,* called his first tennis match—the US Doubles at Longwood Cricket Club. Over the next forty years, Collins became the most identifiable face in tennis coverage. He was enshrined in the International Tennis Hall of Fame in 1994.

---

4. Which of these father-son duos played on the same baseball team at the same time?

a. The Alous

b. The Boones

c. The Raines

d. The Wines

Before Grant Hill was winning championships at Duke or playing in the NBA, his father, Calvin, was a star running back for the Cowboys. The elder Hill, a first-round Dallas draft pick in 1969, played twelve years in the NFL and twice rushed for 1,000+ yards in a season. He also earned a ring when the Cowboys won Super Bowl VI.

---

4. Who is the only Detroit Red Wing to win the Hart Trophy since 1963?

a. Terry Sawchuk

b. Sergei Fedorov

c. Steve Yzerman

d. Nicklas Lidstrom

After taking home the hardware following the 1981-1982 season with the Houston Rockets, Malone won it again in 1982-1983 with the Philadelphia 76ers. What made this second achievement even sweeter was that it was awarded during the year of Malone's only championship.

---

4. Which player holds the record for most receptions in a single Pro Bowl?

a. Tim Brown

b. Jerry Rice

c. Randy Moss

d. Cris Carter

With shock that generated from his sheer lack of size, 5'6" guard Spud Webb defeated his mighty Atlanta Hawks teammate Dominique Wilkins in the finals to become the shortest dunk champion ever. Webb's victory in his hometown of Dallas over "The Human Highlight Reel" was a major surprise.

GAME 19

9. "I got nothing against no Viet Cong. No Vietnamese ever called me a nigger."

a. Muhammad Ali
b. Jim Brown
c. Tommie Smith
d. Terrell Owens

GAME 19 Q8 ANSWER b
Bob Probert spent most of his NHL career earning trips to the penalty box. Unfortunately, his infractions were not limited to the rink. The holder of a lengthy police record, Probert was arrested in 1994 after crashing his motorcycle into a car. When authorities arrived on the scene, he uttered, "Just charge me with the usual."

GAME 39

9. The Minnesota Twins are a spin-off of which defunct baseball franchise?

a. St. Louis Browns
b. Philadelphia Athletics
c. Houston Colt 45's
d. Washington Senators

GAME 39 Q8 ANSWER a
Founded in 1941 by auto tycoon Fred Zollner, the Fort Wayne Zollner Pistons were named after the owner's bread and butter—car parts. After the 1949 season, when the NBL and BAA merged to form the NBA, the Pistons joined the Midwest Division. In 1957, the franchise moved to Detroit, where it has remained ever since.

GAME 59

9. Which company's ads featured O.J. Simpson leaping through the airport?

a. Avis
b. Hertz
c. Federal Express
d. Adidas

GAME 59 Q8 ANSWER a
"It had great results in just under two months," was the line used by Utah Jazz great Karl Malone in one of those late-1990's Rogaine spots. Malone, who has since gone back to the shaved look, was part of a sports promotion that also featured ex-Packers boss Mike Holmgren.

GAME 79

9. Which player was the first to score 51 goals in a season?

a. Maurice Richard
b. Bobby Hull
c. Stan Mikita
d. Dickie Moore

GAME 79 Q8 ANSWER a
After a Stanley Cup win with Detroit in 1950, goaltender Harry Lumley was traded to the Toronto Maple Leafs, where he had one the best netminder seasons ever. He posted 1.89 goals against an average 13 shutouts en route to his only career Vezina Trophy. Lumley was inducted into the Hockey Hall of Fame in 1980.

GAME 2

5. Which horseracing announcer's signature call is "and down the stretch they come!"?

a. Tom Durkin
b. Dave Johnson
c. Mike Battaglia
d. Ross Morton

GAME 2 Q4 ANSWER c
The name might have given it away, but you'd be hard-pressed to find a single Canadian who is not familiar with Don "Grapes" Cherry. A highly popular former coach of the Boston Bruins, Cherry is known for his wild and often humorous musings on the sport of hockey.

GAME 22

5. Besides the Pettys, who is the only father-son duo to win Winston Cup Championships?

a. The Allisons
b. The Labontes
c. The Jarretts
d. The Andrettis

GAME 22 Q4 ANSWER c
Along with the Griffeys, who were the first father and son to play together in 1990 (Mariners), the Raineses—Tim Jr. and Sr.—both played for the Orioles during the last week of the 2001 season. Their first game together saw Tim Sr. go 0 for 1 with a sacrifice, and Tim Jr. go 2 for 4, scoring three runs and stealing a base.

GAME 42

5. Which player has won the most NBA MVP Awards?

a. Kareem Abdul-Jabbar
b. Wilt Chamberlain
c. Michael Jordan
d. Bill Russell

GAME 42 Q4 ANSWER b
Winning the 1993-1994 Hart Trophy, Russian sensation Sergei Fedorov was the only Red Wing to take home the hardware since Gordie Howe (1962-1963 season). Fedorov finished his banner year with 56 goals and 64 assists, leading Detroit to the best record in the Western Conference.

GAME 62

5. Which hurler struck out five consecutive future Hall of Famers in the first All-Star Game in 1934?

a. Carl Hubbell
b. Lefty Gomez
c. Lefty Grove
d. Dizzy Dean

GAME 62 Q4 ANSWER c
Catching nine passes in the 2000 edition, perennial Pro Bowler Randy Moss holds the individual reception mark in the NFL's post-season All-Star Game. His 212 receiving yards in the same game made Moss the only person ever to catch for more than 200 yards in the Bowl.

---

8. "Just charge me with the usual."

a. Randy Moss
b. Bob Probert
c. Steve Howe
d. Dennis Rodman

GAME 19 Q7 ANSWER c
Philadelphia Flyers General Manager Bobby Clarke and estranged star Eric Lindros waged a public war of words following Lindros's sixth career concussion in a playoff game against the Devils in May 2000. Clarke questioned Lindros's desire to play, while Lindros maintained he was injured. Lindros was traded to the Rangers in 2001.

8. Which team did the Fort Wayne NBA franchise become in 1957?

a. Detroit Pistons
b. Cleveland Cavaliers
c. Indiana Pacers
d. Phoenix Suns

GAME 39 Q7 ANSWER b
After moving from Houston for the 1997 season, the franchise was known as the Tennessee Oilers, and played its home games at the 62,000-seat Liberty Bowl in Memphis. The next year, the team called Vanderbilt Stadium home. A year later, the team changed uniforms and logo and moved to its permanent home—the Adelphia Coliseum.

8. Which of the following athletes appeared in a Rogaine commercial?

a. Karl Malone
b. Andre Agassi
c. Matt Williams
d. Wade Boggs

GAME 59 Q7 ANSWER d
In the wake of his June 1988 demolition of Michael Spinks in less than one full round, Tyson appeared in a commercial for Diet Pepsi, which also featured ex-wife Robin Givens and ex-manager Bill Cayton. Tyson's endorsement career went downhill after his street-corner brawl with Mitch Green later that year.

8. Which goalie holds the Toronto record with 13 shutouts in a season?

a. Harry Lumley
b. Turk Broda
c. Terry Sawchuk
d. Curtis Joseph

GAME 79 Q7 ANSWER b
A dynasty in the truest sense of the word, the Montreal Canadiens of the late 1970s rattled off four straight Stanley Cup wins. In the 1976-1977 season, the "Habs" posted 60 wins, 8 losses, and 12 ties with a record point total of 132. Montreal's record during its four consecutive championship seasons was an amazing 229–46–45.

6. Which host called NFL quarterback Jim Everett "Chris Evert" to his face?

a. Jim Rome

b. Scott Ferall

c. Chris Russo

d. Pete Franklin

GAME 2 Q5 ANSWER b
For years, anyone who tuned into a major thoroughbred race on ABC or ESPN would hear the voice of announcer Dave Johnson. Johnson began calling races at the now-defunct Cahokia Downs near St. Louis, and enjoyed more memorable stops at racetracks in New York, California, and New Jersey.

---

6. Who are the only father-son tennis players to win ATP singles titles during the Open Era?

a. The Dents

b. The Mercers

c. The Leaches

d. The Kinseys

GAME 22 Q5 ANSWER c
By winning the 1999 Winston Cup, Dale Jarrett joined his father, Ned, who won the title in 1961 and again in 1965. Lee and Richard Petty first accomplished the elusive NASCAR trick when Richard won the first of his seven titles in 1964, following Lee's three earlier crowns.

---

6. Who is the only closer to win the MVP, Cy Young Award, and World Series all in the same year?

a. Rollie Fingers

b. Mike Marshall

c. Willie Hernandez

d. Dennis Eckersley

GAME 42 Q5 ANSWER a
Kareem Abdul-Jabbar holds the record for best player honors, as the Hall of Famer has walked off with a record six MVP trophies. Winning three with Milwaukee and another three with the Lakers, Kareem can add those accolades to his six NBA Championships, two Finals MVPs and the 1970 Rookie of the Year Trophy.

---

6. Which player scored the most points in an NBA All-Star Game?

a. Allen Iverson

b. Michael Jordan

c. Julius Erving

d. Wilt Chamberlain

GAME 62 Q5 ANSWER a
Using his famed screwball, NY Giants pitcher Carl Hubbell created one of the more memorable All-Star moments in baseball history when he fanned future Cooperstown occupants Babe Ruth, Lou Gehrig, Jimmie Foxx, Al Simmons, and Joe Cronin in the 1934 game at the New York's Polo Grounds. Catcher Bill Dickey ended the streak with a single.

GAME 19

7. "He hurt this organization, I could care less about him.... maybe it will work in New York."

a. Art Howe
b. Bobby Cox
c. Bobby Clarke
d. Robert Kraft

GAME 19 Q6 ANSWER a
The early 1990s saw a New Jersey Nets clubhouse that was filled with egotistical, disrespectful players. Nothing epitomized this attitude better than these infamous words of Derrick Coleman. When asked his feelings about a teammate missing practice, Coleman's response was simply, "Whoop-de-damn-do."

GAME 39

7. In which stadium did the Titans play during their first year in Tennessee?

a. Vanderbilt Stadium
b. Liberty Bowl
c. Neyland Stadium
d. Finley Stadium

GAME 39 Q6 ANSWER a
Spurred by the Patrick Roy trade in December 1995, the Colorado Avalanche capped its first season in Denver by taking home the Stanley Cup. The former Quebec Nordiques were actually the number-one seed in the 1994-1995 NHL Playoffs, but were upset in the first round by the New York Rangers.

GAME 59

7. Which low-calorie soft drink featured Mike Tyson in a 1988 campaign?

a. Diet Sprite
b. Diet Coke
c. Diet 7-Up
d. Diet Pepsi

GAME 59 Q6 ANSWER b
In this clever ad, we see the sleeping tennis star, tossing and turning while muttering the classic lines he is known for on the court, "How can it be out! It can't be out!" But when taken inside the dream, we see Johnny Mac yapping at a bartender whose tap has run dry of Heineken. "It can't be out! You can't be serious!"

GAME 79

7. Which "Original Six" team holds the NHL season record for the most points?

a. Detroit Red Wings
b. Montreal Canadiens
c. Toronto Maple Leafs
d. Chicago Blackhawks

GAME 79 Q6 ANSWER d
As an indication of its stability, the Boston Bruins had only five general managers in its first seventy-seven years. They were Art Ross (1924–1954), Lynn Patrick (1955–1966), Hap Emms (1967–1968), Milt Schmidt (1968–1972), and Harry Sinden (1973–2001).

7. Which NY Giants announcer called baseball's famous "Shot Heard Round the World"?

a. Mel Allen

b. Russ Hodges

c. Red Barber

d. Ernie Harwell

GAME 2 Q6 ANSWER a
In one of the funniest instances of a host provoking an athlete, Jim Rome drew the ire of then-Saints quarterback Jim Everett by calling him "Chris"—the female tennis player with the same-sounding last name—on his ESPN2 talk show in 1994. Rome repeatedly used the name until Everett flipped over a table and knocked the host on his rear.

7. What was the "tasty" nickname of Kobe Bryant's basketball-playing father?

a. "Sugar Daddy"

b. "Tootsie Roll"

c. "Jelly Bean"

d. "Chocolate Thunder"

GAME 22 Q6 ANSWER a
When tennis player Taylor Dent won the 2002 Miller Lite Hall of Fame Championships in Newport, he joined his father, Phil, who won two singles titles during his career. The senior Dent made it to the finals of the 1974 Australian Open, only to lose to Jimmy Connors in 4 sets.

7. Who is the only player to win three straight NCAA Final Four MVP Awards?

a. Bill Russell

b. Bill Walton

c. Jerry Lucas

d. Lew Alcindor

GAME 42 Q6 ANSWER c
An oft-used set-up man before coming to the Tigers in 1984, Hernandez had far and away his best season that year, winning 9 games, converting 32 out of 33 saves, and compiling a 1.92 ERA.

7. Which quarterback threw for a record 274 yards in a Pro Bowl?

a. Peyton Manning

b. Joe Theismann

c. Dan Fouts

d. Drew Bledsoe

GAME 62 Q6 ANSWER d
In addition to his other scoring records, Wilt Chamberlain holds the individual scoring record for NBA All-Star contests with his 42-point output in the 1962 Game at St. Louis, which his East team lost 150–130 to the Western All-Stars. "The Stilt" also holds the career lifetime All-Star Game rebounding record with 197.

6. "Whoop-de-damn-do."

a. Derrick Coleman
b. Shawn Kemp
c. Kevin Garnett
d. Stephon Marbury

Knight was always good at riling up crowds, which is exactly what he did when he spoke these words during Senior Day ceremonies at Indiana University in 1994. "The General" succinctly summed up his attitude in a 1982 magazine article in which he said, "I fortunately have never worried about irritating people."

6. Which team won a Stanley Cup the year after its relocation?

a. Colorado Avalanche
b. Carolina Hurricanes
c. Phoenix Coyotes
d. Calgary Flames

Existing only for the 1969 season, the Seattle Pilots disappeared before anyone got to know them. Playing their games in Sick's Stadium, which was basically a minor league ballpark, the Pilots folded after only 677,000 fans showed up the entire season. They reinvented themselves the next year as the Milwaukee Brewers.

6. Which imported beer did John McEnroe recently push in a "dreamy" ad?

a. Beck's
b. Heineken
c. Foster's
d. Amstel Light

Larry Johnson appeared as "Grandmama" in the ad, making the point that Converse basketball shoes add so much to your game, even your grandmother could beat you when wearing them. LJ parlayed his character into appearances on the 1990's sitcom *Family Matters*.

6. Which team had only five general managers from 1924 to 2001?

a. Chicago Blackhawks
b. New York Rangers
c. Toronto Maple Leafs
d. Boston Bruins

The Red Wings unofficial mascot has been the octopus since a 1952 playoff game in which two fishermen brothers (and devoted fans) tossed one onto the ice. Back then, it took only eight victories to win the Stanley Cup—one win for each tentacle. After the Wings swept the Finals that year, the sea creature was there to stay.

GAME 2

8. Who called George Foreman's legendary knockout of Joe Frazier in 1973?

a. Curt Gowdy

b. Don Dunphy

c. Chuck Hull

d. Howard Cosell

GAME 2 Q7 ANSWER b

It was Russ Hodges who dramatically painted the vocal picture of Bobby Thomson's game-winning home run off Dodger hurler Ralph Branca in 1951. The shot sealed the National League title for the Giants as Hodges gleefully bellowed, "The Giants win the pennant! The Giants win the pennant! The Giants win the pennant!"

GAME 22

8. Who did Joe Frazier's son fight for the heavyweight championship?

a. Mike Tyson

b. Larry Holmes

c. Evander Holyfield

d. Tim Witherspoon

GAME 22 Q7 ANSWER c

In the '70s and early '80s, Joe "Jelly Bean" Bryant played for Philadelphia, San Diego, and Houston. Joe Bryant was a tall, wiry forward who, like his son, excelled at the one-on-one game. In addition to eight seasons with the NBA, Joe played professionally in Italy, where Kobe spent a good portion of his childhood.

GAME 42

8. Who is the only two-time winner of the Heisman Trophy?

a. Tony Dorsett

b. Jay Berwanger

c. Marcus Allen

d. Archie Griffin

GAME 42 Q7 ANSWER d

UCLA's Lew Alcindor (Kareem Abdul-Jabbar) won the awards in 1967, 1968, and 1969. Alcindor's finest year was in 1970, when he averaged 31 points per game and had an incredible field-goal percentage of 67.7.

GAME 62

8. Which NBA player holds the record for most All-Star Game appearances?

a. Jerry West

b. Karl Malone

c. Robert Parish

d. Kareem Abdul-Jabbar

GAME 62 Q7 ANSWER c

In the 1983 game, it was San Diego Chargers signal caller Dan Fouts who threw for the most yardage by any Pro Bowl quarterback. Fouts also holds the record for the most career Pro Bowl yardage (890 yards in six games), most career passing attempts, and most career completions.

5. "When my time on earth is gone, I want that they bury me upside down so my critics can kiss my ass."

a. Billy Martin
b. Terrell Owens
c. Bobby Knight
d. Knute Rockne

GAME 19 Q4 ANSWER a
Spoken near the end of his Hall of Fame career, the always-affable George Brett finally reached the 3,000-hit mark in 1992. He never quite made the 1,000-error plateau—he was more than 600 bungles short when he retired after the 1993 season. Brett entered the legendary ranks at Cooperstown in 1999.

---

5. The Seattle Pilots became which baseball franchise in 1970?

a. Kansas City Royals
b. San Diego Padres
c. Texas Rangers
d. Milwaukee Brewers

GAME 39 Q4 ANSWER b
In another instance of an owner reneging on his pledge to keep his team in its original city, Cleveland Browns owner Art Modell transferred the Browns to Baltimore after the 1995 season, citing a crumbling stadium and a city that couldn't fulfill his needs. The NFL, however, granted Cleveland rights to the Browns' name and colors.

---

5. Which NBA star dressed as an older woman in Converse's "Grandmama" ads?

a. Charles Barkley
b. Kevin Garnett
c. Chris Weber
d. Larry Johnson

GAME 59 Q4 ANSWER b
In 1958, Olympic gold medal decathalon winner Bob Richards was the first athlete to appear on the front of the cereal box. Prior to this, "The Breakfast of Champions" used images of athletes on the *back* of the boxes. The first was clean-cut Yankee great Lou Gehrig in 1934. "Babe" Didrikson Zaharias appeared the following year.

---

5. Which team's good luck charm is an octopus?

a. Detroit Red Wings
b. Chicago Blackhawks
c. Boston Bruins
d. Toronto Maple Leafs

GAME 79 Q4 ANSWER d
The revered Forum, which opened in 1924, featured an endless sea of Canadiens championship banners and nine retired jersey numbers. When the arena closed in 1996, a touching ceremony was held after the final game (a 4–1 Canadiens victory over the Dallas Stars). In it, Montreal greats solemnly passed a lit torch along the ice.

 Answers are in right-hand boxes on page 42.

9. Which college hoops commentator's trademark line is "It's awesome baby!"?

a. Dick Stockton
b. Billy Packer
c. Dick Vitale
d. Jim Nantz

Probably the most memorable boxing call of all time, Howard Cosell's "Down goes Frazier!" will live in infamy. Cosell had picked Foreman to dethrone reigning champion Frazier, but nobody expected it to come in the form of a second round TKO. Cosell repeated the phrase three times, and boxing has yet to see a more dramatic call.

9. Who are the only father-son coaches to win national college football championships?

a. The Bowdens
b. The Osbornes
c. The Tressels
d. The Slocums

While he never came close to mirroring father Joe's skill in the "sweet science," Marvis Frazier did get a shot at the title. In 1983, the son of Smokin' Joe met Larry Holmes in Las Vegas. By the middle of the first round, Holmes had pinned Marvis in the corner and delivered such a pummeling, the fight was stopped.

9. Which NY Islander was known as "the last piece to the puzzle"?

a. Denis Potvin
b. Bob Bourne
c. Clark Gillies
d. Butch Goring

Ohio State running back Archie Griffin won the award in 1974 and 1975. What made the double-win even more incredible was the group of outstanding players in contention, including Pittsburgh's Tony Dorsett. USC's Marcus Allen won the award in 1981; Jay Berwanger from the University of Chicago was the trophy's first recipient in 1935.

9. Which Major Leaguer appeared in fifteen All-Star Games and lost them all?

a. Brooks Robinson
b. George Brett
c. Carl Yastrzemski
d. Jim Palmer

Participating in eighteen All-Star Games over the course of his career, Kareem Abdul-Jabbar holds the record for most appearances. Surprisingly, Kareem never took home an All-Star MVP Award, although he does hold many offensive marks, including blocks in a game (6 in 1980), and several career records.

4. "If I stay healthy, I have a chance to collect 3,000 hits and 1,000 errors."

a. George Brett
b. Robin Yount
c. Rod Carew
d. Paul Molitor

GAME 19 Q3 ANSWER b
Yogi Berra is known for his famous musings, and this classic quote ranks high on the list. The master of stating the obvious in his own unique way, Berra is also the speaker of such gems as "Nobody goes there anymore, it's too crowded" and "A nickel isn't worth a dime today."

4. Who is known as "The most hated man in Cleveland"?

a. Al Lerner
b. Art Modell
c. Mark Shapiro
d. William Davidson

GAME 39 Q3 ANSWER c
Coming into existence in 1945, the Rochester Royals made an instant impact when they joined the NBA in 1949. The franchise moved to Cincinnati in 1957, but despite the presence of Oscar Robertson, received no banners. In 1972, the team moved again, this time to Kansas City. The team settled into its present home, Sacramento, in 1985.

4. Who was the first athlete to appear on the front of a Wheaties box?

a. Dizzy Dean
b. Bob Richards
c. "Babe" Didrikson Zaharias
d. Lou Gehrig

GAME 59 Q3 ANSWER d
This classic ad has a sweaty, battered Greene heading up the runaway when a young kid approaches him and asks, "Aren't you Mean Joe Greene?" After Greene blows him off, the boy offers the football star his Coke and then walks away dejectedly. Greene calls out, "Hey kid," and tosses his game-worn jersey to the child.

4. Which "Original Six" arena opened first?

a. The Boston Garden
b. Maple Leaf Gardens
c. Chicago Stadium
d. The Montreal Forum

GAME 79 Q3 ANSWER c
The taunting "19...40" chant by rival Islander fans came to a sudden end in 1994 as "The Messiah" (Mark Messier) led the long-suffering Rangers to victory after a fifty-four-year drought. After the Game 7 win over Vancouver, an elderly man was sighted holding up a sign in Madison Square Garden that read "Now I Can Die in Peace."

10. Who called the "Miracle on Ice" in the 1980 Winter Olympics?

a. Al Michaels

b. Verne Lundquist

c. Phil Esposito

d. Jim McKay

GAME 2 Q9 ANSWER c
College hoops wouldn't be the same without Dick Vitale. After a successful run of coaching, including a 78–30 record over five seasons at the University of Detroit, Vitale joined ESPN in the network's initial season. His loopy colloquialisms, such as "diaper dandy" and "it's awesome baby!" make viewing a pleasure.

---

10. In which sport did the father of NHL stars Pavel and Valeri Bure compete?

a. Discus

b. Wrestling

c. Weightlifting

d. Swimming

GAME 22 Q9 ANSWER c
Before guiding Ohio State to victory in the 2003 Fiesta Bowl, Jim Tressel had already won four Division I-AA titles with Youngstown State in the early 1990s. His father, Lee, a coaching legend at Baldwin-Wallace College, won the 1978 Division III title.

---

10. Who is the only thoroughbred to win five consecutive Horse of the Year Awards?

a. Seabiscuit

b. Forego

c. Kelso

d. Secretariat

GAME 42 Q9 ANSWER d
It was often said that acquiring Butch Goring from Los Angeles in 1980 gave the Isles everything necessary to win four consecutive championships, hence his nickname. In the '81 NHL playoffs, with 10 goals and 10 assists, Goring led the Islanders to their second straight Stanley Cup and was awarded the Conn Smythe Trophy.

---

10. Who scored the first hat trick in NHL All-Star Game history?

a. Wayne Gretzky

b. Gordie Howe

c. Ted Lindsay

d. Maurice Richard

GAME 62 Q9 ANSWER a
Orioles third baseman Brooks Robinson endured the long American League losing streaks of the '60s and '70s. Conversely, both Willie Mays and Hank Aaron played for seventeen National League winning teams.

---

3. "Always go to other people's funerals; otherwise they won't come to yours."

a. Ralph Kiner
b. Yogi Berra
c. Jack Buck
d. Harry Caray

GAME 19 Q2 ANSWER d
One of the most amusing faux pas in football history was uttered by Notre Dame graduate Joe Theismann when he confused Albert Einstein with some guy named Norman. Theismann's bomb came during one of his mid-1990's NFL telecasts when another announcer called one of the onfield players "a genius."

3. The Rochester Royals are ancestors of which current NBA team?

a. Milwaukee Bucks
b. Houston Rockets
c. Sacramento Kings
d. Dallas Mavericks

GAME 39 Q2 ANSWER b
Beginning as the Boston Red Stockings in the 1870s, the franchise later became the Beaneaters to eliminate confusion with the Cincinnati team. After briefly being known as the Doves in the early 1900s, the team became the Braves. The Braves relocated to Milwaukee in 1953, and to Atlanta in 1966.

3. Which beverage did "Mean" Joe Greene pitch in his 1979 "jersey toss" commercial?

a. 7-Up
b. Pepsi
c. Gatorade
d. Coke

GAME 59 Q2 ANSWER b
Playing for the grand prize of a Big Mac, Jordan and Larry Bird try to one-up each other on the basketball court in this commercial. They eventually get ridiculous with the "off-the-expressway, over-the-river, through-the-window, nothing-but-net" shots, but as Madison Avenue knows, any ad that includes "His Airness" works.

3. Prior to 1994, what was the last year the New York Rangers won the Stanley Cup?

a. 1936
b. 1938
c. 1940
d. 1942

GAME 79 Q2 ANSWER c
With twenty-three Stanley Cups, the Montreal Canadiens are hockey's version of the New York Yankees. The Toronto Maple Leafs rank a distant second, having acquired the Holy Grail thirteen times. The Leafs earned their last victory in 1967.

11. Who called Willis Reed's comeback game during the 1970 NBA Finals?

a. Johnny Most

b. Marv Albert

c. Bill Raftery

d. Kevin Loughery

In an upset of gargantuan proportions, the United States defeated the Soviet Union in a semi-final hockey game at the 1980 Winter Olympics. What many people remember best about that thrilling moment in Lake Placid is Al Michaels' proclamation of the shocker. "Do you believe in miracles? Yes!"

---

11. In which Olympic sport did the father of tennis star Andre Agassi compete?

a. Wrestling

b. Boxing

c. Pole Vault

d. Long Jump

Vladimir Bure was a world-class swimmer who won four medals while competing for the Soviet Union in the 1968, 1972, and 1976 Summer Olympics. Later, he coached swimming at the University of British Columbia.

---

11. Who is the only pitcher to win MVP, Rookie of the Year, and Cy Young Awards?

a. Roger Clemens

b. Dwight Gooden

c. Don Newcombe

d. Steve Carlton

One of the best distance horses ever, Kelso was awarded Horse of the Year honors (the equine version of an MVP award) from 1960 to 1964. Over his sixty-three-race career, Kelso wound up in the winner's circle thirty-nine times, earning almost $2 million in an era of minimal purses.

---

11. Who was the first baseball player to win the All-Star and league MVPs in the same year?

a. Hank Aaron

b. Maury Wills

c. Mickey Mantle

d. Willie Mays

Playing for the defending Stanley Cup Champion Red Wings, forward Ted Lindsay netted the first All-Star hat trick in a 7–1 route. Lindsay, who also won the 1950 Art Ross Trophy for leading the NHL in scoring, would go on to win four Stanley Cups and briefly serve as Detroit's general manager in the late 1970s.

GAME 19

2. "Nobody in football should be called a genius. A genius is a guy like Norman Einstein."

a. Paul McGuire

b. John Madden

c. Terry Bradshaw

d. Joe Theismann

GAME 19 Q1 ANSWER b
Coach Jim Mora uttered these words after a particularly poor 1996 effort with New Orleans. His post-game press-conference tirades—regularly peppered with expressions like "holy crap," "absolutely pitiful," and his trademark "in my opinion, that sucked"—were often hilarious and enjoyed by fans and media alike.

GAME 39

2. What was the original hometown of the Braves baseball franchise?

a. Baltimore

b. Boston

c. Milwaukee

d. Detroit

GAME 39 Q1 ANSWER a
In the early 1990s, Minnesota owners George and Gordon Gund decided to buy the NHL's newest expansion team—the San Jose Sharks. They therefore sold their hockey team, the Stars, to Norman Green, who pledged not to move the team. A mere two years later, after the 1992-1993 season, the Stars packed their sticks and left for Dallas.

GAME 59

2. Who played horse with Michael Jordan in the famous 1993 McDonald's commercial?

a. Charles Barkley

b. Larry Bird

c. Magic Johnson

d. Wilt Chamberlain

GAME 59 Q1 ANSWER c
Looking for a high-profile pitchman, Pfizer recruited Rafael Palmeiro to promote its drug for erectile dysfunction. The Cuban-born player's tagline was, "I take batting practice, I take infield practice, I take Viagra."

GAME 79

2. After Montreal, which "Original Six" franchise has won the most Stanley Cups?

a. Boston Bruins

b. Chicago Blackhawks

c. Toronto Maple Leafs

d. Detroit Red Wings

GAME 79 Q1 ANSWER b
The Flyers and five other teams joined the NHL in 1967 during its first expansion wave. The new franchises joined the "Original Six," which included the Montreal Canadiens, Toronto Maple Leafs, Boston Bruins, Detroit Red Wings, Chicago Blackhawks, and the New York Rangers.

GAME 2	**12.** Which NFL announcer's catch phrase was "Start blow-drying Teddy Koppel's hair"? a. Dan Fouts b. Don Meredith c. Boomer Esiason d. Dennis Miller	**GAME 2 Q11 ANSWER b** In a moment befitting a Hollywood script, "Here comes Willis!" was the phrase uttered by Marv Albert as Willis Reed hobbled onto the court before Game 7 of the 1970 NBA Finals between the NY Knicks and the LA Lakers. Still in pain from an injury sustained in Game 5, Reed, nevertheless, helped the Knicks win the series.
GAME 22	**12.** For which event did Tom Morris, Sr. and Jr. win eight of the first twelve? a. The Boston Marathon b. The BPPA All-Star Bowling Tournament c. The Hambletonian d. The British Open	**GAME 22 Q11 ANSWER b** Iranian-born Mike Agassi was a Golden Gloves boxing champion who represented his country at the 1948 and 1952 Olympic Games. After moving to the United States, the senior Agassi, who always had an interest in tennis, soon became a pro at the Tropicana Hotel in Las Vegas.
GAME 42	**12.** For whom is the NBA's MVP Trophy named? a. James Naismith b. Luther H. Gulick c. Ralph Morgan d. Maurice Podoloff	**GAME 42 Q11 ANSWER c** Taking the National League Rookie of the Year in 1949, Brooklyn's Don Newcombe finished the hat trick in 1956 when he captured both the National League MVP and Cy Young Awards after a stellar campaign in which he won 27 games and struck out 219 batters.
GAME 62	**12.** Since it began in 1951, what was the only year the NBA All-Star Game was *not* played? a. 1959 b. 1968 c. 1971 d. 1999	**GAME 62 Q11 ANSWER b** Maury Wills won the initial All-Star Game MVP award in 1962, and then followed it up with the National League MVP later that year. Wills had a remarkable '62 season. He stole 104 bases, got over 200 hits, batted .299 for the LA Dodgers, and topped it off with a Gold Glove Award.

GAME 19	1. "We couldn't do diddley-poo offensively, we couldn't make a first down . . . we sucked." a. Steve Mariucci b. Jim Mora c. Barry Switzer d. Jerry Glanville	The answer to this question is on: **page 50,** **top frame,** **right side.**
GAME 39	1. Who bought the Minnesota North Stars in the early '90s? a. Norman Green b. Tom Hicks c. George Gund d. Drayton McLayne	The answer to this question is on: **page 50,** **second frame,** **right side.**
GAME 59	1. Which of the following Major Leaguers appeared in a Viagra commercial? a. Roger Clemens b. Wade Boggs c. Rafael Palmeiro d. Matt Williams	The answer to this question is on: **page 50,** **third frame,** **right side.**
GAME 79	1. Which of the following teams is not an "Original Six" franchise? a. Chicago Blackhawks b. Philadelphia Flyers c. Detroit Red Wings d. Boston Bruins	The answer to this question is on: **page 50,** **bottom frame,** **right side.**

GAME 3

"Awards and Trophies"

How Well Do You Know Sports Hardware?

*Turn to page 55
for the first question.*

Turn to page 55
for the first question.

GAME 2 Q12 ANSWER d
During his short and controversial tenure as a *Monday Night Football* announcer, comedian Dennis Miller often signified the end of a game by signaling the crew to get the *Nightline* host ready for the set. Throughout his two seasons in the booth, Miller amused some and confused most with his satirical barbs.

GAME 23

"Singing Jocks"

Remember These Crooning Athletes?

*Turn to page 55
for the first question.*

Turn to page 55
for the first question.

GAME 22 Q12 ANSWER d
From 1861 through 1872, the father-son Morris duo captured eight British Opens. The elder Morris, who helped set up the Open, lost the inaugural 1860 match, but went on to capture titles in 1861, 1862, 1864, and 1867. Morris, Jr. won four Claret Jugs consecutively from 1868 to 1872 (the Open wasn't held in 1871).

GAME 43

"Super Streaks"

Whether for a Week, Month, or Years, These Athletes Were "In the Zone"

*Turn to page 55
for the first question.*

Turn to page 55
for the first question.

GAME 42 Q12 ANSWER d
Rarely called the Maurice Podoloff Trophy, the award is named for the man who worked out the 1949 merger between the Basketball Association of America and the National Basketball League. The Yale-educated, Russian-born lawyer also served as the NBA's first commissioner, and helped implement the 24-second clock.

GAME 63

"Foreign Stars"

International Athletes Who Made Their Presence Felt

*Turn to page 55
for the first question.*

Turn to page 55
for the first question.

GAME 62 Q12 ANSWER d
Due to a lockout, which resulted in the shortening of the 1998-1999 NBA schedule to fifty games, that year's All-Star Game was cancelled. The condensed slate of games began in early February, right around the time the league's All-Star Game would have normally been held, and ended in early May, leaving no time for the annual contest.

GAME 19

"Who Said It"?

Remember Who Uttered These Memorable Words?

Turn to page 52 for the first question.

GAME 18 Q12 ANSWER c

Marvin Webster, a talented center who blocked everything that came his way, played a few seasons with the Nuggets and Sonics before bolting to the Knicks as a free agent in 1978. He ranks third on the Knicks all-time blocks list with 542, just 1 behind second-place occupant Bill Cartwright.

GAME 39

"Moving Franchises"

Teams that Change Cities Like We Change Socks

Turn to page 52 for the first question.

GAME 38 Q12 ANSWER b

A star at the University of Detroit in the early 1960s, DeBusschere decided to play both pro baseball and basketball, and pitched for the Chicago White Sox from 1962 to 1965. But DeBusschere's hoop skills were always superior, and he eventually played with the Knicks, winning two titles and cementing his Hall of Fame credentials.

GAME 59

"Sell it, Baby!"

Commercials and Your Favorite Sports Stars

Turn to page 52 for the first question.

GAME 58 Q12 ANSWER b

German track star Luz Long gave the American hero jumping advice, openly congratulated him at the medals ceremony, and walked with him past the Fuhrer's box. Owens said, "You could melt down all these medals, and they wouldn't be plating for the 24-karat friendship I felt for Luz Long." Long was killed in World War II.

GAME 79

"The Original Six"

Are You in Tune with the NHL's Original Franchises?

Turn to page 52 for the first question.

GAME 78 Q12 ANSWER d

At the 2000 Olympics in Sydney, Australia, little-known American wrestler Rulon Gardner dethroned living legend Alexander Karelim to take the gold in Greco-Roman's heavyweight division. Karelin had lost only one match in 1987, and had not been scored against in the ten years prior to Gardener's stunning 1–0 victory.

GAME 3	**1. Which NHL position player is eligible to receive the Vezina Trophy?** a. Defenseman b. Goaltender c. Right wing d. Center	The answer to this question is on: **page 57, top frame, right side.**
GAME 23	**1. Which NHL star sang lead vocal on the "Hockey Sock Rock"?** a. Wayne Gretzky b. Bobby Orr c. Phil Esposito d. Mario Lemieux	The answer to this question is on: **page 57, second frame, right side.**
GAME 43	**1. Whose consecutive-games-played streak did Lou Gehrig break?** a. Everett Scott b. Ty Cobb c. Honus Wagner d. Tris Speaker	The answer to this question is on: **page 57, third frame, right side.**
GAME 63	**1. Which foreign-born NFL kicker holds the all-time record for points scored?** a. Jan Stenerud b. Gary Anderson c. Pete Stoyanovich d. Morten Andersen	The answer to this question is on: **page 57, bottom frame, right side.**

12. "The Human Eraser"

a. Jack Sikma
b. Kevin Duckworth
c. Marvin Webster
d. Mark Eaton

GAME 18 Q11 ANSWER d
A pure goal scorer, Pavel Bure had four seasons in which he scored at least 58 goals. His best was in 1993-1994, when he led the NHL with 60 lamp-lighters. That season he also had 47 assists, and led the overmatched Vancouver Canucks to Game 7 of the Stanley Cup Finals, which they ultimately lost to the New York Rangers.

12. Which early '60s White Sox pitcher went on to win two NBA Championships?

a. Gail Goodrich
b. Dave DeBusschere
c. Gary Peters
d. Bill Sharman

GAME 38 Q11 ANSWER d
Excelling in both hockey and baseball in his native Massachusetts, Tom Glavine was selected by the Los Angeles Kings in the fourth round of the 1984 NHL Entry Draft. Strangely, the Kings drafted the top lefty ahead of sure-bet hockey Hall of Famer, Luc Robitaille, who was selected in the ninth round of the same draft.

12. Which German athlete befriended Jesse Owens at the 1936 Summer Games in Berlin?

a. Konrad Frey
b. Luz Long
c. Alfred Schwarzmann
d. Matthias Volz

GAME 58 Q11 ANSWER c
During the 1920 Summer Games in Antwerp, Belgium, American sportsman Edward Eagan won the gold medal in boxing as a light heavyweight. Twelve years later, he won a second gold medal at the Winter Games in Lake Placid, New York, as a member of the US four-man bobsled team.

12. Which American wrestler upset the dominant Alexander Karelin at the 2000 Olympics?

a. Kendall Cross
b. Kurt Angle
c. Kenny Monday
d. Rulon Gardner

GAME 78 Q11 ANSWER b
With a team batting average of .248, the weak-hitting 1988 Dodgers faced the powerful Oakland A's with a lineup that included Alfredo Griffin (.199), Franklin Stubbs (.223), Mike Davis (.196), and Jeff Hamilton (.236). Excellent pitching and a miracle home run by the injured Kirk Gibson were key in helping LA win the title.

2. The champion of which event receives the Borg Warner Trophy?

a. The Masters

b. The French Open

c. The Indy 500

d. The British Open

GAME 3 Q1 ANSWER b
Named after legendary goaltender Georges Vezina, the award is presented annually to the league's top goalie. Nicknamed "The Chicoutimi Cucumber," Vezina was famous for his ability to remain cool under fire.

2. Which NFL coach once sang "Groovin'" in a Tostitos commercial?

a. Bill Parcells

b. Mike Ditka

c. George Seifert

d. Mike Shanahan

GAME 23 Q1 ANSWER c
New York Rangers Greatest Hits, put out by several members of the team in the early 1980s, included a number of forgettable athlete anthems, including "Hockey Sock Rock." The tune featured some dreadful vocals by Hall of Famer Phil Esposito and Ranger teammates Ron Duguay, John Davidson, and Dave Maloney.

2. Which NBA player holds the record for scoring 30+ points in consecutive games?

a. Michael Jordan

b. Oscar Robertson

c. Rick Barry

d. Wilt Chamberlain

GAME 43 Q1 ANSWER a
Most baseball fans know that in 1995, Cal Ripkin, Jr. passed Lou Gehrig's consecutive-games record of 2,130 (and didn't stop until his total reached 2,632). In 1925, Gehrig had broken the 1,307 record of shortstop Everett Scott, who played with the Red Sox and Yankees for most of his career.

2. Who was the first Australian-born baseball player to win a World Series?

a. Graeme Lloyd

b. Mark Hutton

c. Dave Nilsson

d. Craig Shipley

GAME 63 Q1 ANSWER b
Still kicking in 2002 at the age of 43, kicker Gary Anderson is the league's all-time leader in points scored, with 2,223 to date. The South African-born Anderson began his career in 1982 with the Pittsburgh Steelers, and completed his twenty-first season with the Minnesota Vikings.

11. "The Russian Rocket"

a. Alexei Yashin
b. Sergei Fedorov
c. Alexander Mogilny
d. Pavel Bure

GAME 18 Q10 ANSWER b
A temperamental Red Sox hurler, Dennis Boyd can boast one of the best nicknames in baseball history. Growing up in Mississippi, Boyd would spend long days in the hot southern sun perfecting his craft. His refreshment of choice was always beer, or as it was known in Boyd's hometown, oil.

11. Which Cooperstown-bound pitcher did the LA Kings draft in 1984?

a. Greg Maddux
b. Randy Johnson
c. Curt Schilling
d. Tom Glavine

GAME 38 Q10 ANSWER a
After finishing his college football career at Florida State, Deion Sanders jumped sports lines and joined the New York Yankees, playing in 14 games. During a 1990 game after striking out, Sanders shook hands with his teammates in the dugout and left—in the middle of the game—to join the Falcons.

11. Who is the only person to win Olympic medals in both Summer and Winter Games?

a. Jim Thorpe
b. "Babe" Didrikson
c. Edward Eagan
d. Ulrich Salchow

GAME 58 Q10 ANSWER a
Thirty-six years after winning the gold as an Olympic boxer, Muhammad Ali was given the honor of lighting the 1996 Olympic flame in Atlanta. Just twelve years earlier, Ali had run in the 1984 Los Angeles Olympics torch relay; but in 1996, Parkinson's disease had taken its toll, and the boxer trembled as he ignited the torch.

11. Which World Series team started Alfredo Griffin and his .199 average at shortstop?

a. Toronto Blue Jays
b. Los Angeles Dodgers
c. Kansas City Royals
d. Philadelphia Phillies

GAME 78 Q10 ANSWER c
In 1984, the NBA began its current playoff seeding format, and for ten years, no eighth-seeded team had ever upended a number-one team. But in 1994, the Denver Nuggets, led by Dikembe Mutombo, stunned the Seattle Sonics in a best-of-five series after decisively losing the first two games.

GAME 3

3. Who is the only person to have won the Heisman Trophy twice?

a. Archie Griffin
b. O.J. Simpson
c. Herschel Walker
d. George Rogers

GAME 3 Q2 ANSWER c
Originally awarded in 1936 by the Borg Warner Automobile Company, this trophy goes to the Indianapolis 500 champion. Due to its height of over 51 inches and its weight of over 80 pounds, the original trophy permanently resides in the Indy Speedway Hall of Fame. But each year, the winner of the race gets a 14-inch-high replica.

GAME 23

3. Which NFL team recorded "The Super Bowl Shuffle"?

a. New York Giants
b. Chicago Bears
c. San Francisco 49ers
d. Dallas Cowboys

GAME 23 Q2 ANSWER a
While guiding the New York Jets in 1998, Bill Parcells appeared in the commercial, singing both "Groovin'" and a quick version of "Kumbaya." Parcells is not the only NFL coach to sing in a commercial. In a 1995 Visa ad, George Seifert of the 49ers tried to croon "Blame it on the Bossa Nova."

GAME 43

3. Which boxing heavyweight champ had a streak of twenty-five successful title defenses?

a. John L. Sullivan
b. Joe Louis
c. Rocky Marciano
d. Tommy Burns

GAME 43 Q2 ANSWER d
Dropping in at least 30 points in a mind-boggling 65 consecutive games in the 1961-1962 season, Wilt Chamberlain holds the record. He also went 126 straight games scoring 20+ points, 14 consecutive games scoring 40+ points, and most impressive of all, 7 straight contests scoring 50 points or more.

GAME 63

3. Korean-born hockey player Jim Paek won a Stanley Cup with which NHL team?

a. Montreal Canadiens
b. Calgary Flames
c. Pittsburgh Penguins
d. New Jersey Devils

GAME 63 Q2 ANSWER a
After an August 1996 trade with the Milwaukee Brewers, pitcher Graeme Lloyd became a Yankee. Later that year, he became the first native from "Down Under" to play in a World Series game and take home a ring. Craig Shipley of the Dodgers was the first Australian to play in the Major Leagues when he debuted in 1986.

10. "Oil Can"

a. Al Nipper
b. Dennis Boyd
c. Floyd Youmans
d. Dennis Lamp

GAME 18 Q9 ANSWER a
One of the best welterweights to step into the ring, Roberto Duran threw punches that were so strong, it was said that he once punched out a horse back in his native Panama. Duran may be best known for his "No Mas" (no more) match, in which he quit after taking a pounding from Sugar Ray Leonard. He retired from boxing at age 50.

10. What was the first Major League team for which Deion Sanders played?

a. New York Yankees
b. Cincinnati Reds
c. San Francisco Giants
d. Atlanta Braves

GAME 38 Q9 ANSWER b
Chris Drury's Little League team from Trumbull, Connecticut made it all the way to Williamsport in 1989, when the future hockey hero pitched his team to victory over Taiwan. That success was a harbinger of things to come, as he won a collegiate National Championship with Boston University in 1995, and the Stanley Cup with Colorado in 2001.

10. Who lit the Olympic flame, signifying the beginning of the 1996 Summer Games?

a. Muhammad Ali
b. Bill Clinton
c. Dexter King
d. Ted Turner

GAME 58 Q9 ANSWER c
An American highlight at the 1992 Barcelona Games was the appearance of professionals on the US basketball squad. The "Dream Team," which included NBA stars like Michael Jordan, Magic Johnson, and Larry Bird, romped to a gold medal, defeating Croatia in the final game 117–85.

10. Which eighth-seeded team was the first to knock off a number-one seed in the NBA playoffs?

a. New York Knicks
b. Houston Rockets
c. Denver Nuggets
d. Portland Trailblazers

GAME 78 Q9 ANSWER d
What most people don't realize is that the "Miracle on Ice" was a semifinal game in which the US team shocked the world by knocking off the seemingly unbeatable Soviet Union team 4–3. The anticlimactic gold medal game was held two days later, when the Americans took out Finland 4–2.

GAME 3

4. Which sport awards the Little Brown Jug?

a. Bowling

b. Lacrosse

c. Track and Field

d. Harness Racing

GAME 3 Q3 ANSWER a

Called "the greatest player that I have ever coached" by Ohio State football coach Woody Hayes, Archie Griffin was a powerful running back known for his ability to break multiple tackles on a single play. Winning the award in his junior and senior years, Griffin rushed for over 100 yards in a remarkable string of 31 consecutive games.

GAME 23

4. What was the title of the song recorded by the 1986 New York Mets?

a. "World Series Boogaloo"

b. "Mets Mack Down"

c. "Gettin' Funky in Flushing"

d. "Get Metsmerized"

GAME 23 Q3 ANSWER b

The dominating 1985 Bears took to the recording studio and put together the "Super Bowl Shuffle." The January 1986 release of the song (and accompanying video) coincided with the Super Bowl XX matchup between the Bears and the New England Patriots. Chicago won the 46–10 contest easily, thereby justifying the song.

GAME 43

4. Which NFL player had an 18-game touchdown-scoring streak?

a. Gale Sayers

b. Emmitt Smith

c. Lenny Moore

d. Frank Gifford

GAME 43 Q3 ANSWER b

After winning the title from James J. Braddock in 1937, Joe Louis went on to successfully defend his title a record twenty-five straight times, before retiring as champion in 1948. "The Brown Bomber" had one more championship fight after briefly coming out of retirement in 1950, but lost in a 15-round decision to Ezzard Charles.

GAME 63

4. Who was the first hockey player to appear on a Swedish postage stamp?

a. Peter Forsberg

b. Borje Salming

c. Anders Kallur

d. Wayne Gretzky

GAME 63 Q3 ANSWER c

In addition to being the first Korean player ever to appear in an NHL game, Jim Paek also holds the distinction of becoming the first Korean native ever to win a Stanley Cup, which he did twice with the Pittsburgh Penguins in 1991 and 1992.

9. "Hands of Stone"

a. Roberto Duran
b. Alexis Arguello
c. Marvin Hagler
d. Archie Moore

GAME 18 Q8 ANSWER b
A defensive back for the Raiders and Oilers, Jack Tatum delivered a brutal (yet legal) hit to Patriots receiver Daryl Stingley during a 1978 *exhibition* game that left the wide out paralyzed. After the game, most members of both teams visited Stingley in the hospital, with the most notable exception being "The Assassin" himself.

---

9. Who is the only player to win both a Stanley Cup and a Little League World Series?

a. Chris Chelios
b. Chris Drury
c. Scott Young
d. Tom Barrasso

GAME 38 Q8 ANSWER a
Playing for three AFL teams during his eight-year football career, the 315-pound 6'9" Ernie "Big Cat" Ladd was the largest player in the league at the time. Ladd was always at odds with AFL officials, whether it was over salary or his desire to wear a beard. After football, he became a professional wrestler.

---

9. Which year saw the first appearance of the basketball "Dream Team"?

a. 1984
b. 1988
c. 1992
d. 1996

GAME 58 Q8 ANSWER d
During the 1904 Summer Games in St. Louis, American distance runner Fred Lorz began to experience cramps from the stifling heat. He jumped into a car and drove to the stadium, where he got out and finished the race. After accepting congratulations from President Roosevelt, Lorz admitted his act, and was promptly suspended.

---

9. Which team did the United States defeat to win the 1980 Olympic Hockey gold medal?

a. Sweden
b. Soviet Union
c. Czechoslovakia
d. Finland

GAME 78 Q8 ANSWER b
In his first full year on the PGA Tour, little known Jack Fleck defeated the legendary Ben Hogan after coming back from a 9-stroke deficit. After his "big" win, Fleck appeared on the *Today* show, met President Eisenhower at the White House, and attended baseball games as a guest of Joe DiMaggio.

GAME 3

5. Which league offers the Grey Cup as its championship trophy?

a. Women's National Basketball Association

b. Canadian Football League

c. Arena Football League

d. International League

GAME 3 Q4 ANSWER d

The initial Little Brown Jug was run at the Delaware County Fairgrounds in Ohio. In 1956, the race became the third and final leg of harness racing's Pacing Triple Crown, along with the Cane Pace and the Messenger Stakes.

GAME 23

5. Which NBA star released a rap song titled "What's Up Doc?"

a. Allen Iverson

b. Chris Webber

c. Steve Francis

d. Shaquille O'Neal

GAME 23 Q4 ANSWER d

Yes, it's true. The New York Mets totally ripped off the Chicago Bears by releasing a mid-1986 song titled, "Get Metsmerized." Like the Bears, the Mets won their league's championship that year, but unlike the Chicago recording, the lyrics of "Get Metsmerized" were totally lame.

GAME 43

5. Who holds the NHL record for consecutive complete games by a goaltender?

a. Glenn Hall

b. Gump Worsley

c. Terry Sawchuk

d. Bill Durnan

GAME 43 Q4 ANSWER c

In 18 consecutive contests from 1963 to 1965, Baltimore Colts flanker/running back Lenny Moore took the ball in for a touchdown. Moore has often said that he was unaware that his streak even existed; it was only later, when statistics came into focus, that his achievement was noticed. Moore received his invitation to Canton in 1975.

GAME 63

5. In which country was top golfer Vijay Singh born?

a. India

b. Western Samoa

c. Pakistan

d. Fiji

GAME 63 Q4 ANSWER a

After scoring the medal-clinching goal on a penalty shot in the 1994 Winter Olympics, Peter Forsberg was elevated to icon status in Sweden. The image of that goal, which gave the Nordic nation its first hockey gold medal, was depicted on a national stamp, making "Foppa" the first hockey player to appear on Swedish postage.

8. "The Assassin"

a. Ray Nitschke

b. Jack Tatum

c. Dick Butkus

d. Lyle Alzado

GAME 18 Q7 ANSWER d
One of the most feared enforcers in recent NHL history, Stu Grimson earned his ghoulish nickname after pummeling countless foes into oblivion. He once accrued 397 penalty minutes over 72 games while playing in the IHL. In a career spanning over fourteen years, Grimson has never scored more than 3 goals in a season.

---

8. Football player/wrestler Ernie Ladd did *not* play on which of the following teams?

a. New York Jets

b. San Diego Chargers

c. Kansas City Chiefs

d. Houston Oilers

GAME 38 Q7 ANSWER b
An all-around athlete, Zaharias was given the nickname "Babe" because she hit home runs that were as long as Mr. Ruth's. Her many accomplishments included winning two gold and one silver medal at the 1932 Summer Olympics. After taking up golf at the age of 24, Zaharias won three US Open titles and was a founding member of the LPGA.

---

8. Which athlete fraudulently completed the Olympic Marathon in 1904?

a. Thomas Hicks

b. Felix Carvajal

c. Michael Spring

d. Fred Lorz

GAME 58 Q7 ANSWER c
During the final week of the 1972 Summer Games in Munich, Germany, eight Arab terrorists stormed into the complex that housed Israeli athletes, killing two and holding nine more captive. The next day, all nine were killed in a shootout between the terrorists and West German police at a military airport.

---

8. Which golfer defeated Ben Hogan in a playoff to take the 1955 US Open?

a. Ed Furgol

b. Jack Fleck

c. Cary Middlecoff

d. Ed Oliver

GAME 78 Q7 ANSWER b
By upsetting the number-one seeded Georgetown team in the 1985 NCAA Championship Game, Villanova's eighth-seeded Wildcats became the lowest ranked team to win the national title. Known for its close finishes, Villanova dethroned the defending champs by a 66–64 margin.

---

6. Besides Randy Johnson, which pitcher has won four consecutive Cy Young Awards?

a. Jim Palmer

b. Greg Maddux

c. Roger Clemens

d. Sandy Koufax

GAME 3 Q5 ANSWER b
Originally an amateur award intended for presentation to the Canadian senior hockey champions, the cup was donated in 1909 by Lord Albert Earl Grey, Governor General of Canada, and was earmarked for the top senior amateur football team. Since 1954, only teams in the Canadian Football League have competed for the prized bowl.

6. Which former Major Leaguer's son is a country music star?

a. Tug McGraw

b. Bobby Brooks

c. Lou Jackson

d. Bud Black

GAME 23 Q5 ANSWER d
Collaborating with the popular early '90s hip-hop group the Fu Schnickens, Shaquille O'Neal jumped in to rap a verse or two in "What's Up Doc (Can We Rock)?" Not too bad as far as athlete jams go, especially when Shaq belts out, "Forget Tony Danza, I'm the boss."

6. Which Major League pitcher has lost the most consecutive games?

a. Roger Craig

b. Mike Maroth

c. Anthony Young

d. Cliff Curtis

GAME 43 Q5 ANSWER a
In a streak that spanned seven years, and with two different teams, goaltender Glenn Hall started and finished an astonishing 502 consecutive games, from the beginning of the 1955-1956 season through November of 1962. A cranky back forced him to leave his 503rd straight game in the first period.

6. Which former NFL player was known as "The Throwin' Samoan"?

a. Esera Tuaolo

b. Jack Thompson

c. Mark Tuinei

d. Nuu Faaola

GAME 63 Q5 ANSWER d
Making his name on the international golf circuit before enjoying success in America, Fijian Vijay Singh has won tournaments in over ten nations. He is consistently among the top PGA money winners, and is always a contender, no matter which tournament he enters.

GAME 18

7. "The Grim Reaper"

a. Dave Schultz
b. Dave Williams
c. Bob Probert
d. Stu Grimson

GAME 18 Q6 ANSWER c
Known for his falling-down pitch delivery and uncanny ability to throw outside the strike zone, Major Leaguer Mitch Williams was appropriately dubbed "Wild Thing." Living up to his nickname, Williams is the only pitcher with over 250 career innings who allowed more walks than hits—issuing 544 walks and 537 hits in 691 innings.

GAME 38

7. What was "Babe" Didrikson Zaharias's real first name?

a. Margaret
b. Mildred
c. Catherine
d. Ruth

GAME 38 Q6 ANSWER b
Prior to his baseball career, Brian Jordan went through a football phase so productive that many were surprised when he jumped to baseball. Selected in the 1989 NFL Draft by Buffalo, Jordan was released and quickly snapped up by Atlanta, where he earned a 1992 Pro Bowl invitation. Jordan moved to baseball later that year.

GAME 58

7. Which city's Olympics were marred by terrorist violence?

a. Helsinki
b. Moscow
c. Munich
d. Sapporo

GAME 58 Q6 ANSWER c
Before the 1968 Games in Mexico City, the long-jump world record was 27 feet, 4.75 inches. American Bob Beamon set a new world record at 29 feet, 2.5 inches. Beamon's mark stood for twenty-three years until countryman Mike Powell became the new record holder in 1991 with a jump of 29 feet, 4.5 inches.

GAME 78

7. What was the lowest-seeded team to win an NCAA basketball tournament?

a. North Carolina State
b. Villanova
c. Marquette
d. Loyola (Illinois)

GAME 78 Q6 ANSWER c
The upstart 1987 Twins rocked their way to the World Series by first defeating the powerful Detroit Tigers in the ALCS, and then dethroning the favored Cardinals to capture the franchise's first crown in Minnesota. The Twins won only 85 regular season games, the lowest victory total for a World Series titlist.

7. The Stanley Cup was found at the bottom of which super-star's pool?

a. Mario Lemieux

b. Wayne Gretzky

c. Peter Forsberg

d. Mike Modano

GAME 3 Q6 ANSWER b
By winning the National League Cy Young Award in 2002, Randy Johnson became the second pitcher to receive the award for four straight seasons. He joined Greg Maddux, who took home the trophy from 1992 to 1995. Roger Clemens has been a six-time winner, but has never taken home the hardware more than two years in a row.

7. Hip-hop star Master P played briefly for which NBA team?

a. Cleveland Cavaliers

b. Denver Nuggets

c. Los Angeles Clippers

d. Charlotte Hornets

GAME 23 Q6 ANSWER a
At age 11, country singer Tim McGraw discovered he was the son of baseball legend Frank Edwin "Tug" McGraw. A colorful star pitcher for the Mets and Phillies, Tug coined the phrase "You Gotta Believe" with the Mets during their improbable pennant run in 1973. He spent nineteen seasons in the majors.

7. Which NCAA football powerhouse recorded the most consecutive winning seasons?

a. Nebraska

b. Notre Dame

c. Alabama

d. Texas A&M

GAME 43 Q6 ANSWER c
Beating Cliff Curtis's then-record of 23 consecutive losses might have seemed impossible, but enter Anthony Young. Beginning the 1992 season, Young won his first two starts, and then proceeded to lose every decision from May 28th of that year to June 24th of the *following* year.

7. Who was the first Czech player to be taken first overall in the NHL Entry Draft?

a. Petr Nedved

b. Jaromir Jagr

c. Roman Hamrlik

d. Radek Bonk

GAME 63 Q6 ANSWER b
Going down as one of the best quarterbacks in Washington State University history, Jack "The Throwin' Samoan" Thompson set many Cougar standards during his Pullman tenure in the late '70s. Taken third overall by Cincinnati in the 1979 NFL Draft, Thompson fared much better in college than he did in the NFL.

GAME 18

6. "Wild Thing"

a. Bruce Sutter
b. Rod Beck
c. Mitch Williams
d. Billy Wagner

GAME 18 Q5 ANSWER c
The sixth man on the Detroit Pistons championship squads of '89 and '90, Vinnie Johnson was called "The Microwave" because he could come off the bench, heat up in seconds, and provide instant offense. Johnson was best known for coming through in the clutch.

GAME 38

6. Which NFL team drafted future defensive back Brian Jordan?

a. Miami Dolphins
b. Buffalo Bills
c. Tampa Bay Buccaneers
d. Atlanta Falcons

GAME 38 Q5 ANSWER c
Playing from 1979 to 1981 as a utility man for the Toronto Blue Jays, Ainge realized his true calling was in basketball. The Wooden Award winner as top collegiate player in 1981, Ainge found himself as the starting point guard on the Celtics' championship teams in 1984 and 1986. Later, he had coaching stints with Portland and Phoenix.

GAME 58

6. In which event did Bob Beamon set a world record during the 1968 Summer Olympics?

a. Pole Vault
b. High Jump
c. Long Jump
d. Discus

GAME 58 Q5 ANSWER b
With his likeable personality and silly grin, British athlete Eddie "The Eagle" Edwards burst on the scene with his horridly poor jumps at the 1988 Winter Olympics in Calgary. Edwards, who easily finished last in his two events, used his fame to record a song in 1991 called "My Name Is Eddie"—a number-two hit in Finland.

GAME 78

6. Which World Series winner had a regular season record of only 85–77?

a. Toronto Blue Jays
b. Kansas City Royals
c. Minnesota Twins
d. New York Mets

GAME 78 Q5 ANSWER a
Leading the Western Conference, the Detroit Red Wings were expected to have an easy time with the bumbling team from San Jose. But the Sharks upset Detroit in 7 games, just one year after losing an NHL record 71 regular season games. San Jose also took second-round opponent Toronto to Game 7, but did not strike gold twice.

8. Which nation won the first World Cup championship?

a. Brazil
b. France
c. Germany
d. Uruguay

8. Which Olympic medalist was booed while singing the National Anthem before an NBA game?

a. Michael Johnson
b. Carl Lewis
c. Dan Jansen
d. Brian Boitano

8. Which NFL franchise has lost the most consecutive games in a single season?

a. New Orleans
b. Tampa Bay
c. Cincinnati
d. Carolina

8. In which country was NFL's Martin Gramatica born?

a. Colombia
b. Uruguay
c. Argentina
d. Peru

GAME 3 Q7 ANSWER a
Hockey's "Holy Grail" is a distinctive trophy in that each member of the winning team is allowed to spend one day with the cup during the off-season. When the Pittsburgh Penguins took home the prize after the 1990-1991 season, the cup was found at the bottom of Mario Lemieux's pool.

GAME 23 Q7 ANSWER d
Master P, who's real name is Percy Miller, was a member of the Charlotte Hornets during training camp in the strike-shortened 1998-1999 season. Although he was cut before the start of the season, Miller impressed then-coach Dave Cowens with his desire and love of the game.

GAME 43 Q7 ANSWER a
By going 7–7 in the 2002 season, the Nebraska Cornhuskers endured their first non-winning season since going 3–6–1 in 1961, ending the nation's longest college football winning-season streak at forty years. It also marked only the fourth time in fifty-three seasons that the Huskers had lost that many games.

GAME 63 Q7 ANSWER c
Selected by the Tampa Bay Lightning in the 1992 NHL Entry Draft, standout defenseman Roman Hamrlik became the first Czech player taken first overall, and only the second European to be drafted in the top spot since Mats Sundin broke the barrier in 1989.

Answers are in right-hand boxes on page 71.

5. "The Microwave"

a. Rick Mahorn

b. Trent Tucker

c. Vinnie Johnson

d. Byron Scott

"Sweetness" described the spirit and character of Chicago legend Walter Payton. Known for a lethal combination of speed and agility, Payton sliced his way across 16,726 yards over thirteen seasons. He was the all-time NFL rushing leader until 2002, when his mark was shattered by Emmitt Smith. "Sweetness" died of cancer in 1999 at 45.

---

5. Before joining the Boston Celtics, for which baseball team did Danny Ainge play?

a. Chicago White Sox

b. San Diego Padres

c. Toronto Blue Jays

d. Philadelphia Phillies

A veteran of the old USBL's Lakeland Ducks, Jones later attended the training camp of the NBA Developmental League's Mobile Revelers. Nevertheless, his right hook is better than his sky hook.

---

5. What was the name of the memorable British ski jumper at the 1988 Games?

a. Eric Edgewood

b. Eddie Edwards

c. Evan Eschmeyer

d. Emil Evans

At the 1976 Summer Games in Montreal, 14-year old Nadia Comaneci stole the show by becoming the first gymnast to receive a perfect score, followed by six more flawless grades. She took home three gold medals (individual all-around, balance beam, and uneven bars), one silver (team all-around), and one bronze (floor exercise).

---

5. Which eighth-seeded team upset a number-one seed in the 1994 NHL playoffs?

a. San Jose Sharks

b. Pittsburgh Penguins

c. Florida Panthers

d. Ottawa Senators

Despite its 11–0 home playoff record, and quarterback Brett Favre posting a 35–0 record in temperatures below 34 degrees, the Packers were stunned by the Falcons in a 27–7 thrashing during a 2002 NFL Wild Card game. Behind Michael Vick and a spirited defense, Atlanta jumped to a 24–0 halftime lead and never looked back.

---

9. Who is the only player to take home the NBA All-Star Game MVP after retiring?

a. Larry Bird
b. Magic Johnson
c. Michael Jordan
d. Kareem Abdul-Jabbar

GAME 3 Q8 ANSWER d

In 1930, host country Uruguay bested Argentina 4–2 to take the first World Cup. There were no qualifying competitions for the event. The thirteen participating teams entered by invitation, and the final draw was not made until the teams arrived in Uruguay. Through 2002, the host country has won six of the nineteen World Cups.

9. Which former Cy Young Award winner belongs to a band called "Stick Figure"?

a. Bret Saberhagen
b. Pat Hentgen
c. Mark Davis
d. Jack McDowell

GAME 23 Q8 ANSWER b

During Carl Lewis's painfully embarrassing performance prior to a 1993 Bulls-Nets game, his voice even cracked "at the rockets' red glare." At that point, the nine-time medalist promised the sold-out crowd it would get better. It didn't, and he was booed and heckled by the fans. Even Michael Jordan was laughing when Lewis finished.

9. Who holds the NHL "Ironman" record for most consecutive games played?

a. Steve Larmer
b. Doug Jarvis
c. Tony Amonte
d. Garry Unger

GAME 43 Q8 ANSWER d

Although the 1976-1977 Tampa Bay Buccaneers set the futility record with 26 consecutive defeats, the schedule was only 14 games. Therefore, the single-season consecutive-loss mark goes to the 2001 Carolina Panthers, who beat Minnesota on Opening Day and then lost their last 15 games, sending head coach George Seifert into retirement.

9. Which foreign-born pitcher has won the most Major League games?

a. Bert Blyleven
b. Dennis Martinez
c. Juan Marichal
d. Pedro Martinez

GAME 63 Q8 ANSWER c

Martin Gramatica, winning kicker for the Tampa Bay Buccaneers in Super Bowl XXXVII, was born in Argentina. He spent his college years kicking for Kansas State, and is the older brother of fellow booters Bill and Santiago Gramatica.

4. "Sweetness"

a. Emmitt Smith

b. Walter Payton

c. Gale Sayers

d. Jim Brown

GAME 18 Q3 ANSWER d

His determination and "never-take-it-easy" attitude earned Pete Rose the nickname "Charlie Hustle." Never was this name more appropriate than when he got his record-breaking hit number 4,192. After his line-drive single off Eric Show, Rose ran out the hit, making sure he couldn't get an extra base, before breaking down with joy.

4. Outside of boxing, in what other sport does Roy Jones, Jr. show talent?

a. Football

b. Track and Field

c. Basketball

d. Baseball

GAME 38 Q3 ANSWER b

Originally drafted by the Baltimore Orioles in 1969, Winfield decided to attend college instead. A multi-sport star at the University of Minnesota, Winfield was drafted by the San Diego Padres, Minnesota Vikings, and Atlanta Hawks, as well as the ABA's Utah Stars. The 2001 Baseball Hall of Fame inductee played for twenty-two seasons.

4. Who was the first female gymnast to receive a perfect score in an Olympic event?

a. Nadia Comaneci

b. Mary Lou Retton

c. Olga Korbut

d. Ludmila Turishcheva

GAME 58 Q3 ANSWER d

In a game of controversy, the US led the USSR team 50–49 with 3 seconds left, but the Soviets were given *three* chances to inbound the ball after several controversial plays. When Aleksandr Belov dropped the winning shot, a disgusted US team refused its silver medals and filed protests, which were ruled in favor of the Russians.

4. Which team was the first to beat the Packers in a playoff game at Lambeau Field?

a. Minnesota Vikings

b. Tampa Bay Buccaneers

c. Philadelphia Eagles

d. Atlanta Falcons

GAME 78 Q3 ANSWER c

A classic example of David slaying Goliath occurred during the tournament when the number-one ranked Virginia Cavaliers lost to the tiny Division II Chaminade Sillverswords. In stunning fashion, Chaminade pulled off the miracle 77–72 victory against Virginia and a less-than-100-percent Ralph Sampson.

GAME 3	
10. Which award is presented to the outstanding NCAA hockey player? a. Scotty Bowman Award b. Jack Parker Award c. Bob Johnson Award d. Hobey Baker Award	GAME 3 Q9 ANSWER b On November 7, 1991, Magic Johnson became the first prominent athlete to publicly disclose that he had the HIV virus. Johnson retired immediately, but returned in February 1992 to make a special appearance at that year's All-Star Game. There, he recorded game highs of 25 points and 9 assists, winning the Most Valuable Player Award.
GAME 23	
10. Which former New York Giants star once sang at Carnegie Hall? a. Roosevelt Grier b. Y.A. Tittle c. Sam Huff d. Harry Carson	GAME 23 Q9 ANSWER d Aptly named because of the tall lanky frame of McDowell (AL Cy Young winner in 1993), the rock band was formed in 1992 and has recorded more than five albums to date.
GAME 43	
10. Who is the only golfer to capture four consecutive Majors? a. Ben Hogan b. Gary Player c. Tiger Woods d. Jack Nicklaus	GAME 43 Q9 ANSWER b Playing in 964 consecutive games, from opening night in 1975 until October 10, 1987, Doug Jarvis currently sits atop the NHL Ironman throne. He achieved the record while playing with Montreal, Washington, and Hartford.
GAME 63	
10. In which country was NBA's Pau Gasol born? a. Turkey b. Greece c. Spain d. Germany	GAME 63 Q9 ANSWER a With 287 career game wins, the Holland-born Bert Blyleven holds the record. He also lost 250 games in a twenty-two year career that saw him pitch until the age of 42.

Answers are in right-hand boxes on page 75.

GAME 18

3. "Charlie Hustle"

a. Charles Barkley

b. Ty Cobb

c. Charlie Joiner

d. Pete Rose

GAME 18 Q2 ANSWER d
Similar to "Golden Jet" (the nickname of his famous father Bobby), "Golden Brett" was the name given to Brett Hull early in his NHL career. Living up to the accomplishments of his dad, the junior Hull once scored 86 goals in a season with the St. Louis Blues. He also won multiple Stanley Cup championships.

GAME 38

3. Which baseball Hall of Famer was drafted by four pro teams after college?

a. Luke Appling

b. Dave Winfield

c. Ernie Banks

d. Lou Brock

GAME 38 Q2 ANSWER b
Angering Raiders and Royals fans alike, Jackson called his off-season football playing "just a hobby." Not a bad "hobby" for a man who won the 1985 Heisman Trophy while a member of the Auburn Tigers. Jackson played his best football during a Monday night game in 1988, when he ran right through Seattle's Brian Bosworth.

GAME 58

3. To whom did the US Men's Basketball Team lose in the 1972 gold medal game?

a. China

b. Yugoslavia

c. Greece

d. Soviet Union

GAME 58 Q2 ANSWER c
Six countries battled it out for the first-ever Olympic gold medal in Women's Ice Hockey at the 1998 Games in Nagano, Japan. Led by Captain Cami Granato, the United States defeated heavily favored Canada to take home the gold.

GAME 78

3. Which unknown college hoops team upset top-ranked Virginia in the 1982 Maui Invitational?

a. Florida Atlantic

b. Prairie View

c. Chaminade

d. Rice

GAME 78 Q2 ANSWER b
In his twenty-one career starts, Man o' War had only one loss—to Upset in the 1919 Sanford Stakes at Saratoga. In the stretch, Upset's jockey, Johnny Loftus, boxed in Man o' War, and eventually posted a half-length victory over the legendary thoroughbred. Man o' War faced Upset six more times, defeating him soundly each time.

GAME 3

11. Who is the only rookie to win the NFL's Defensive Player of the Year Award?

a. Lawrence Taylor

b. "Mean" Joe Greene

c. Reggie White

d. Mike Singletary

GAME 3 Q10 ANSWER d
Named in honor of one of the original college hockey greats, the Hobey Baker Award is presented annually to the top college hockey player in the United States. Playing for Princeton in the early part of the twentieth century, Baker excelled not only in hockey, but also in golf, football, swimming, and track and field.

GAME 23

11. Which boxer put out a rap CD in 2002 titled *Round One, The Album*?

a. Lennox Lewis

b. Chris Byrd

c. Roy Jones, Jr.

d. Oscar de la Hoya

GAME 23 Q10 ANSWER a
Because fearsome defensive lineman Rosey Grier always had an interest in singing, one of his Giants teammates introduced him to a talent agent in the early 1960s. By February of 1963, Grier was on stage at New York's famed Carnegie Hall—one of the many prestigious concert arenas in which he performed throughout the country.

GAME 43

11. Which NBA team has won the most consecutive games?

a. Boston Celtics

b. New York Knicks

c. Los Angeles Lakers

d. Detroit Pistons

GAME 43 Q10 ANSWER c
Tiger won the 2000 US and British Opens, the 2000 PGA Championship, and then the following year's Masters.

GAME 63

11. Ruslan Salei was the lone NHL representative for which national team at the 2002 Olympics?

a. Kazakhstan

b. Belarus

c. Ukraine

d. Latvia

GAME 63 Q10 ANSWER c
Taken third overall by the Memphis Grizzlies in the 2001 NBA Draft, Rookie of the Year winner Paul Gasol was born July 6, 1980 in Barcelona, Spain. He averaged 17.6 points and 8.9 rebounds per game in his initial season while playing for the woeful Grizzlies, who finished the season with a 23–59 record.

GAME 18

2. "Golden Brett"

a. Brett Boone

b. Brett Favre

c. George Brett

d. Brett Hull

GAME 18 Q1 ANSWER c
Dubbed the "Dinner Bell," due to his huge appetite, NBA player Mel Turpin lasted only five seasons before eating his way out of the league. Selected sixth overall in the 1984 draft by the Washington Bullets, Turpin, a legend at the University of Kentucky, failed to continue his collegiate success with the NBA.

GAME 38

2. "It's just a hobby" was a phrase spoken by which two-sport star?

a. Randy Moss

b. Bo Jackson

c. Deion Sanders

d. Brian Jordan

GAME 38 Q1 ANSWER c
Although he played in only 12 games, "Papa Bear" could say he had been a member of the NY Yankees. Compiling a soft .091 average, Halas was a participant in the May 1919 game against the Senators, which saw Walter Johnson retire 28 straight batters over 12 innings. Later that year, he was a founding father of the NFL.

GAME 58

2. Which Olympics first introduced Women's Ice Hockey as a medal event?

a. 1992

b. 1994

c. 1998

d. 2002

GAME 58 Q1 ANSWER a
After shattering the 100-meter dash world record during the Summer Games in Seoul, Korea, Canada's Ben Johnson tested positive for steroids. His time of 9.79 seconds was erased and he was stripped of his gold medal. After being reinstated in 1991, Johnson again tested positive for steroid use, and was banned from the Olympics for life.

GAME 78

2. Which thoroughbred was handed his only career loss by the aptly named "Upset"?

a. Citation

b. Man o' War

c. Secretariat

d. War Admiral

GAME 78 Q1 ANSWER d
In spite of Cincinnati's pesky lineup and stellar bullpen, few people believed the team had a shot at dethroning the defending World Champion Oakland A's. So, when the Reds *swept* Oakland in four straight, the baseball world was stunned. Most shocking was that they outscored the mighty A's 22–8 in the series.

GAME 3

12. Which company sponsors Major League Baseball's annual Gold Glove awards?

a. Everlast

b. Rawlings

c. Ringside

d. Wilson

GAME 3   Q11   ANSWER a
Viewed by many as the best linebacker ever to play the sport, Lawrence Taylor burst upon the scene in 1981 and led the New York Giants to a pair of championships in the next ten seasons. Besides winning the Defensive Player of the Year Award as a rookie, Taylor won the same award in 1982 and 1986 as well.

GAME 23

12. Which NFL star was once the opening act for Boyz II Men?

a. Deion Sanders

b. Andre Rison

c. Jerry Rice

d. Rodney Peete

GAME 23   Q11   ANSWER c
In addition to once dominating the ring as a middleweight, Roy Jones, Jr. is a pretty capable musician as well. His 2002 release actually received favorable reviews and has been compared to the work of such popular artists as DMX.

GAME 43

12. Who is the only ML player with two streaks of at least 650 consecutive games each?

a. Pete Rose

b. Steve Garvey

c. Nellie Fox

d. Sandy Alomar, Jr.

GAME 43   Q11   ANSWER c
Taking a record 33 straight games in the 1971-1972 season, the Lakers squad, led by Chamberlain, West, Goodrich, McMillian, and Hairston, established an NBA standard that has yet to be touched. The team's 69-13 season was capped by its first NBA Championship since moving to the West Coast.

GAME 63

12. Who was the first Japanese player to appear in a Major League game?

a. Hideo Nomo

b. Masanori Murakami

c. Shigetoshi Hasegawa

d. Hiroshi Takahashi

GAME 63   Q11   ANSWER b
Representing his home nation of Belarus, defenseman Ruslan Salei competed on the national team, which pulled off one of the most stunning upsets in Olympic history by knocking off the far-superior Swedish team 4–3 in the quarterfinals. Belarus lost out on a medal when they were defeated 7–2 by Russia for the bronze.

GAME 18

1. "Dinner Bell"

a. Gilbert Brown
b. Mickey Lolich
c. Mel Turpin
d. Turk Broda

The answer to this question is on: **page 76, top frame, right side.**

GAME 38

1. Besides football, which pro sport did George Halas play?

a. Hockey
b. Golf
c. Baseball
d. Tennis

The answer to this question is on: **page 76, second frame, right side.**

GAME 58

1. Ben Johnson, whose world record was stripped in the 1988 Games, represented which country?

a. Canada
b. United Kingdom
c. Jamaica
d. United States

The answer to this question is on: **page 76, third frame, right side.**

GAME 78

1. Which team knocked off the heavily favored Oakland A's in the 1990 World Series?

a. Pittsburgh Pirates
b. Los Angeles Dodgers
c. St. Louis Cardinals
d. Cincinnati Reds

The answer to this question is on: **page 76, bottom frame, right side.**

GAME 4

"Retired Numbers"

Do You Remember the Digits on the Stars' Backs?

Turn to page 81 for the first question.

GAME 3 Q12 ANSWER b
Baseball equipment manufacturer Rawlings has presented the awards since 1957. The honor was initially bestowed on just nine baseball players, tops in each position. But a year later, the company decided to give out trophies to the top nine position players in each of the two major leagues, for a total of eighteen awards.

GAME 24

GRAB BAG

Turn to page 81 for the first question.

GAME 23 Q12 ANSWER a
Getting his start in music with M.C. Hammer's "2 Legit to Quit" in 1991, Deion Sanders developed a singing career that included performing as the opening act for the 1994 Boyz II Men tour.

GAME 44

"Michael Jordan"

All About "His Airness"

Turn to page 81 for the first question.

GAME 43 Q12 ANSWER a
Lost in the shuffle of the Ripken and Gehrig streaks is a feat accomplished only by Pete Rose. During his career, "Charlie Hustle" had two separate streaks of 745 and 678 consecutive games played. This means that in eleven straight seasons, he missed only about ten games.

GAME 64

GRAB BAG

Turn to page 81 for the first question.

GAME 63 Q12 ANSWER b
Prior to 1964 spring training, the San Francisco Giants signed three Japanese players and assigned them to their minor league teams. Masanori Murakami, Tatsuhiko Tanaka, and Hiroshi Takahashi were the first Japanese ball players to compete on American teams. In September of '64, left-handed reliever Murakami debuted for the Giants.

GAME 18

"Nicknames, Part I"

Does Your "Nickname Knowledge" Cut the Mustard?

*Turn to page 78
for the first question.*

GAME 17 Q12 ANSWER b

No, Tiger Woods is *not* the youngest Major winner. That honor goes to Gene Sarazen, the 1922 US Open Champion. "The Squire," who passed away in 1999 at age 97, took home his first Major at age 20, and proceeded to capture six more during his career. He has also been credited with inventing the first "true" sand wedge in 1931.

GAME 38

"Two-Sport Stars"

Athletes Who Excel at Two Sports

*Turn to page 78
for the first question.*

GAME 37 Q12 ANSWER c

Prior to serving in the US House of Representatives in 1994, J.C. Watts was a star quarterback for the Oklahoma Sooners, leading the team to Orange Bowl victories in 1980 and 1981. After college, Watts went on to play with the Canadian Football League's Ottawa Rough Riders, and won the 1981 Grey Cup Offensive MVP Award.

GAME 58

"Olympic Scrapbook"

Remember These Memorable Olympic Moments?

*Turn to page 78
for the first question.*

GAME 57 Q12 ANSWER c

After rallying from 2 runs down in the bottom of the ninth with 1 out left, the Mets stood in position to win the game on a hit. Incredibly, Mookie Wilson's routine grounder got past Red Sox first baseman Bill Buckner, and Ray Knight came skipping home with the winning run. No one has to remind Boston fans who took Game 7.

GAME 78

"Memorable Upsets"

Everybody Loves an Underdog

*Turn to page 78
for the first question.*

GAME 77 Q12 ANSWER b

Growing up in French Lick, with the scant population of 2,100, "Larry Legend" drew over 4,000 spectators to Springs Valley High School to watch him play his last secondary school contest. At Indiana State, Bird led the Sycamores to the NCAA Championship Game in 1979, which they dropped to rival Magic Johnson's Michigan State squad.

GAME 4	**1. Who is the only baseball player to have his number retired by every team?** a. Babe Ruth b. Hank Aaron c. Jackie Robinson d. Ted Williams	The answer to this question is on: **page 83,** **top frame,** **right side.**
GAME 24	**1. Who were the first black head coaches to meet in an NFL playoff game?** a. Art Shell/Dennis Green b. Tony Dungy/Herman Edwards c. Dennis Green/Tony Dungy d. Art Shell/Terry Robiskie	The answer to this question is on: **page 83,** **second frame,** **right side.**
GAME 44	**1. In which state was Michael Jordan born?** a. New Jersey b. South Carolina c. New York d. North Carolina	The answer to this question is on: **page 83,** **third frame,** **right side.**
GAME 64	**1. Who was the last active Major League player from the Negro Leagues?** a. Satchel Paige b. Hank Aaron c. Jackie Robinson d. Larry Doby	The answer to this question is on: **page 83,** **bottom frame,** **right side.**

GAME 17	12. Who is the youngest golfer ever to win a major championship? a. Jack Nicklaus b. Gene Sarazen c. Tiger Woods d. Ben Hogan	**GAME 17 Q11 ANSWER a** Making his Major League debut in 1953 at age 18, Al Kaline set a standard in 1955, when, at age 20, he led the American League in batting (.340) and hits (an even 200). As good as his season was, Kaline finished second in MVP voting to Yankees' catcher Yogi Berra.
GAME 37	12. Which school did former Representative J.C. Watts attend? a. Oklahoma State b. Texas A&M c. Oklahoma d. Texas	**GAME 37 Q11 ANSWER c** After retiring from wrestling in 1987, Jesse Ventura served as a commentator, and then decided to run for the mayoral seat in his hometown of Brooklyn Park, Minnesota. Ventura held that office for four years, and then shocked the political world by successfully running for the state's governorship in 1998.
GAME 57	12. Which player scored the Mets' winning run in Game 6 of the '86 World Series? a. Gary Carter b. Howard Johnson c. Ray Knight d. Kevin Mitchell	**GAME 57 Q11 ANSWER b** In a controversial World Cup goal, midfielder Diego Maradona deflected a ball into the net with his hand (proven later by video replay) during Argentina's quarterfinal match with England. Minutes later, he scored the game-winning goal. When asked how the first ball went in, he replied, "Must have been the hand of God."
GAME 77	12. Larry Bird a. Indianapolis, Indiana b. French Lick, Indiana c. Bloomington, Indiana d. Terre Haute, Indiana	**GAME 77 Q11 ANSWER d** The man known as "St. Patrick" was born on October 5, 1965 in Quebec City. His amazing goaltending skills derailed the law career he had planned. Roy's butterfly style revolutionized the goalie position. As a rookie, Roy practically lived on French fries, earning him the nickname "Casseau," the box in which fries are served.

2. Which basketball franchise has retired the most player's numbers?

a. Boston Celtics
b. Los Angeles Lakers
c. New York Knicks
d. Philadelphia 76ers

GAME 4 Q1 ANSWER c
On April 15, 1997—fifty years after Jackie Robinson broke the color barrier in Major League Baseball—President Clinton gave a stirring speech paying tribute to the man. Bud Selig then announced that all teams would jointly retire Robinson's number 42, joining the Los Angeles Dodgers, who had done so years earlier.

2. By how many lengths did Secretariat win the 1973 Belmont Stakes?

a. 15
b. 24
c. 28
d. 31

GAME 24 Q1 ANSWER b
When the New York Jets and Indianapolis Colts met in a first-round playoff game at Giants Stadium, history was made. The January 3, 2003 meeting marked the first time in NFL history that two black head coaches have met in a playoff game. The event was more exciting than the game, as Edwards' Jets blitzed Dungy's Colts, 41–0.

2. Which North Carolina teammate was Jordan's college roommate?

a. Sam Perkins
b. Chris Brust
c. Jeb Barlow
d. Buzz Peterson

GAME 44 Q1 ANSWER c
Knicks fans probably don't want to hear this, but Michael Jordan was born February 17, 1963 in good old Brooklyn, New York. The Jordan family migrated to Wilmington, North Carolina, very early in Michael's life, and quickly realized that he was talented in basketball, football, and baseball.

2. Which of the following NBA headmen has won Coach of the Year with three different teams?

a. Bill Fitch
b. Gene Shue
c. Pat Riley
d. Cotton Fitzsimmons

GAME 64 Q1 ANSWER b
After playing for the Indianapolis Clowns in the Negro Leagues, "Hammerin'" Hank Aaron began his Major League career with the Milwaukee Braves in 1954, and ended it in 1976 with the Milwaukee Brewers. In 1974, he hit his 715th home run, breaking Babe Ruth's record.

11. Who is the youngest winner of a Major League Baseball batting title?

a. Al Kaline
b. Ty Cobb
c. Honus Wagner
d. Harvey Kuenn

GAME 17 Q10 ANSWER b
By defeating Trevor Berbick on November 22, 1986 to capture the WBC Heavyweight Championship, Mike Tyson became the youngest fighter to claim a major title. At just 20 years and 144 days old, Tyson needed only two rounds to knock out his formidable opponent. He continued his winning streak until he met James "Buster" Douglas in 1990.

---

11. What was former wrestler Jesse Ventura's first elected office?

a. Councilman
b. Representative
c. Mayor
d. Congressman

GAME 37 Q10 ANSWER d
Nicknamed "Whizzer," White was an All-American running back at the University of Colorado before joining the Pittsburgh Steelers in 1938. After signing for a then-record $15,800, White led the league with 567 rushing yards. He accepted a Rhodes Scholarship a year later, but returned to the NFL in 1940, joining the Lions.

---

11. Who scored the controversial "Hand of God" goal in soccer's 1986 World Cup?

a. Lothar Matteus
b. Diego Maradona
c. Paolo Rossi
d. Steve Hodge

GAME 57 Q10 ANSWER c
In one of the all-time great playoff performances, goalie Ron Hextall led his Philadelphia Flyers to Game 7 of the 1987 Stanley Cup Finals against the dominant Edmonton Oilers. Despite losing, Hextall became only the fourth player on a losing team to be named MVP.

---

11. Patrick Roy

a. Montreal, Quebec
b. Ottawa, Ontario
c. Oakville, Ontario
d. Quebec City, Quebec

GAME 77 Q10 ANSWER a
Born on June 11, 1956, Montana first displayed baseball skill by tossing three perfect games as a Little Leaguer. When offered a basketball scholarship to NC State, Joe chose football instead and headed to Notre Dame. He joins other quarterback greats from Western Pennsylvania, including Dan Marino, Joe Namath, and Johnny Unitas.

GAME 4

3. Which NFL team retired the number 12 in honor of its fans?

a. Miami Dolphins

b. San Francisco 49ers

c. Atlanta Falcons

d. Seattle Seahawks

GAME 4 Q2 ANSWER a
With a record twenty numbers hanging from the rafters of the Fleet Center, the Boston Celtics lead the way in this category. The team with the second highest number of honored numerals is the Portland Trail Blazers, who have a mere nine jerseys out of circulation.

GAME 24

3. Which coaches won a combined six Grey Cups but were winless in their Super Bowls?

a. Dan Reeves/Bobby Ross

b. Raymond Berry/Sam Wyche

c. Bud Grant/Marv Levy

d. Ray Malavasi/Forrest Gregg

GAME 24 Q2 ANSWER d
Celebrated thoroughbred Secretariat completed his Triple Crown romp by blowing out the 1973 Belmont Stakes field by an astounding 31 lengths. The horse affectionately known as "Big Red" won sixteen out of twenty-one career starts. He finished off the board just once, after being badly bumped at the outset of his first career start.

GAME 44

3. Which city hosted the Olympics in which Jordan won his first gold medal?

a. Atlanta

b. Los Angeles

c. Seoul

d. Barcelona

GAME 44 Q2 ANSWER d
During their playing days at North Carolina in the early '80s, Jordan's roomie was none other than Robert "Buzz" Peterson. In his senior year at Asheville High School, Peterson actually beat out "His Airness" for North Carolina Player of the Year and North Carolina Athlete of the Year.

GAME 64

3. Who is the only thoroughbred trainer to lead the nation in earnings ten years straight?

a. Bob Baffert

b. Charlie Whittingham

c. Laz Barrera

d. D. Wayne Lukas

GAME 64 Q2 ANSWER c
Pat Riley's awards have come with the Lakers (1990), Knicks (1993), and Heat (1997). The Armani-attired coach won four titles with Los Angeles in the '80s, but after leaving Southern California, he has managed only one trip to the finals (Knicks in 1994), which he lost.

---

10. Who is the youngest boxer to win a heavyweight title?

a. Sonny Liston

b. Mike Tyson

c. Joe Louis

d. Rocky Marciano

By winning the 1989 French Open—his only Major championship—Michael Chang surpassed Boris Becker as the youngest male player to capture a Grand Slam title. At 17 years and 3 months, Chang beat his German rival's record by 4 months.

---

10. Which Supreme Court Justice once led the NFL in rushing?

a. Clarence Thomas

b. Antonin Scalia

c. Tom Clarke

d. Byron White

Gerald Ford began his gridiron career as an All-State selection at Grand Rapid's South High School, and while attending the University of Michigan, played on the Wolverines' 1932 and 1933 championship teams. After graduation, the future President was offered tryouts by the Packers and Lions, but opted for law school instead.

---

10. Who won the 1987 NHL Playoff MVP despite being on the losing Finals team?

a. Bobby Clarke

b. Cam Neely

c. Ron Hextall

d. Ray Bourque

With the sixteenth overall pick in the 1985 NFL Draft, the 49ers chose Jerry Rice from Mississippi Valley State. The athlete would go on to become the best wide receiver in the history of the NFL. Rice, who has appeared in four Super Bowls with both the 49ers and the Raiders, has shown amazing resiliency, playing well beyond his 40th birthday.

---

10. Joe Montana

a. New Eagle, Pennsylvania

b. Fort Wayne, Indiana

c. Sandusky, Ohio

d. Schaumburg, Illinois

George Kenneth Griffey, Jr. was born on November 21, 1969, in Cincinnati, where his dad was an outfielder for the "Big Red Machine." He arrived in Seattle amid much fanfare after being selected first overall in the 1987 Baseball Amateur Draft. In 2000, "Griff" became the youngest player ever to hit 400 home runs.

4. Who is the only baseball manager to have his number retired by two different teams?

a. John McGraw
b. Miller Huggins
c. Sparky Anderson
d. Casey Stengel

GAME 4 Q3 ANSWER d
In football, retiring the number 12 signifies the importance of a loud, supportive home crowd, which some teams refer to as the "Twelfth Man" (11 position players, 1 crowd). Texas A&M University is a big follower of Twelfth Man traditions, and even has "Home of the Twelfth Man" emblazoned on its stadium's facade.

4. Actress Ashley Judd married which CART driver in 2001?

a. Michael Andretti
b. Dario Franchitti
c. Alex Zanardi
d. Patrick Carpentier

GAME 24 Q3 ANSWER c
Coaches Bud Grant and Marv Levy combined six championships in the Canadian Football League before moving south, where they went a collective 0 for 8 in their Super Bowl appearances with Minnesota and Buffalo, respectively. Grant won four Grey Cups with the Winnipeg Blue Bombers; Levy captured a pair with the Montreal Alouettes.

4. Who was taken before Michael Jordan as the second pick in the 1984 NBA Draft?

a. Mel Turpin
b. Terence Stansbury
c. Sam Bowie
d. Lancaster Gordon

GAME 44 Q3 ANSWER b
Jordan shone as co-captain of the 1984 US Men's Basketball Team, leading the American squad to an 8–0 record and the gold medal. Those 8 games saw Jordan lead the team in scoring with 17.8 points per game, while shooting over 54 percent from the field. Later that year, Jordan made his NBA debut.

4. Who was the first pro golfer to average 300-yard drives over the course of a season?

a. Tiger Woods
b. John Daly
c. Davis Love III
d. Jack Nicklaus

GAME 64 Q3 ANSWER d
Lukas led the nation in earnings for an astounding fourteen of fifteen straight years from 1983 to 1997 (Bobby Frankel edged him out in 1993). Lukas oversaw a national powerhouse that included horses in every major racing market. He had six straight wins in Triple Crown races from 1984 to 1996.

9. Who is the youngest male tennis player to win a Grand Slam title?

a. Michael Chang

b. Boris Becker

c. Ken Rosewall

d. Jimmy Connors

In the 1979-1980 season, a 19-year-old Wayne Gretzky amassed 137 points (51 goals, 86 assists), which actually only tied him for the league lead with Marcel Dionne. However, due to Gretzky's explosiveness and unbelievable playmaking ability, voters saw fit to award him the trophy.

---

9. Former President Gerald Ford starred on which college football team?

a. Michigan

b. Notre Dame

c. Northwestern

d. Yale

Best known in political circles as Bob Dole's running mate in the 1996 Presidential election, Jack Kemp had an illustrious thirteen-year football career, quarterbacking for San Diego and Buffalo. Co-founder of the AFL Players' Association, Kemp got a head start on his political career by serving five years as president of the group.

---

9. Which small college did Jerry Rice attend?

a. Jackson State

b. Mississippi Valley State

c. Delta State

d. Alcorn State

One of baseball's premier pitchers, Houston's J.R. Richard had won at least 18 games in the four seasons prior to 1980, and was well on his way to a fifth when he suffered a devastating stroke in July of 1980 at age 30. The 6'8" hurler who had twice struck out over 300 batters never pitched in the Major Leagues again.

---

9. Ken Griffey, Jr.

a. Port Angeles, Washington

b. Mamaroneck, New York

c. Cincinnati, Ohio

d. Lexington, Kentucky

Born on March 6, 1972 in a depressed area of Newark, New Jersey, "Shaq" was raised with strict Army discipline—courtesy of his adoptive father. Due to his pop's livelihood, O'Neal bounced from base to base before settling in San Antonio, where he became a high school All-American, and led his team to a Texas state title.

5. Which Major League team has retired the number 455?

a. Cleveland Indians

b. Los Angeles Dodgers

c. New York Mets

d. Boston Red Sox

"The old perfesser" had his number 37 retired by both the New York Yankees and the New York Mets. Stengel did far better with the Yanks, winning the World Series seven times. With the Mets, he never finished better than last place.

---

5. Which is the only university to use a Disney character as its mascot?

a. Washington State

b. Florida State

c. University of Oregon

d. UCLA

Wed at a picturesque castle in Scotland, actress Ashley Judd and Scottish race-car driver Dario Franchitti tied the knot in December 2001. Dario, whose solid racing career has been marred by injuries, appeared in the Sylvester Stallone auto-racing movie *Driven* (2001).

---

5. Which player threw down "The Dunk" in the 1993 NBA playoffs?

a. Reggie Miller

b. John Starks

c. Rik Smits

d. Xavier McDaniel

After the Rockets took Hakeem Olajuwon as first draft pick, Portland chose oft-injured center Sam Bowie—a surprising choice, especially with Jordan still on the board. Needless to say, the Bulls were thrilled to snatch up Michael with the third pick.

---

5. Who ended Pete Sampras's three-year winning streak at Wimbledon in 1996?

a. MaliVai Washington

b. Cedric Pioline

c. Goran Ivanisevic

d. Richard Krajicek

Known for his insanely long drives, John Daly first led the nation in driving in 1991, when he averaged a mere 288.9 yards. In 1997, he broke the 300-yard barrier, averaging 302 yards per drive. With the exception of 1994, Daly, has led the tour in driving every year since 1991.

---

8. Who is the youngest player to win the Hart Trophy as the NHL's MVP?

a. Nels Stewart
b. Gordie Howe
c. Eric Lindros
d. Wayne Gretzky

GAME 17 Q7 ANSWER c
Making a brief appearance on June 10, 1944 for the Cincinnati Reds, Joe Nuxhall, at age 15 years and 10 months, threw two-thirds of an inning. He gave up 2 hits and 5 runs in a game that saw his Reds get shellacked 18–0 by the St. Louis Cardinals. Nuxhall didn't return to the Majors until 1952, when he was the ripe old age of 23!

8. Which member of Congress was a quarterback on back-to-back AFL Championship teams?

a. Daryle Lamonica
b. Len Dawson
c. Jack Kemp
d. George Blanda

GAME 37 Q7 ANSWER d
On April 14, 1910, President William H. Taft attended the Washington Senators initial game, and started a tradition by tossing the ball to Walter Johnson. Taft, who was a huge baseball fan, was also the first president to attend two games in one day, catching both a Browns and a Cardinals game while in Saint Louis later that year.

8. Which talented Houston Astros pitcher suffered a career-ending stroke in 1980?

a. Vern Ruhle
b. Ken Forsch
c. Joaquin Andujar
d. J.R. Richard

GAME 57 Q7 ANSWER b
Larry Holmes won the championship in 1978 from Ken Norton, and went on to defend his title in twenty bouts over an eight-year period. His reign ended in 1985 after losing a unanimous 15-round decision to Michael Spinks. In the years that followed, Holmes would continue to retire and un-retire, even fighting in 2002 at age 52.

8. Shaquille O'Neal

a. Newark, New Jersey
b. New Orleans, Louisiana
c. Brooklyn, New York
d. Shreveport, Louisiana

GAME 77 Q7 ANSWER b
Born August 12, 1971 in Washington DC, to the son of Greek immigrants, a toddling Pete Sampras spent his days hitting tennis balls against the basement wall of his home. The family relocated to the tennis-friendly state of California in the late '70s to give Pete a better opportunity to develop his craft.

GAME 4

6. Who is the only NBA player to have his number retired by three different teams?

a. Kareem Abdul-Jabbar
b. Oscar Robertson
c. Wilt Chamberlain
d. Moses Malone

GAME 4 Q5 ANSWER a
Franchises have retired numbers for players, coaches, fans, and even owners, but only one team has retired a number for consecutive home sellouts. From June 12, 1995 to April 2, 2001, not a single seat was available in Jacobs Field, new home of the Cleveland Indians. This illustrates how a new stadium can revitalize a franchise.

GAME 24

6. Which favored soccer team did not score a single goal at the 2002 Men's World Cup?

a. France
b. Argentina
c. Mexico
d. Croatia

GAME 24 Q5 ANSWER c
Oregon's early students called themselves "Webfoots," which eventually became "Ducks." The school's first mascot—a live duck named Puddles—drew complaints from the Humane Society, ending its career. In 1947, athletic director Leo Harris reached an agreement with Walt Disney to make Donald Duck the school's official mascot.

GAME 44

6. What did Jordan always wear underneath his uniform?

a. His high school jersey
b. His JV jock strap
c. His North Carolina shorts
d. His father's tank top

GAME 44 Q5 ANSWER b
In a play so shocking it is simply known as "The Dunk," John Starks took a baseline drive over the heads of a prone Horace Grant and Michael Jordan in the 1993 Eastern Conference Finals. Jordan had the last laugh, though, as his Bulls took out the Knicks in 6 games, and cruised to the NBA Championship.

GAME 64

6. Which university had the most players selected in a single NFL draft?

a. Notre Dame
b. Texas
c. USC
d. Miami

GAME 64 Q5 ANSWER d
Pete Sampras took an amazing seven out of eight Wimbledon men's singles titles from 1992 to 2000, with his only defeat coming in the '96 quarterfinals when he faced Richard Krajicek, the eventual tournament champion. Sampras would go on to win the next four Wimbledon titles. Krajicek has not reached a Major final since his '96 win.

---

7. Who is the youngest baseballer to appear in a twentieth-century Major League game?

a. Eddie Gaedel
b. Andruw Jones
c. Joe Nuxhall
d. Jim Bagby

GAME 17 Q6 ANSWER c
At age 14, swimmer Kusuo Kitamura of Japan won the gold in the 1,500-meter freestyle at the 1932 Games held in Los Angeles.

7. Who was the first US president to throw an opening day first pitch?

a. Woodrow Wilson
b. Teddy Roosevelt
c. William McKinley
d. William Taft

GAME 37 Q6 ANSWER a
After winning back-to-back national championships with Nebraska in 1994 and 1995, and splitting a third with Michigan in 1997, coach Tom Osborne decided it was time to give something back to the community. So in 2000, he ran for and won a congressional seat, representing Nebraska's third district.

7. To which fighter did Larry Holmes lose his eight-year Heavyweight Title?

a. Mike Tyson
b. Michael Spinks
c. Tim Witherspoon
d. "Bonecrusher" Smith

GAME 57 Q6 ANSWER c
After making racist remarks about black athletes, long-time gambling prognosticator Jimmy "The Greek" Snyder saw his career as a football analyst come to an end. He had said, "Blacks are bred to be better athletes, and this goes back to the Civil War when the slave owner would breed his big woman so they would have big, black kids."

7. Pete Sampras

a. Palo Alto, California
b. Washington D.C.
c. Orlando, Florida
d. Corpus Christi, Texas

GAME 77 Q6 ANSWER c
The native of Cypress, California, entered the world on December 20, 1975, and demonstrated early on that he would become a golf force to be reckoned with. While playing in the World Junior Golf Championships at age 8, Woods went into the final day 5 strokes off the pace. He calmly shot 5 under par to win the tournament.

GAME 4

7. Who is the first Pittsburgh Steeler to have his number retired?

a. "Mean" Joe Greene

b. Ernie Stautner

c. Franco Harris

d. Terry Bradshaw

GAME 4 Q6 ANSWER c
Wilt Chamberlain's jersey was retired by the Philadelphia/San Francisco Warriors, Philadelphia 76ers, and Los Angeles Lakers. A dominant NBA player, Chamberlain will always be remembered for his performance on March 2, 1962, when he scored 100 points for the Philadelphia Warriors while playing against the NY Knicks.

GAME 24

7. Which Grand Slam event has tennis great Pete Sampras *not* won?

a. Wimbledon

b. The Australian Open

c. The French Open

d. The US Open

GAME 24 Q6 ANSWER a
Coming into the 2002 FIFA World Cup, the defending champion French team was one of the heavy favorites. Three matches and zero goals later, the French were on their way back home after being unceremoniously ousted in the first round. They were shut out by Senegal and Denmark, and battled Uruguay to a 0–0 tie.

GAME 44

7. How many scoring titles did Jordan win?

a. 7

b. 8

c. 9

d. 10

GAME 44 Q6 ANSWER c
Fiercely loyal to his alma mater, Jordan always wore his North Carolina shorts under his uniform as a good luck charm. Jordan's superstition paid off in the form of six NBA Championships, five MVP awards, three All-Star MVP trophies, etc., etc.

GAME 64

7. Who is boxing's *heaviest* heavyweight champion?

a. Primo Carnera

b. Larry Holmes

c. George Foreman

d. Tony Galento

GAME 64 Q6 ANSWER b
During the 1984 NFL Draft, seventeen players from the University of Texas were selected.

---

6. Who is the youngest *male* athlete to win an Olympic gold medal?

a. Buster Crabbe
b. Tony Nieminen
c. Kusuo Kitamura
d. Magnar Solberg

GAME 17 Q5 ANSWER d
Competing in the springboard diving event for the United States at the 1936 Summer Games in Munich, Germany, Marjorie Gestring took home the gold when she was just 13 years and 268 days old. When she was in her prime, the 1940 and 1944 Games were cancelled due to World War II. Gestring's 1948 comeback at age 25 was fruitless.

---

6. Which football coach won both a national championship and a congressional seat?

a. Tom Osborne
b. Don James
c. Bill McCartney
d. Gene Stallings

GAME 37 Q5 ANSWER d
After a Hall of Fame-caliber pitching career that saw him win 224 games and strike out almost 3,000 batters, Jim Bunning decided to enter politics in 1977. The Kentucky resident worked his way up through the ranks of city councilman, state senator, and state representative before being elected a US Senator in 1998.

---

6. Which CBS television sportscaster was fired in 1988 after making racist remarks?

a. Howard Cosell
b. Beano Cook
c. Jimmy Snyder
d. Roger Twibell

GAME 57 Q5 ANSWER b
In 1986, Greg Lemond became the first American to capture the world's most prestigious cycling event. Lemond, who would also go onto win the race in 1989 and 1990, set the stage for future triumphs by fellow countryman Lance Armstrong in the late '90s. Unfortunately, a muscle disorder forced Lemond into early retirement in 1994.

---

6. Tiger Woods

a. Bangkok, Thailand
b. La Jolla, California
c. Cypress, California
d. Sherman Oaks, California

GAME 77 Q5 ANSWER a
Then known as Ferdinand Lewis Alcindor, Jr., Kareem Abdul-Jabbar was born on August 16, 1947 in New York City, and first rose to prominence at Power Memorial High School. The three-time high school All-American led his team to a record of 95–6 during his secondary school tenure.

GAME 4

8. Besides Jackie Robinson, who is the only MLB player to have his number retired by three different teams?

a. Babe Ruth

b. Frank Robinson

c. Nolan Ryan

d. Willie Mays

GAME 4 Q7 ANSWER b
When a franchise can boast that twenty-two of its former players are enshrined in the Pro Football Hall of Fame, it is quite surprising that only one of those twenty-two has had his number retired. Such is the case of former Steeler Ernie Stautner, the defensive tackle who played from 1950 to 1962.

GAME 24

8. Who is the first baseballer to hit 50 home runs and 50 doubles in the same season?

a. Greg Vaughn

b. Albert Belle

c. Alex Rodriguez

d. Barry Bonds

GAME 24 Q7 ANSWER c
Arguably the most dominant male tennis player of the 1990s, Pete Sampras won two Australian Opens, seven Wimbledons, and five US Opens during his career. Sampras's obvious dislike of the clay surface at Roland Garros, which is notorious for slowing down serves, is the likely reason he never advanced to a French Open final.

GAME 44

8. Before Nike's Air Jordan ads, in which movie did Spike Lee's character Mars Blackmon debut?

a. *Do the Right Thing*

b. *School Daze*

c. *Mo' Better Blues*

d. *She's Gotta Have It*

GAME 44 Q7 ANSWER d
Walking off with an NBA-record ten scoring titles, M.J. took the honors each year he played a full season with the Bulls, beginning in 1986. The only times he didn't win in the twelve-year period were 1993-1994 (he was playing baseball) and 1994-1995, when he came back for only the last 17 games of the regular season.

GAME 64

8. Who was the first baseball player to have his uniform number retired?

a. Walter Johnson

b. Babe Ruth

c. Cy Young

d. Lou Gehrig

GAME 64 Q7 ANSWER a
Though some heavyweight champs have come close, 6'7" Italian boxer Primo Carnera, at 270 pounds, remains the heaviest. The "Ambling Alp" beat Jack Sharkey for the title in 1933. After defending it twice, Carnera lost the title in 1934 to Max Baer. The 1956 Humphrey Bogart movie *The Harder They Fall* is loosely based on Carnera's life.

Answers are in right-hand boxes on page 97.

5. Who is the youngest athlete to win an Olympic gold medal?

a. Nadia Comaneci

b. Tara Lipinski

c. Dominique Monceau

d. Marjorie Gestring

GAME 17 Q4 ANSWER a
Just 19 years and 5 months old when he started the 1998 All-Star Game in New York, Kobe Bryant took away the youngest player honor from Magic Johnson. Bryant made a decent showing, leading the Western Conference with 18 points in a 135–144 loss.

5. Which baseball Hall of Famer has been a senator from Kentucky?

a. Jim Hunter

b. Carl Hubbell

c. Robin Roberts

d. Jim Bunning

GAME 37 Q4 ANSWER b
After winning the Heisman Trophy in 1958, Army halfback Pete Dawkins went on to an illustrious career in the service, ascending to the rank of Brigadier General. Dawkins, who also received a PhD from Princeton, failed in his 1988 bid to win the New Jersey senatorship.

5. Who was the first American cyclist to capture the Tour de France?

a. Lance Armstrong

b. Greg Lemond

c. Stephen Roche

d. Roger Pingeon

GAME 57 Q4 ANSWER d
In 1986, Maryland basketball star Len Bias died in his dorm room after using cocaine with friends. A mere two days earlier, the Boston Celtics had selected Bias with the second overall pick in the 1986 Draft. The incident ultimately cost longtime Maryland coach Lefty Driesell his job and sent the Celtics franchise into a tailspin.

5. Kareem Abdul-Jabbar

a. New York, New York

b. Philadelphia, Pennsylvania

c. Hartford, Connecticut

d. Boston, Massachusetts

GAME 77 Q4 ANSWER c
Born October 20, 1931 in Spavinaw, Oklahoma, Hall of Famer Mickey Mantle learned the craft of baseball from "Mutt," his miner father, and Charles, his grandfather. "The Mick" honed his switch-hitting skills by batting left-handed against his righty father, and right-handed against his lefty grandpa.

GAME 4

9. Which NHL team retired the numbers of all three members of its "French Connection" line?

a. Montreal Canadiens
b. Toronto Maple Leafs
c. Buffalo Sabres
d. Edmonton Oilers

GAME 4 Q8 ANSWER c
Nolan Ryan's jersey has been retired by the California Angels, Houston Astros, and Texas Rangers. The "Ryan Express" pitched in the big leagues for twenty-seven seasons (1966–1993). During that time, he amassed 324 wins, 5,714 strikeouts, and his most impressive achievement, 7 no-hitters.

GAME 24

9. Who is the shortest player to win an NBA scoring championship?

a. Nate Archibald
b. Allen Iverson
c. Jerry West
d. Bernard King

GAME 24 Q8 ANSWER b
Finishing the 1995 season with 50 runs and 52 doubles, Albert Belle became the first player to achieve the 50/50 club in the two statistical categories. Many believe the surly Belle should have been named American League MVP that year, but he lost votes to Mo Vaughn, the friendlier Red Sox slugger.

GAME 44

9. How many NBA Finals MVP Awards did Michael Jordan win?

a. Six
b. Five
c. Four
d. Two

GAME 44 Q8 ANSWER d
It was the film *She's Gotta Have It* (1986) that brought attention to independent filmmaker Spike Lee. For Nike, it spawned the popular Mars Blackmon character, which was used successfully in the Air Jordan sneaker advertisements of the late 1980s.

GAME 64

9. What was the real first name of Jack Dempsey "The Manassa Mauler"?

a. Liam
b. William
c. Jacob
d. Wallace

GAME 64 Q8 ANSWER d
In 1939, the New York Yankees retired Gehrig's Number 4, making him the first player to receive such an honor. The "Iron Horse" died in 1941 after a long and courageous battle with amyotrophic lateral sclerosis, which is more commonly known as Lou Gehrig's disease.

4. Who is the youngest player to start an NBA All-Star Game?

a. Kobe Bryant
b. Magic Johnson
c. Shaquille O'Neal
d. Kevin Garnett

GAME 17 Q3 ANSWER c
Dan Fortmann began playing football for Colgate University at age 17. After graduating in 1936 at age 20, he became the youngest player ever to sign an NFL contract. Later that year, Fortmann debuted as a guard for the Chicago Bears, and played until 1943, when he left football to pursue a career in surgical medicine.

4. Which former Heisman Trophy winner once ran for senator of New Jersey?

a. Dick Kazmaier
b. Pete Dawkins
c. Ernie Davis
d. John Lattner

GAME 37 Q3 ANSWER c
Known for his days with Detroit, Red Kelly was later traded to the Toronto Maple Leafs, during which time he served two terms as a member of the Canadian Parliament. Kelly was once quoted as saying "I thought the greatest stick handlers were in hockey, but I found out they were in Parliament."

4. Which school did basketball player Len Bias star for?

a. Duke
b. North Carolina
c. Georgia Tech
d. Maryland

GAME 57 Q3 ANSWER b
Under coach Danny Ford, the Clemson Tigers defeated Nebraska in the January 1982 Orange Bowl to claim the 1981 National Championship. Eleven months later, the NCAA placed the school on three year's probation (two years without bowls and televised games) for doling out money and other perks to players on its football team.

4. Mickey Mantle

a. Oklahoma City, Oklahoma
b. Commerce, Oklahoma
c. Spavinaw, Oklahoma
d. Tulsa, Oklahoma

GAME 77 Q3 ANSWER b
Spending his early years in a two-room shack without indoor plumbing, NBA legend Karl Malone and his eight siblings were raised by his mother in this northern Louisiana town. Young Karl honed his hoops skills on a makeshift basket court, and parlayed his talents into a scholarship from Louisiana State.

10. Which of the numbers that Michael Jordan wore for the Bulls was *not* retired?

a. 33

b. 6

c. 17

d. 45

The Buffalo Sabres' famed "French Connection" line of the 1970s included Gilbert Perrault, Rick Martin, and Rene Robert—all of French-Canadian origin. The French Connection dominated the league from 1972 to 1979. Its most successful season was 1974-1975, when it led the Sabres to their first Stanley Cup Finals.

---

10. Which kicker is tied with Tom Dempsey for the longest field goal in NFL history?

a. Morten Andersen

b. Gary Anderson

c. Mike Vanderjagt

d. Jason Elam

Even though Nate Archibald's nickname is "Tiny," multiple-scoring champ Allen Iverson is the shortest individual ever to lead the league in scoring. At an even 6 feet tall, Iverson's best season came in 2000-2001 when he won the scoring crown, led the Sixers to their first NBA Finals in eighteen years, and was voted the league's MVP.

---

10. Who was Jordan's co-star in his first full-length feature film?

a. Brian Dennehy

b. Denzel Washington

c. Bugs Bunny

d. Spike Lee

Each time Michael Jordan's Bulls won the NBA Championship, Jordan walked away with the Finals MVP Award—six trophies. With the all-time highest NBA playoff scoring average of 33.6 points per game, Jordan really turned it on in the finals—like the 1993 championship round against Phoenix in which he averaged 41 points per game!

---

10. Who was the first black man to play in the NHL?

a. Tony McKegney

b. Tommy Williams

c. Willie O'Ree

d. Bud Kelly

Like his older professional boxer brothers, William Harrison Dempsey called himself "Jack" in honor of previous boxing great Jack Dempsey ("The Nonpareil"). Born in Manassa, Colorado, he began fighting professionally in 1914. A colorful character of the "Roaring Twenties," Dempsey reigned as heavyweight champ from 1919–1926.

---

3. Who is the youngest man ever to play in the NFL?

a. Red Grange
b. Bronko Nagurski
c. Dan Fortmann
d. Emlen Tunnell

GAME 17 Q2 ANSWER d
Leading the Montreal Canadiens to the 1986 Stanley Cup, Patrick Roy, who was a rookie at the wee age of 20, remains the youngest starting goaltender to hoist Lord Stanley's trophy. Due to his stellar play in the 1986 postseason, Roy is also the youngest player to win the Conn Smythe Award for playoff MVP.

3. Which NHL standout served in Canada's House of Parliament while still playing?

a. Terry Sawchuk
b. Eddie Bower
c. Red Kelly
d. Marcel Pronovost

GAME 37 Q2 ANSWER a
Hall of Famer Steve Largent retired from the NFL after spending fourteen seasons with the Seattle Seahawks, and hauling in 100 touchdown receptions. Largent went on to serve Oklahoma in the House of Representatives, and made a failed attempt at winning the state's governorship in 2002.

3. Which school received probation less than a year after winning football's NCAA Title?

a. Alabama
b. Clemson
c. USC
d. Nebraska

GAME 57 Q2 ANSWER a
The Cubs installed lights around the stadium in 1988, and on August 8th the bulbs went on for the first time as the Cubbies hosted the Phillies. Rain, however, shortened the game after an unofficial four innings. The following day, the NY Mets came to town and lost to Chicago 6–4 in the stadium's first completed evening affair.

3. Karl Malone

a. Dothan, Alabama
b. Summerfield, Louisiana
c. Pensacola, Florida
d. Bay St. Louis, Mississippi

GAME 77 Q2 ANSWER a
The pride of Floral, Saskatchewan, was born in 1928. At age 18, he made his Detroit Red Wings debut. "Mr. Hockey" hung up his skates in 1980 at age 53, but returned to the ice in 1997 to play one shift for the IHL's Detroit Vipers at age 69. He was the first person to play in six separate decades.

11. Through 2004, which of the following NFL teams has not officially retired any numbers?

a. Dallas Cowboys

b. Denver Broncos

c. Washington Redskins

d. San Diego Chargers

GAME 4 Q10 ANSWER d
After returning from his baseball sojourn in 1995, Michael Jordan donned number 45 for the season's final 17 regular games and 5 Chicago playoff games. This was the same number that Jordan had donned for the Birmingham Barons in 1994, during his ill-fated attempt at a baseball career.

11. Which team won the most ABA Championships?

a. Indiana Pacers

b. New York Nets

c. Kentucky Colonels

d. Utah Stars

GAME 24 Q10 ANSWER d
On October 25, 1998, Denver Broncos kicker Jason Elam booted his way into the record book by kicking a 63-yard field goal. The kick tied him with Tom Dempsey of the Saints, who managed a field goal of the same distance in 1970. Elam's kick was supposed to be a 58-yard attempt, but a 5-yard penalty was added for delay of game.

11. Which team did Jordan's Tar Heels beat to win his only NCAA Championship?

a. Georgetown

b. Houston

c. Kentucky

d. Georgia

GAME 44 Q10 ANSWER c
While Jordan had been in several basketball action videos—*Come Fly With Me* (1989), *Above and Beyond* (1995), *Journey of the African-American Athlete* (1996)—and had an uncredited cameo in *Malcolm X* (1992), his first full-length flick was *Space Jam* (1996), featuring co-stars Bugs Bunny, Daffy Duck, and the rest of the Looney Toons.

11. Who was the first designated hitter to win a World Series MVP award?

a. Cecil Fielder

b. Paul Molitor

c. Don Baylor

d. Tim Salmon

GAME 64 Q10 ANSWER c
Unlike the mass hysteria surrounding Jackie Robinson's first Major League game, the reaction to Willie O'Ree hitting the ice for the Boston Bruins on January 18, 1958 was calm. O'Ree bounced between the pros and minors for a few years until finally scoring his first goal, on New Years Day in 1961 against Montreal.

2. Who is the youngest starting goaltender to win the Stanley Cup?

a. Martin Brodeur

b. Terry Sawchuk

c. Ken Dryden

d. Patrick Roy

At age 19, Sergio Garcia competed in the 1999 Ryder Cup Matches, making him the youngest player to compete in the European-USA competition (beating Nick Faldo's 1977 Ryder Cup age record by just over 5 months). During the match, Garcia posted a 3–1–1 record. Even earlier, at age 15, he won the 1995 European Amateur.

---

2. Which top NFL receiver went on to represent Oklahoma in the House?

a. Steve Largent

b. Don Maynard

c. Brian Brennan

d. John Jefferson

Quite a sharpshooter before his political days, Bill Bradley still holds the record for most points in an NCAA Final Four game, dumping 58 on Wichita State in the 1965 third-place game while playing for Princeton. Bradley, of course, went on to win a pair of titles with the Knicks, and become a major player in the Democratic Party.

---

2. Which team did the Cubs host in the first "completed" night game at Wrigley Field?

a. New York Mets

b. Los Angeles Dodgers

c. Philadelphia Phillies

d. St. Louis Cardinals

Led by the outstanding play of goaltender Mike Vernon and stellar defenseman Al MacInnis, the Calgary Flames captured the city's only Stanley Cup by defeating the formidable Montreal Canadiens in the Finals, 4 games to 2. MacInnis took home the Conn Smythe Trophy after scoring 31 points in the playoffs—a rare feat for a defender.

---

2. Gordie Howe

a. Floral, Saskatchewan

b. Red Deer, Alberta

c. Surrey, British Columbia

d. Winnipeg, Manitoba

The most famous football player ever to come out of Kiln, Brett Favre was also one of the better Mississippi high school baseball players in the late 1980s, as he was the leading batter for Hancock High School every year he played. He moved onto football stardom at Southern Miss before bringing his magic to the NFL.

GAME 4

12. Which single-digit retired number in Major League Baseball has been used the least?

a. 2

b. 3

c. 6

d. 7

GAME 4 Q11 ANSWER a
Circling the facade of Texas Stadium is the legendary Dallas Cowboys' "Ring of Honor," which pays tribute to ten of the franchise's greatest players, including Hall of Famers Tony Dorsett, Bob Lilly, Mel Renfro, Roger Staubach, Randy White, and, of course, coach Tom Landry. The Cowboys have never officially retired any jersey numbers.

GAME 24

12. Which boxer was the subject of a Warren Zevon song?

a. Ray Mancini

b. Marvin Hagler

c. Sugar Ray Leonard

d. Gerry Cooney

GAME 24 Q11 ANSWER a
Led by two-time league MVP Mel Daniels, the Pacers captured three titles in the ABA's nine-year existence. Julius Erving's New York Nets were second with a pair of championships, while the Pittsburgh Pipers, Oakland Oaks, Utah Stars, and Kentucky Colonels each claimed a single crown.

GAME 44

12. Who was Jordan's first pro coach?

a. Stan Albeck

b. Kevin Loughery

c. Paul Westhead

d. Doug Collins

GAME 44 Q11 ANSWER a
In the only NCAA Championship game of his college career, Jordan found himself matching up against future rival Patrick Ewing. Jordan, who scored only 16 points, got the ball with less than 30 seconds to play and his Tar Heels down 1 point. M.J. drained the bucket and, after a bad Georgetown turnover, NC sealed the deal.

GAME 64

12. Who is the youngest coach to win a Super Bowl?

a. Jon Gruden

b. John Madden

c. Joe Gibbs

d. Chuck Noll

GAME 64 Q11 ANSWER b
Taking home the World Series MVP honor in 1993, Toronto's Paul Molitor became the first DH to win the best player award in the Fall Classic. The longtime Brewer hit .500 in the series with 2 home runs and 8 RBIs.

GAME 17	1. Who is the youngest player ever to compete in the Ryder Cup Matches? a. Tiger Woods b. Sergio Garcia c. Nick Faldo d. Jack Nicklaus	The answer to this question is on: **page 102, top frame, right side.**
GAME 37	1. Which college did presidential candidate and NY Knick Bill Bradley attend? a. Harvard b. Princeton c. Yale d. Penn	The answer to this question is on: **page 102, second frame, right side.**
GAME 57	1. Which Canadian hockey franchise won its only Stanley Cup in 1989? a. Winnipeg Jets b. Calgary Flames c. Vancouver Canucks d. Quebec Nordiques	The answer to this question is on: **page 102, third frame, right side.**
GAME 77	1. Brett Favre a. Biloxi, Mississippi b. Kiln, Mississippi c. Tupelo, Mississippi d. Jackson, Mississippi	The answer to this question is on: **page 102, bottom frame, right side.**

GAME 5

"Remarkable Rookies"

Are You Familiar with These Fantastic Freshmen?

Turn to page 107 for the first question.

Turn to page 107 for the first question.

GAME 4 Q12 ANSWER d
Only Yankee legend Mickey Mantle wore retired number 7. Next in line are the numbers 2 and 6, which have each been worn by four players. Who said 7 is a lucky number?

GAME 25

"The 1940s"

The Decade of FDR and World War II

Turn to page 107 for the first question.

Turn to page 107 for the first question.

GAME 24 Q12 ANSWER a
In a tragic 1982 boxing match between Ray "Boom Boom" Mancini and Korean fighter Duk Koo Kim, Kim suffered a brain injury and died five days later. After Mancini received some negative press following the fight, boxing fan Warren Zevon shot back in defense of the American fighter with the haunting tune "Boom Boom Mancini."

GAME 45

"The Sweet Science"

Notable Boxers, Fights, and Ring Personalities

Turn to page 107 for the first question.

Turn to page 107 for the first question.

GAME 44 Q12 ANSWER b
The coach of the Bulls for Jordan's rookie year (1984-1985), Kevin Loughery often held practice games in which the first squad to hit 10 points would win. If one team got too far ahead, he would switch Jordan to the losing group. With M.J.'s ultra-competitive nature, the team usually wound up winning.

GAME 65

"The 1990s"

Grunge, Clinton, and a Great Decade for Sports

Turn to page 107 for the first question.

Turn to page 107 for the first question.

GAME 64 Q12 ANSWER a
By winning Super Bowl XXVII as coach of the Tampa Bay Buccaneers, Jon Gruden eclipsed John Madden's record as the youngest coach to hoist the Lombardi Trophy. The 39-year-old Gruden accomplished the feat in his first year on the job.

GAME 17

"Under 21"

They Shocked the World at a Young Age

Turn to page 104 for the first question.

GAME 16 Q12 ANSWER c
One of the most recognizable and treacherous holes in golf is Hole 17 at the TPC at Sawgrass, in Ponte Vedra Beach, Florida. The Players Championship is held there every March. According to the superintendent, over 100,000 balls are pulled from the surrounding lake each year.

GAME 37

"Sports and Politics"

From Sportsman to Politician—or Vice Versa

Turn to page 104 for the first question.

GAME 36 Q12 ANSWER d
An actual referee, Lou Filippo was recruited to play parts in all five *Rocky* films. Playing a fight announcer in the first film, *Rocky* (1976), Filippo went on to serve as referee in the next four movies. He also had guest roles on 1980s television shows *Moonlighting*, *The A-Team*, and *The Fall Guy*.

GAME 57

"The 1980s"

Junk Bonds, Rambo, and "Reaganomics"

Turn to page 104 for the first question.

GAME 56 Q12 ANSWER c
Prior to being known as Apollo Creed, film star Carl Weathers had a brief CFL career with the British Columbia Lions. After coming out of San Diego State as a linebacker, Weathers had a cup of coffee with the Oakland Raiders, and then moved up north, where he played three seasons in the CFL from 1971 to 1973.

GAME 77

"Superstar Hometowns"

Do You Know Where They Were Reared?

Turn to page 104 for the first question.

GAME 76 Q12 ANSWER b
Brian Bosworth was chosen in the 1987 NFL Supplemental Draft, which cost the Seattle Seahawks a 1988 first-round pick. "The Boz" had his most notable moment in a 1988 Monday night game, when he was embarrassingly carried into the end zone while trying to tackle Bo Jackson. A shoulder injury ended his career after three seasons.

GAME 5	1. Which is the last NBA team to have back-to-back Rookie of the Year winners? a. Orlando Magic b. Buffalo Braves c. San Antonio Spurs d. Rochester Red Wings	The answer to this question is on: **page 109, top frame, right side.**
GAME 25	1. Which teams participated in the first NBA game? a. Boston and New York b. Minneapolis and Boston c. Minneapolis and St. Louis d. New York and Toronto	The answer to this question is on: **page 109, second frame, right side.**
GAME 45	1. After Mike Tyson's release from prison, whom did he dispose of in his first fight? a. Buster Mathis, Jr. b. Peter McNeely c. Bert Cooper d. Lou Savarese	The answer to this question is on: **page 109, third frame, right side.**
GAME 65	1. Who did Minnesota defeat in the 1991 "Worst to First" World Series? a. Pittsburgh b. Atlanta c. San Diego d. Cincinnati	The answer to this question is on: **page 109, bottom frame, right side.**

107

12. Which golf course is known for its seventeenth-hole island green?

a. Oakland Hills
b. Pebble Beach
c. TPC at Sawgrass
d. Oakmont

GAME 16 Q11 ANSWER d
Debuting at the 1984 Denver All-Star Game, the first NBA slam-dunk contest included nine of the best dunk artists. The finals saw Dr. J. competing against Larry Nance, with both getting 3 dunks each. While Julius Irving was the first player to receive a perfect score of 50, Nance won the trophy due to Irving's botched second dunk.

12. Which boxing figure was the featured ref in *Rocky II, III, IV,* and *V*?

a. Stu Nahan
b. Ferdie Pacheco
c. Eddie Lopez
d. Lou Filippo

GAME 36 Q11 ANSWER b
Parlaying his notoriety from the bizarre boxing match into his own television show, *Judge Mills Lane,* the famous ringsman actually had a career in law before his small screen debut. Aside from law, boxing is his great passion.

12. For which Canadian Football League team did actor Carl Weathers once play?

a. Edmonton
b. Winnipeg
c. British Columbia
d. Montreal

GAME 56 Q11 ANSWER b
While all of the listed teams have had disappointing seasons at some point, no regular season team can match the futility of the 76ers in the 1972-1973 season. The team accumulated a pitiful record of 9 wins and 73 losses for a record low winning percentage of .123.

12. Which NFL draft flop starred in the film *Stone Cold* (1991)?

a. Cade McNown
b. Brian Bosworth
c. Keith McCants
d. Steve Emtman

GAME 76 Q11 ANSWER b
Forever known as the man who was taken ahead of both Michael Jordan and Charles Barkley with the second overall pick in the 1984 NBA Draft, Sam Bowie actually had his number 31 jersey retired by the Kentucky Wildcats. A 7-foot center, Bowie's biggest honor of his senior season was being named to the UPI's SEC second team.

GAME 5

2. Who is the only rookie besides Ichiro Suzuki to win baseball's MVP Award?

a. Fernando Valenzuela

b. Mark McGwire

c. Fred Lynn

d. Jose Canseco

GAME 5 Q1 ANSWER b
When Bob McAdoo and Ernie DiGregorio took home the hardware in the 1972-1973 and 1973-1974 seasons, respectively, it was as members of the now-defunct Buffalo Braves. McAdoo led the NBA in scoring for three consecutive seasons (from 1973-1974 through 1975-1976). He took home the league MVP trophy in the 1974-1975 season.

GAME 25

2. Which team ended Joe DiMaggio's hitting streak in 1941?

a. Boston Red Sox

b. Cleveland Indians

c. Detroit Tigers

d. Philadelphia Athletics

GAME 25 Q1 ANSWER d
The Toronto Huskies hosted the New York Knicks for the first NBA game, which was held at Toronto's Maple Leaf Gardens on November 1, 1946. The visitors won 68–66. To kick off the NBA's Fiftieth Anniversary season (1996-1997), the game was again held in Toronto, but this time the Toronto Raptors hosted the Knicks.

GAME 45

2. Which boxing figure is known as "The Fight Doctor"?

a. Teddy Atlas

b. Eddie Futch

c. Ferdie Pacheco

d. Angelo Dundee

GAME 45 Q1 ANSWER b
This highly anticipated match proved to be a major letdown as Tyson, even after being incarcerated for over three years, was far superior to McNeely. The bout was less than a warm-up for Iron Mike, as McNeely trainer Vinnie Vecchione stopped the fight in the first round.

GAME 65

2. Which female skater won the gold medal in the wake of the Harding-Kerrigan incident?

a. Kristi Yamaguchi

b. Midori Ito

c. Oksana Baiul

d. Lu Chen

GAME 65 Q1 ANSWER b
The 1991 Series pit the previous season's last-place teams—the Minnesota Twins and the Atlanta Braves—against each other in an exciting matchup. Three games went into extra innings. Four ended with a team scoring the winner in its final at-bat. Five games were decided by one run. Minnesota won the series in Game 7.

11. Who won the NBA's first slam-dunk competition?

a. Dominique Wilkins

b. Michael Jordan

c. Julius Irving

d. Larry Nance

GAME 16 Q10: ANSWER c

Playing the stressed-out best friend of Ferris Bueller (Matthew Broderick) in John Hughes' flick about teens skipping a day of school, Cameron Frye (Alan Ruck) is often attired in a Gordie Howe, number 9, Detroit Red Wings jersey. Sports fans may also remember the scene in which Ferris catches a foul ball in Wrigley Field.

---

11. Who refereed the famous Tyson-Holyfield ear-biting match?

a. Richard Steele

b. Mills Lane

c. Eddie Cotton

d. Octavio Meyran

GAME 36 Q10 ANSWER a

It took selectors over thirty-five years to find an umpire worthy of Hall of Fame induction. And Evans was one of the all-time best. He joined the AL staff in 1906 at age 22, becoming the youngest Major League umpire. He was known for his fairness and integrity.

---

11. Which team posted the worst winning percentage in NBA regular season history?

a. Dallas Mavericks

b. Philadelphia 76ers

c. Denver Nuggets

d. Vancouver Grizzlies

GAME 56 Q10 ANSWER a

In June of 1998, Chicago Cubs' "Slammin' Sammy Sosa hit 20 home runs, breaking the sixty-year-old record held by Rudy York, who had hit 18 homers in August of 1937.

---

11. For which college did 1984 draft choice Sam Bowie play in the 1980s?

a. Duke

b. Kentucky

c. Ohio State

d. Wake Forest

GAME 76 Q10 ANSWER c

Taken before Barry Sanders and Deion Sanders, Tony Mandarich held out his rookie year for a huge salary, which he got. After three miserable seasons, he contracted a parasitic infection, suffered a major concussion, and developed a thyroid condition. He appeared on a *Sports Illustrated* cover under the headline "Incredible Bust."

GAME 5

3. Who holds the NFL rookie record for most rushing yards in a single game?

a. Corey Dillon
b. Walter Payton
c. Edgerrin James
d. Mike Anderson

The 1975 season was a memorable one for Red Sox rookie outfielder Fred Lynn, as he not only captured the American League Rookie of the Year Award, but also took home the league's MVP. Lynn hit .331 that year, with 21 homers and 105 runs batted in.

GAME 25

3. Who was the first quarterback to throw for 7 touchdowns in a game?

a. Sammy Baugh
b. Bob Waterfield
c. Sid Luckman
d. Norm Van Brocklin

Over 67,000 fans packed Cleveland's Municipal Stadium on July 17, 1941, to watch Joe DiMaggio extend his hitting streak to 57 games. It didn't happen. Twice robbed by Indians' third baseman Ken Keltner, DiMaggio's 56-game hit parade came to an end. The very next day, he started a new 16-game streak.

GAME 45

3. Which Latino fighter was called "El Flaco Explosivo" (The Skinny Explosive)?

a. Alexis Arguello
b. Bobby Chacon
c. Danny Lopez
d. Wilfredo Vazquez

Best known as the personal physician to Muhammad Ali, Ferdie Pacheco has been a lifelong fan of the sweet science. After his doctoring days were complete, he made a switch to the broadcast booth.

GAME 65

3. Which thoroughbred won 16 straight races in the mid-'90s?

a. Kelso
b. Sumac Lad
c. Strike the Gold
d. Cigar

After the incident in which Tonya Harding's "associates" tried to knock Nancy Kerrigan out of the 1994 Olympics, teenager Oksana Baiul of the Ukraine swept to the gold medal platform in Lillehammer. Kerrigan, who miraculously competed, took home the silver, while Harding finished a disappointing eighth.

GAME 16

10. Which hockey jersey did Cameron Frye wear in *Ferris Bueller's Day Off* (1986)?

a. Chicago Blackhawks

b. Boston Bruins

c. Detroit Red Wings

d. Minnesota North Stars

GAME 16 Q9 ANSWER a
In 1965, Cleveland Indians outfielder Rocky Colavito was the first and only player to accomplish this feat. He was on the field for all 162 games with 265 put outs, 9 assists, and no errors.

GAME 36

10. Who was the first umpire inducted into the Baseball Hall of Fame?

a. Billy Evans

b. Cal Hubbard

c. Jocko Conlon

d. Al Barlick

GAME 36 Q9 ANSWER c
One of the most colorful and well-liked umpires of all time, Ron Luciano was as clever with the pen as with the whistle. The late Luciano also produced works entitled *Strike Two* (1984) and *The Fall of the Roman Umpire* (1986).

GAME 56

10. Who holds the record for the most home runs in a single month?

a. Sammy Sosa

b. Mark McGwire

c. Babe Ruth

d. Rudy York

GAME 56 Q9 ANSWER a
By tallying 48 markers for the Edmonton Oilers in the 1985-1986 season, Hall of Famer Paul Coffey holds the record for most goals in a season by a defenseman. The three-time Norris Trophy winner played for nine different NHL teams, and won four Stanley Cups. He retired in 2001 with 396 goals, 1,135 assists, and 1,531 total points.

GAME 76

10. Which disappointing selection did Green Bay make second over-all in the 1989 NFL Draft?

a. Aundray Bruce

b. Bennie Blades

c. Tony Mandarich

d. Sammie Smith

GAME 76 Q9 ANSWER a
After some flashes of brilliance, Quebec product Alexandre Daigle fizzled with the Senators, and has since bounced around between several minor league and NHL clubs. Ottawa fans cringe when they realize that Chris Pronger, Paul Kariya, and Jason Arnott were all selected behind Daigle.

4. Which NHL star scored 76 goals in his rookie campaign?

a. Teemu Selanne

b. Wayne Gretzky

c. Alexander Mogilny

d. Jari Kurri

GAME 5 Q3 ANSWER d
Built more like a Sherman Tank than a running back, Denver Broncos' Mike Anderson exploded for 251 yards in a December 2000 game against New Orleans, besting Corey Dillon's 1997 standard of 246 yards in a game. Anderson also scored four touchdowns that day.

---

4. Which NHL goaltender won five Vezina Trophies during the 1940s?

a. Frank Brimsek

b. Bill Durnan

c. Turk Broda

d. Johnny Mowers

GAME 25 Q3 ANSWER c
Quarterbacking the Chicago Bears' "Monsters of the Midway" teams, Sid Luckman had his best afternoon on November 14, 1943 at the Polo Grounds. The master of the "T-Formation" blitzed his hometown Giants 56–7, and tossed 7 TDs in the process. Luckman was the league MVP that year and led the Bears to the NFL Championship.

---

4. Which fighter retired after he was denied a rematch for Sugar Ray Leonard's middleweight belt?

a. Thomas Hearns

b. Marvin Hagler

c. Frank Tate

d. Wilfred Benitez

GAME 45 Q3 ANSWER a
Standing 5'10" and weighing only 130 pounds, the Nicaraguan fighter blazed a path through the lightweight divisions in the late 1970s after his possessions were seized by the Sandinista regime. Arguello moved to Miami and began to win titles in the flyweight, junior lightweight, and lightweight divisions.

---

4. In 1997, which NBA player's assault on his coach resulted in a costly suspension?

a. Vernon Maxwell

b. Isaiah Rider

c. Latrell Sprewell

d. J.R. Reid

GAME 65 Q3 ANSWER d
In fall of 1994, Cigar began his famous 16-race winning streak, which would tie the record of legendary racehorse Citation. Cigar, whose wins included the 1995 Breeders' Cup Classic and the Dubai World Cup, would have his streak stopped in the August 1996 Pacific Classic, in which he finished second to a horse named Dare and Go.

---

9. Which post-expansion era baseballer played all 162 season games in the field without making a single error?

a. Rocky Colavito
b. Steve Garvey
c. Brett Butler
d. Paul Blair

GAME 16 Q8 ANSWER a
The first Rose Bowl, held in Pasadena's Tournament Park in 1902, featured Michigan pummeling Stanford 49–0. The game moved to its present home, the aptly named Rose Bowl, in 1923. It has been held there ever since, except for 1942 when the game was played at Duke University Stadium due to war concerns.

9. Which ump authored the successful 1982 book *The Umpire Strikes Back*?

a. Bruce Froemming
b. Doug Harvey
c. Ron Luciano
d. Harry Wendelstedt

GAME 36 Q8 ANSWER a
Just hearing the name Ben Dreith makes older Patriots fans cringe, as his questionable "roughing the passer" call against New England's Ray Hamilton cost them a trip to the Super Bowl. After the hit on Oakland quarterback Ken Stabler was enforced, the Raiders rallied for the winning score, knocking the Patriots out of the playoffs.

9. Which hockey player holds the record for most goals in a season by a defenseman?

a. Paul Coffey
b. Denis Potvin
c. Bobby Orr
d. Ray Bourque

GAME 56 Q8 ANSWER d
A title achieved by less than 100 men, Yokozuna is the highest ranking in sumo wrestling. A Yokozuna is differentiated from other competitors by his hair, which is worn in the shape of a gingko plant. The first non-Japanese wrestler to achieve the sport's top honor was the Hawaiian-born Akebono, who tipped the scales at 500 pounds.

9. Which regrettable 1993 draft pick did the Ottawa Senators make first overall?

a. Alexandre Daigle
b. Radim Bicanek
c. Ryan Sittler
d. Phil Bourque

GAME 76 Q8 ANSWER c
In a draft that was one of the deepest for quarterbacks, Kansas City scored a major bust with Penn State signal caller Todd Blackledge, who was chosen ahead of Jim Kelly and Dan Marino. In his first two years as the Chiefs' starter, Blackledge threw 12 touchdowns and 25 interceptions.

5. Who was the last jockey to lead the sport in victories and win the top apprentice award in the same year?

a. Steve Cauthen

b. Laffit Pincay, Jr.

c. Kent Desormeaux

d. Angel Cordero, Jr.

GAME 5 Q4 ANSWER a
The days of 76 goals in a season seem a distant memory now, with the current defensive style of NHL play, but back in the 1992-1993 season, the "Finnish Flash," Teemu Selanne, found the back of the net a record 76 times while playing for the Winnipeg Jets.

---

5. How many thoroughbreds won the Triple Crown during the 1940s?

a. 1

b. 2

c. 3

d. 4

GAME 25 Q4 ANSWER b
In a decade that belonged to rival Toronto, a Montreal goaltender shined the brightest. Bill Durnan took home five Vezina Trophies during the decade, along with two Stanley Cups. Playing only seven NHL seasons, Durnan was awarded the top goalie prize in six of those campaigns, and posted 34 shutouts in 383 career starts.

---

5. Which boxing promoter once received a four-year prison sentence?

a. Bob Arum

b. Dan Duva

c. Cedric Kushner

d. Don King

GAME 45 Q4 ANSWER b
Marvin Hagler received his shot at the middleweight belt in 1979, battling champion Vito Antuofermo to a draw. A year later, he wrestled the title from Alan Minter and held the championship until 1987, when a previously retired Sugar Ray Leonard took him down in a questionable split decision. He was denied a rematch.

---

5. Which college football team did Colorado defeat in the 1990 "5ᵗʰ Down Game"?

a. Missouri

b. Michigan

c. Oklahoma

d. Texas

GAME 65 Q4 ANSWER c
Fed up with what he called constant verbal abuse, an angry Latrell Sprewell choked and then threatened to kill Golden State head coach P.J. Carlesimo. Sprewell, who was suspended one full year by the NBA and had his $32 million contract terminated by the Warriors, eventually signed with the Knicks in 1998.

GAME 16

8. Which is the oldest (the "Granddaddy") of all the college bowl games?

a. Rose Bowl

b. Orange Bowl

c. Cotton Bowl

d. Sugar Bowl

GAME 16 Q7 ANSWER d
Deciding that it would be better to alternate the Winter and Summer Games every two years rather than having both in the same year, the International Olympic Committee scheduled the Lillehammer Winter Olympics in 1994, just two years after the 1992 games were held in Albertville, France.

GAME 36

8. Which ref hit New England with a "roughing the passer" penalty in the 1976 playoffs?

a. Ben Dreith

b. Gerry Austin

c. Dick Hantak

d. Bob McLwee

GAME 36 Q7 ANSWER d
With the St. Louis Cardinals holding a 1–0 lead in the ninth inning of Game 6, Kansas City outfielder Jorge Orta hit a ground ball towards first base and was out by a decent margin. Umpire Don Denkinger clearly blew the call, and probably cost the Cards the title, as Kansas City rallied to win the game and clinch the series a day later.

GAME 56

8. What is the title given to the Grand Champion of sumo wrestling?

a. Yumiori

b. Yasumi

c. Yobidashi

d. Yokozuna

GAME 56 Q7 ANSWER b
The annual tournament that decides Canada's National Curling Champion, the Brier is held at various Canadian cities, and features curlers from each province. Played on ice, the game involves sliding a 42-pound granite stone toward a 12-foot archery-style target, as sweepers furiously polish the ice ahead of the rock for better glide.

GAME 76

8. Which team selected Todd Blackledge seventh overall in the 1983 NFL Draft?

a. New England Patriots

b. Green Bay Packers

c. Kansas City Chiefs

d. Houston Oilers

GAME 76 Q7 ANSWER a
Looking for a big man to eventually replace the aging Patrick Ewing, the Knicks selected French center Frederick Weis with the fifteenth overall pick. The first and last draft choice of New York's brief-tenured general manager Ed Tapscott turned out to be an oft-injured player who never appeared in a single NBA game.

6. Which player holds the rookie record for home runs in a season?

a. Mark McGwire

b. Mickey Mantle

c. Roger Maris

d. Ken Griffey, Jr.

GAME 5 Q5 ANSWER c
Racing primarily on the Maryland circuit, Kent Desormeaux took home the Eclipse Award as the nation's top apprentice jockey in 1987, while also leading the sport in races won, with an astounding 450 victories in just over 2,200 mounts. Desormeaux continued his winning ways the next year, topping the victory chart with 474 wins.

6. Which fighter besides Joe Louis held the NBA Heavyweight Title in the 1940s?

a. Ezzard Charles

b. Rocky Marciano

c. Jersey Joe Walcott

d. Buddy Baer

GAME 25 Q5 ANSWER d
The 1940s was the decade that produced the most Triple Crown winners, as four of the eleven horses to win racing's most coveted prize competed during that tenure. Whirlaway kicked things off in 1941, followed by Count Fleet in 1943. Assault captured the triple in 1946, and Citation was the 1948 winner.

6. Who is the only cartoonist to be inducted into the Boxing Hall of Fame?

a. Jim Davis

b. Bill Gallo

c. Charles Schulz

d. Gary Trudeau

GAME 45 Q5 ANSWER d
Once serving time for non-negligent homicide in his early days, the legendary Don King has always said he used his time in the slammer to build up his intelligence. Studying the writings of Aristotle, Homer, and Freud, he cited his favorite author as William Shakespeare, once commenting, "He was some bad dude."

6. Fans of which NHL team once threw toy rats on the ice after goals were scored?

a. Los Angeles Kings

b. Florida Panthers

c. Dallas Stars

d. Phoenix Coyotes

GAME 65 Q5 ANSWER a
In an amazing blunder, the officials of the 1990 Colorado-Missouri game mistakenly gave the Buffaloes an extra down when the sideline marker wasn't changed from 2nd to 3rd down. The bonus down resulted in a hollow 33–31 Colorado victory after a Charles Johnson touchdown run and a share of the national championship with Georgia Tech.

7. Which city hosted the Winter Olympics only two years after the previous one?

a. Lake Placid, New York
b. Albertville, France
c. Calgary, Alberta
d. Lillehammer, Norway

GAME 16 Q6 ANSWER c
In Game 1 of the 1923 Series, the Yankees and Giants headed into the ninth inning all tied up at 4–4. With 2 outs, Giants veteran outfielder Charles Dillon "Casey" Stengel stepped up to the plate and lined one into center field. The ball rolled to the wall as Stengel made it around the bases for an in-the-park home run.

7. Which umpire is best known for blowing a crucial call in the 1985 World Series?

a. Dutch Rennert
b. Ken Kaiser
c. Dave Pallone
d. Don Denkinger

GAME 36 Q6 ANSWER a
One of the few refs in the NHL who does not wear a helmet, Kerry Fraser is known to many NHL fans by his always-perfect hair. Never getting mussed, even after a triple-overtime playoff game, Fraser's do is the stuff of legends. He has also become one of hockey's most respected "zebras."

7. "The Brier" is the championship event of which sport?

a. Table Tennis
b. Curling
c. Badminton
d. Logrolling

GAME 56 Q6 ANSWER d
By coaching Italy to victories in the 1934 and 1938 World Cups, coach Vittorio Pozzo is the only man to be credited with having more than one title. Even though Brazil had three championships between 1958 and 1970, there was a different coach for each appearance.

7. Which disappointing choice did the Knicks make in the first round of the 1999 Draft?

a. Frederick Weis
b. Vonteego Cummings
c. Rico Hill
d. Leon Smith

GAME 76 Q6 ANSWER b
The Bengals chose promising quarterback Akili Smith ahead of Ricky Williams and Daunte Culpepper. The Oregon legend played in just a handful of games since 1999. As of the 2003 season, he has thrown just 5 career touchdowns.

GAME 5

7. Who is the only member of the Utah Jazz to have been named Rookie of the Year?

a. Karl Malone

b. John Stockton

c. Darrell Griffith

d. Mark Eaton

GAME 5 Q6 ANSWER a
Mark McGwire belted a record 49 round-trippers in his initial season for the Oakland Athletics in 1987. While he struggled through injuries and inconsistencies in the following years, in 1997, McGwire was the second player since Babe Ruth to hit at least 50 home runs in consecutive seasons.

GAME 25

7. In which year was the last .400 batting average achieved in baseball?

a. 1940

b. 1941

c. 1944

d. 1945

GAME 25 Q6 ANSWER a
After long-time champ Joe Louis retired in 1948, Ezzard Charles won the 15-round decision against Joe Walcott in June of 1949. When Louis "un-retired" in 1950, Charles beat him in 15 rounds (by decision) to become the undisputed champ. He held the belt until July 1951, when Walcott finally got the better of him in Round 7.

GAME 45

7. Who was the first boxer to hold three world championships simultaneously?

a. Tony Zale

b. Henry Armstrong

c. Kid Gavilan

d. Willie Pep

GAME 45 Q6 ANSWER b
After creating satirical sports cartoons for over forty years, *New York Daily News* cartoonist Bill Gallo was inducted into the Boxing Hall of Fame in 2002. The World War II veteran's most notable boxing cartoon came in the late 1970s. It featured an aging, obese Muhammad Ali with his stomach flopping into a wheelbarrow.

GAME 65

7. Which player called a devastating "time-out" in the 1993 NCAA Men's Basketball title game?

a. Ray Jackson

b. Glenn Robinson

c. Jalen Rose

d. Chris Webber

GAME 65 Q6 ANSWER b
The brief mid-'90s tradition of littering the Florida Panthers home rink with toy rats began after team captain, Scott Mellanby found and destroyed a rat in the locker room before the home opener. Mellanby went on to score a pair of goals that night, including the game winner, in a performance that was dubbed "The Rat Trick."

Answers are in right-hand boxes on page 121.   **119**

6. Who hit the very first World Series home run at Yankee Stadium?

a. Lou Gehrig
b. Bob Meusel
c. Casey Stengel
d. Babe Ruth

GAME 16 Q5 ANSWER a
A holder of many records, the "Georgia Peach" Ty Cobb is also the holder of the single-season home steals mark. Swiping the plate 8 times in 1912 as a member of the Detroit Tigers, Cobb set the league standard, which still stands. Cobb also holds the career record, with 55 total steals of home.

6. Which current NHL referee is known simply by his hairdo?

a. Kerry Fraser
b. Bill McCreary
c. Shane Heyer
d. Kevin Collins

GAME 36 Q5 ANSWER b
After twelve years behind the plate in the Atlanta organization, ex-catcher Benedict—who began calling junior high and high school games while still playing baseball—switched to blowing a whistle in NCAA basketball games. The year 2002 marked an officiating milestone for Benedict, as he called his first NCAA tournament game.

6. Who is the only soccer coach to have more than one World Cup title?

a. Aime Jacquet
b. Alf Ramsey
c. Helmut Schoen
d. Vittorio Pozzo

GAME 56 Q5 ANSWER c
Winning NASCAR's top honor in 1975, 1976, and 1977, legendary speedster Cale Yarborough remains the only driver to take three straight Winston Cups. A four-time Daytona 500 victor, Yarborough remains firmly in fifth place all-time, with eighty-three career wins —one behind both Bobby Allison and Darrell Waltrip.

6. Which team chose Akili Smith third overall in the 1999 NFL Draft?

a. Dallas Cowboys
b. Cincinnati Bengals
c. Miami Dolphins
d. Chicago Bears

GAME 76 Q5 ANSWER d
Taken with the sixth overall pick by Dallas, portly forward Robert "Tractor" Traylor was quickly traded to Milwaukee for the rights to Dirk Nowitzki and Pat Garrity. In the following years, Traylor played for three different franchises, but was never more than a bench player.

8. Which team boasted five consecutive National League Rookie of the Year Awards in the 1990s?

a. St. Louis Cardinals

b. Los Angeles Dodgers

c. Montreal Expos

d. Oakland Athletics

GAME 5 Q7 ANSWER c
Selected second overall in the 1980 draft, Darrell Griffith came to Utah after leading Louisville to the NCAA Championship and being named College Player of the Year. Dubbed "The Golden Griff" by announcer Hot Rod Hudley, Griffith topped all rookies in the 1980-1981 campaign by averaging 20.6 points per game.

8. Which university had three Heisman Trophy winners during the 1940s?

a. Ohio State

b. Army

c. Southern Methodist

d. Notre Dame

GAME 25 Q7 ANSWER b
Ted Williams finished the 1941 season hitting .406. He was batting .399 when heading into the final day's doubleheader against Philadelphia. As the number would have rounded up to .400, manager Joe Cronin suggested that Williams take the day off. Teddy insisted on playing and went 6 for 8 on the day, raising the number to .406.

8. Who is the only person to defeat Gene Tunney?

a. Jack Dempsey

b. Harry Greb

c. Battling Siki

d. Max Schmeling

GAME 45 Q7 ANSWER b
"Hurricane Henry" won the featherweight title in 1937. In 1938, he beat Barney Ross for the welterweight title. Three months later, he dropped back down to take the lightweight title from Lou Ambers.

8. Which American stadium hosted the 1994 FIFA Men's World Cup Final?

a. Rose Bowl

b. RFK Stadium

c. Giants Stadium

d. Soldier Field

GAME 65 Q7 ANSWER d
With his team down 2 against North Carolina in the waning seconds of the game, Michigan's Chris Webber had the ball and called a time-out. Michigan, however, had already used up its allotted stoppages. Webber's blunder resulted in a technical foul, which gave the Tar Heels the ball and ended any hopes of a Wolverines victory.

5. Who holds the single-season record for stealing home?

a. Ty Cobb

b. Rickey Henderson

c. Max Carey

d. Pete Reiser

GAME 16 Q4 ANSWER d
According to the rules, the honor goes to the last player to win a hole or take the least number of strokes. For confirmation of this rule, refer to the scene in *Caddyshack* (1980) in which Lou Loomis, speaking to Judge Smails at the beginning of a match, exclaims, "Your honor, Your Honor."

---

5. Which Major League catcher became a successful NCAA Basketball referee?

a. Rich Gedman

b. Bruce Benedict

c. Ron Karkovice

d. Ron Hassey

GAME 36 Q4 ANSWER d
Taking the field for the Washington Senators' opener on April 4, 1966, Emmett Ashford became the first black umpire to call a Major League game. Ashford, who was hired at the age of 51 and worked only the requisite five years necessary to get a pension, was also known for his sense of style.

---

5. Who was the only NASCAR driver to take three straight Winston Cups?

a. Richard Petty

b. Jeff Gordon

c. Cale Yarborough

d. David Pearson

GAME 56 Q4 ANSWER a
Sonny Liston was convicted of armed robbery in 1950 after he and a number of accomplices robbed several gas stations and other businesses. While serving two years of a three-to-five sentence, Liston learned how to box. He won his first professional fight in 1952 by knocking out Don Smith in a mere 33 seconds.

---

5. Which 1998 Dallas Mavericks first-round pick was a major disappointment?

a. Cherokee Parks

b. Randolph Childress

c. George Zidek

d. Robert Traylor

GAME 76 Q4 ANSWER b
Selected by the New York Yankees first overall in baseball's 1991 amateur draft, pitcher Brien Taylor received a fat signing bonus of $1,550,000. Sidelined by injuries and various other problems, Taylor never made it higher than Double-A ball.

GAME 5

9. Who was the last player to win both the Vezina and Calder Trophies in the same year?

a. Patrick Roy
b. Dominik Hasek
c. Ed Belfour
d. Martin Brodeur

GAME 5 Q8 ANSWER b
From 1992 to 1996, whenever the award was handed out, a Los Angeles Dodger was there to take home the trophy. In chronological order, the winners were Eric Karros, Mike Piazza, Raul Mondesi, Hideo Nomo, and Todd Hollandsworth. Piazza and Mondesi were both unanimous winners in their respective years.

GAME 25

9. What was the line called that featured Detroit Red Wings Howe, Abel, and Lindsay?

a. The HAL Line
b. The Production Line
c. The Power Line
d. The Octopus Line

GAME 25 Q8 ANSWER d
Along with their four national championships in the 1940s, Notre Dame also had three members of its squad take home the coveted Heisman Trophy. They were quarterback Angelo Bertelli in 1943; his successor, John Lujack, in 1947; and receiver Leon Hart in 1949.

GAME 45

9. Which boxer/trainer pair is a mismatch?

a. Muhammad Ali/Angelo Dundee
b. Joe Louis/Jack Blackburn
c. Mike Tyson/Teddy Atlas
d. Evander Holyfield/Mickey Goldmill

GAME 45 Q8 ANSWER b
Gene Tunney and Rocky Marciano are considered the only undefeated heavyweight champions. But Tunney actually lost a bout as a light heavyweight to Harry Greb in 1922.

GAME 65

9. Who was the MVP when the Giants defeated Buffalo in Super Bowl XXV?

a. Jeff Hostetler
b. Lawrence Taylor
c. Ottis Anderson
d. Mark Ingram

GAME 65 Q8 ANSWER a
The memorable 1994 FIFA World Cup Final between Brazil and Italy was held at the Rose Bowl in Pasadena, California. Over 100,000 fans packed the stadium to watch the two nations battle to a scoreless tie in a game that was decided by penalty kicks. Brazil ultimately triumphed.

4. In golf, a player allowed to hit first off a particular tee has the:

a. Privilege

b. Right

c. Advantage

d. Honor

GAME 16 Q3 ANSWER b
Lowe's Motor Speedway in Charlotte, North Carolina, is home to the Charlotte 600—the longest annual NASCAR race. The race is considered one of the most grueling on the schedule.

---

4. Who was Major League Baseball's first black umpire?

a. Billy Donaldson

b. Eric Gregg

c. William Embry

d. Emmett Ashford

GAME 36 Q3 ANSWER c
The 1960-1961 NBA Finals between the Boston Celtics and St. Louis Hawks was the only one in history that featured the same two referees working all 7 games. Earl Strom and Mendy Rudolph are viewed as role model NBA officials, and in 1995, Strom was posthumously enshrined in the Basketball Hall of Fame.

---

4. For what crime was former heavyweight champion Sonny Liston sent to prison?

a. Armed Robbery

b. Tax Evasion

c. Forgery

d. Murder

GAME 56 Q3 ANSWER d
Edmonton head coach Craig MacTavish was in a bad mood as he watched his Oilers getting thumped by Calgary, their archrival. So when Flames mascot, Harvey the Hound, leaned over the glass to glare at MacTavish, the aggravated head man reached over and ripped the character's felt tongue from its mouth and threw it into the stands.

---

4. Who was the first baseball amateur draft pick to be given a million-dollar signing bonus?

a. Phil Nevin

b. Brien Taylor

c. Todd van Poppel

d. Paul Wilson

GAME 76 Q3 ANSWER d
Penn State running back Blair Thomas was heralded as the back who would take the Jets to the next level. He showed some promise during his first two years, rushing for 620 yards in 1990 and then 728 in 1991, but after injuries limited him to 9 games and 440 yards in 1992, Thomas's career was virtually over.

10. Which of the following NBA superstars did *not* win the NBA Rookie of the Year Award?

a. Magic Johnson
b. Larry Bird
c. Kareem Abdul-Jabbar
d. Oscar Robertson

GAME 5 Q9 ANSWER c
What a season 1990-1991 was for Ed Belfour! He posted an amazing record of 43–19–7, while keeping his goals against average down to 2.47. "The Eagle" added four shutouts to further solidify his rookie credentials.

10. Who is the only pitcher to throw a no-hitter on opening day?

a. Bob Feller
b. Warren Spahn
c. Bucky Walters
d. Johnny Vander Meer

GAME 25 Q9 ANSWER b
Debuting in 1948, Detroit's "Production Line" led the Red Wings to seven straight regular season titles. Howe spent most of his first season injured, but rebounded in time for the playoffs, and led the "Line" to a romp over Montreal in the first round. They were swept by Toronto in the Finals.

10. Who was the original "Great White Hope"?

a. Jim Jeffries
b. Jack Johnson
c. Jess Willard
d. Jack Dempsy

GAME 45 Q9 ANSWER d
Although Mickey Goldmill was, indeed, connected with boxing, it was as Rocky Balboa's trainer (played by Burgess Meredith) in the *Rocky* movie series. Don Turner was the trainer of four-time heavyweight champ Evander Holyfield.

10. Which NHL team won a record 62 games during the 1995-1996 season?

a. Colorado Avalanche
b. Philadelphia Flyers
c. Detroit Red Wings
d. New Jersey Devils

GAME 65 Q9 ANSWER c
The Super Bowl remembered most for Scott Norwood's "wide right" kick as time expired also featured an excellent performance from veteran running back Ottis Anderson, who carried the ball 21 times for 104 yards and a crucial third-quarter touchdown. Anderson retired in 1992 after totaling over 10,000 rushing yards.

3. Which annual NASCAR race is held at Lowe's Motor Speedway?

a. The Daytona 500

b. The Charlotte 600

c. The Brickyard 400

d. The Talladega 500

GAME 16 Q2 ANSWER c
Hall of Fame trainer Woody Stephens saddled winners of the Triple Crown from 1982 to 1986. Laffit Pincay, Jr. rode the first three winners (Conquistador Cielo, Caveat, and Swale); while Eddie Maple piloted Crème Fraiche to a half-length win; and Chris McCarron rode Stephens' final winner, Danzig Connection.

3. What was the 1961 feat of NBA refs Earl Strom and Mendy Rudolph?

a. Worked every game together.

b. Never had a day off.

c. Worked all 7 NBA Final games.

d. Never called a technical foul.

GAME 36 Q2 ANSWER a
Calling time just a few pitches into the Reds contest against Montreal, home plate umpire John McSherry stumbled backwards and collapsed, dying of an apparent heart attack. Reds owner Marge Schott seemed more upset about the game's cancellation than McSherry's passing, "First snow this morning, and now this. I feel cheated."

3. Which NHL mascot had its tongue pulled out by an irate coach in 2003?

a. SpartaCat

b. ThunderBug

c. Sparky the Dragon

d. Harvey the Hound

GAME 56 Q1 ANSWER b
On November 14, 1970, a plane carrying seventy-five passengers, including thirty-seven Marshall University football players, crashed in Huntington, West Virginia. Struggling for years to recover, the Thundering Herd rebounded to prosperity in the 1990s behind players such as NFL stars Randy Moss and Chad Pennington.

3. Which disappointing choice did the Jets make second over-all in the 1990 NFL Draft?

a. Jeff Lageman

b. Johnny "Lam" Jones

c. Dave Cadigan

d. Blair Thomas

GAME 76 Q2 ANSWER b
The New York Islanders drafted Saskatoon product Scott Scissons ahead of standout defensemen Darryl Sydor and Derian Hatcher. Not to be confused with the NFL kicker of the same name, Scissons managed to appear in only 2 career NHL contests with the Isles in the early 1990s.

11. Which running back holds the record for most rushing yards by a rookie?

a. Barry Sanders
b. Walter Payton
c. Eric Dickerson
d. Ricky Williams

GAME 5 Q10 ANSWER a
The only thing that kept Magic Johnson from becoming the NBA Rookie of the Year in the 1979-1980 season was the fact that he entered the league at the same time as Larry Bird. At any other time, Johnson's 18.3 points, 10.5 rebounds, and 9.4 assists per game should have been more than enough to secure the trophy.

11. Which team won the most lopsided NFL playoff ever?

a. Green Bay Packers
b. Chicago Bears
c. Washington Redskins
d. Cleveland Browns

GAME 25 Q10 ANSWER a
Cleveland Indian Bob Feller kicked off the 1940 season with a "no-no" against the Chicago White Sox. During the game, which ended in a 1–0 win for the Tribe, Luke Appling of the Sox fouled off 15 pitches in row, but eventually took a seat. Feller tossed 3 no-hitters during his eighteen-year career.

11. During which Olympic Games did the United States win nine boxing gold medals?

a. 1968
b. 1972
c. 1976
d. 1984

GAME 45 Q10 ANSWER a
Former heavyweight champion Jeffries was brought out of retirement to take the crown back from Jack Johnson—the first black heavyweight champ—in the "Fight of the Century," which took place on July 4, 1910. He failed.

11. How old was Nolan Ryan when he threw his seventh and final no-hitter?

a. 43
b. 44
c. 45
d. 46

GAME 65 Q10 ANSWER c
Posting an amazing 62–13–7 record, the Detroit Red Wings established a new standard for wins in a season. The Wings, who were eliminated in the Western Conference Finals by Colorado, fell 1 point short of the Montreal Canadiens' record of 132 points in a season, which they set in their 1976-1977 Stanley Cup Championship season.

Answers are in right-hand boxes on page 129.

2. Which trainer won five consecutive Belmont Stakes in the 1980s?

a. Jack Van Berg

b. Ron McAnally

c. Woody Stephens

d. D. Wayne Lukas

GAME 16 Q1 ANSWER c
During Sanders' 12-year NFL career, the seven-time Pro Bowl cornerback went to the Super Bowl with San Francisco in 1994 and Dallas in 1995, earning rings both times. In 1992, he went to the World Series with the Atlanta Braves.

2. Which umpire died on the field during the 1996 Cincinnati season opener?

a. John McSherry

b. Eric Gregg

c. Ken Kaiser

d. Ron Luciano

GAME 36 Q1 ANSWER b
The first American to achieve the position of Senior NHL Official, Bill Chadwick will be forever known by his nickname, "The Big Whistle." Credited with inventing the hand signals still used by NHL refs, Chadwick was inducted into the Hockey Hall of Fame in 1964.

2. Which college team lost thirty-seven players in a 1970 plane crash?

a. Fresno State

b. Marshall

c. Oklahoma State

d. Wake Forest

GAME 56 Q2 ANSWER c
While playing for the AFL's Houston Oilers in 1962, George Blanda set the modern mark by throwing an amazing 42 interceptions. Blanda, who had led Houston to titles in the first two AFL seasons, went on to play football until the age of 48, throwing 247 career interceptions in both the AFL and the NFL.

2. Which team selected Scott Scissons sixth overall in the 1990 NHL Entry Draft?

a. Washington Capitals

b. New York Islanders

c. Montreal Canadiens

d. Quebec Nordiques

GAME 76 Q1 ANSWER c
The biggest bust of the NBA's 1994 first round was 7-foot-tall Yinka Dare, who was selected fourteenth overall by the New Jersey Nets. The Nigerian-born prospect played only 3 minutes during his rookie campaign. During his 110-game NBA career, Dare never averaged better than 2.8 points per game.

GAME 5

12. Who was the last player over age 30 to win Rookie of the Year in any major sport?

a. Sergei Makarov

b. Ichiro Suzuki

c. Hideo Nomo

d. Wes Unseld

GAME 25

12. Which team won the first NBA Championship?

a. Chicago

b. Syracuse

c. Minneapolis

d. Philadelphia

GAME 45

12. Who were the first undefeated heavy-weights to meet in a championship bout?

a. Bob Fitzsimmons/James J. Corbett

b. Jack Dempsey/Luis Firpo

c. Rocky Marciano/Archie Moore

d. Muhammad Ali/Joe Frazier

GAME 65

12. The all-time leading Summer Olympic medal winner is a gymnast from which country?

a. USSR

b. Romania

c. Germany

d. United States

GAME 5 Q11 ANSWER c
Coming out of Southern Methodist University in 1983, Eric Dickerson joined the LA Rams and proceeded to carry the ball 390 times for 1,808 yards, easily the best total by a rookie. Nicknamed "ET" for "Eric Touchdown," Dickerson's best year came in 1984, when he set the single season rushing yards mark by grinding out 2,105 yards.

GAME 25 Q11 ANSWER b
The Chicago Bears captured the 1940 NFL Championship after pummeling the Washington Redskins 73–0. The Bears, who had lost 7–3 to the Skins earlier in the season, utilized George Halas's "T" formation. The strategy left the Redskins scratching their heads, as the Bears rushed for 381 yards and picked off 8 of Sammy Baugh's passes.

GAME 45 Q11 ANSWER d
The American team, trained by Emanuel Steward, took home nine of the possible twelve gold medals in boxing at the 1984 Olympics held in Los Angeles. Medalists included Paul Gonzales, Steve McCrory, Meldrick Taylor, Jerry Page, Pernell Whitaker, Mark Breland, Frank Tate, Ray Mercer, and Tyrell Biggs.

GAME 65 Q11 ANSWER b
In a masterful performance at the age of 44, Nolan Ryan struck out sixteen Blue Jays on May 1, 1991, when he tossed the seventh and final no-hitter of his illustrious career. Ryan allowed just two walks, and interestingly enough, the feat occurred on the same day Rickey Henderson broke Lou Brock's all-time stolen base record.

Answers are in right-hand boxes on page 131.

1. Who is the only person in pro sports to play in both a World Series and Super Bowl?

a. Michael Jordan

b. Bo Jackson

c. Deion Sanders

d. Brian Jordan

The answer to this question is on:

page 128, top frame, right side.

1. Which NHL official was known as "The Big Whistle"?

a. Chaucer Elliott

b. Bill Chadwick

c. Matt Pavelich

d. Frank Udvari

The answer to this question is on:

page 128, second frame, right side.

1. Which pro quarterback threw the most interceptions in a single season?

a. Dan Fouts

b. Norm Van Brocklin

c. George Blanda

d. Vinny Testaverde

The answer to this question is on:

page 128, third frame, right side.

1. Which NBA franchise drafted center Yinka Dare in 1994?

a. Indiana Pacers

b. Denver Nuggets

c. New Jersey Nets

d. Los Angeles Clippers

The answer to this question is on:

page 128, bottom frame, right side.

GAME 6

"The New York Yankees"

Have You Boned Up on the Bronx Bombers?

*Turn to page 133
for the first question.*

Turn to page 133
for the first question.

GAME 5 Q12 ANSWER a
The late 1980s was a period of change not only in Eastern Europe but also in the NHL, as handfuls of Russian players started trickling into the league. One of those in the first wave was Soviet legend Sergei Makarov, who won the Rookie of the Year trophy at age 31.

GAME 26

"O Canada!"

Are You Familiar with Your Athletic Neighbors to the North?

*Turn to page 133
for the first question.*

Turn to page 133
for the first question.

GAME 25 Q12 ANSWER d
By defeating the Chicago Stags 4 games to 1 in the 1947 NBA (then called the BAA) Finals, the Philadelphia Warriors captured the championship. Led by guard Jumpin' Joe Fulks, who led the league in scoring (23.2 ppg), the Warriors knocked off the St. Louis Bombers and New York Knicks before manhandling Chicago for the title.

GAME 46

"NCAA Champions"

They Won It All at the College Level

*Turn to page 133
for the first question.*

Turn to page 133
for the first question.

GAME 45 Q12 ANSWER d
On March 8, 1971 in Madison Square Garden, Muhammad Ali gave Joe Frazier everything in his arsenal, but a smiling Smokin' Joe seemed unfazed. Almost knocking out Ali in the final round, Frazier took the unanimous decision, winning the title, and handing Ali his first professional defeat.

GAME 66

"Cover to Cover"

Books and the World of Sports

*Turn to page 133
for the first question.*

Turn to page 133
for the first question.

GAME 65 Q12 ANSWER a
Tiny Larissa Latynina is the winningest Olympian in history. Born in the Ukraine, Latynina competed in the 1956, 1960, and 1964 Games. She took home a total of eighteen medals—nine gold, five silver, and four bronze.

GAME 16

GRAB BAG

*Turn to page 130
for the first question.*

GAME 15 Q12 ANSWER a
While I was playing with the Warriors, Nate Thurmond was my teammate for four seasons. I have admired him both as a player and a person, and was honored to have him present me at the Hall of Fame induction. We still get together for great conversation and ribs at his San Francisco restaurant, Big Nate's Barbeque.

GAME 36

"Refs and Umps"

Do You Recall These Men in Stripes?

*Turn to page 130
for the first question.*

GAME 35 Q12 ANSWER a
Muhammad Ali's first win was over Sonny Liston in 1964—but he was stripped of his belt after refusing to enter the Armed Forces. The second came in 1974, when he beat George Foreman in the "Rumble in the Jungle." After losing to Leon Spinks in 1978, he quickly regained the belt in a rematch seven months later.

GAME 56

GRAB BAG

*Turn to page 130
for the first question.*

GAME 55 Q12 ANSWER c
Earning the nickname "Mad Stork," due to his long, flailing arms and tall frame (6'7"), linebacker Ted Hendricks spent fifteen years in the NFL, winning four Super Bowls with the Baltimore Colts and the Oakland/Los Angeles Raiders. The last game Hendricks played was a 38–9 victory over the Redskins in Super Bowl XVIII.

GAME 76

"First-Round Busts"

Remember These Highly Drafted Disasters?

*Turn to page 130
for the first question.*

GAME 75 Q12 ANSWER b
Before Detroit's Mike Maroth accrued 21 losses in 2003, the last hurler to drop 20 season games was Oakland A's starter Brian Kingman, who posted 8 wins and 20 losses in 1980. Between 1980 and 2003, no fewer than eight pitchers had lost 19 decisions before unofficially shutting it down to avoid the mystical 20-loss mark.

GAME 6	1. Which of the following jersey numbers has *not* been retired by the Yankees? a. 23 b. 2 c. 37 d. 9	The answer to this question is on: **page 135, top frame, right side.**
GAME 26	1. Who was the first Canadian-born player to win baseball's MVP award? a. Jake Daubert b. Dale Murphy c. Larry Walker d. Bob O'Farrell	The answer to this question is on: **page 135, second frame, right side.**
GAME 46	1. As of 2004, who was the last college football coach to win consecutive NCAA Championships? a. Bear Bryant b. Bobby Bowden c. Tom Osborne d. Steve Spurrier	The answer to this question is on: **page 135, third frame, right side.**
GAME 66	1. Which former pitcher wrote the controversial *Ball Four* in 1970? a. Phil Linz b. Jim Bouton c. Larry Dierker d. Joe Horlen	The answer to this question is on: **page 135, bottom frame, right side.**

12. Who was my presenter for induction into the Naismith Basketball Hall of Fame?

a. Nate Thurmond
b. Alex Hannum
c. Lou Carnesecca
d. George Yardley

GAME 15 Q11 ANSWER c
When I was young and learning how to play baseball, my dad taught me how to catch fly balls using the "basket catch." The next year, Willie Mays, a rookie with the NY Giants, used the same technique. From that point on, he was my favorite sports hero. Amazingly, we both wound up playing in San Francisco and became friends.

12. Who was the first boxer to win the heavyweight championship three separate times?

a. Muhammad Ali
b. Evander Holyfield
c. Floyd Patterson
d. George Foreman

GAME 35 Q11 ANSWER d
Showing tremendous resolve in searing heat, Al Geiberger shot 59 in the second round of the 1977 Danny Thomas Classic on a sweltering June day in Memphis. Geiberger's standard has been matched only twice on the PGA Tour—by Chip Beck in 1991 and David Duval in 1999. Annika Sorenstam shot an LPGA-record 59 in 2001.

12. "Mad Stork"

a. Ben Davidson
b. Lyle Alzado
c. Ted Hendricks
d. Todd Christensen

GAME 55 Q11 ANSWER a
The original name of the band Pearl Jam—"Mookie Blaylock"—was eventually changed to reflect the nickname of this flashy NBA guard. The band even titled its first significant album *Ten,* after the former New Jersey Net's uniform number. Blaylock strung eleven seasons averaging at least 11 points a game.

12. Prior to 2003, who was the last Major League pitcher to lose 20 games in a season?

a. Jose DeLeon
b. Brian Kingman
c. Scott Erickson
d. Omar Daal

GAME 75 Q11 ANSWER a
In two seasons, George Kingston, the first coach in Shark's history, saw his team compile an embarrassing 28 wins, 129 losses, and 7 ties. After losing only 58 games during their first season, the Sharks went backwards, losing a record 71 in 1992-1993. A year later, they were one win away from the Western Conference semifinals.

2. Who is the only Yankee hurler to pitch a no-hitter and lose?

a. Ron Guidry
b. Andy Hawkins
c. Tommy John
d. Joe Cowley

GAME 6 Q1 ANSWER b
Leading all Major League teams in retired numbers with fourteen jerseys out of circulation, the Yankees have not yet retired number 2. As for the other numbers mentioned, 23 was worn by '80s icon Don Mattingly, 37 was donned by manager supreme Casey Stengel, and 9 graced the back of Roger Maris.

---

2. Who is the only Canadian player to be inducted into baseball's Hall of Fame?

a. Tommy McCarthy
b. Harmon Killebrew
c. Robin Roberts
d. Ferguson Jenkins

GAME 26 Q1 ANSWER c
During Larry Walker's 1997 legendary season, he batted .366 with 49 homers and 130 runs batted in, chasing baseball's Triple Crown down to the season's last week. Some feel his numbers were skewed because he played in hitter-friendly Coors Field. Regardless, Walker is down as the best Canadian hitter of all time.

---

2. Who is the only college freshman to win the Hobey Baker Award?

a. Scott Pellerin
b. Paul Kariya
c. Chris Drury
d. Neal Broten

GAME 46 Q1 ANSWER c
Nebraska coaching legend Tom Osborne led his teams to back-to-back NCAA victories in 1994 and 1995. Osborne's squad won 35 of the 36 games during the two seasons, with its only loss coming in a 19–0 shutout at Arizona State in the second game of the 1996 season.

---

2. Which author's books usually include a horseracing scandal?

a. Dick Francis
b. Dick Young
c. Dick Irvin
d. Dick Schapp

GAME 66 Q1 ANSWER b
In a shocking exposé, Jim Bouton revealed some not-so-wonderful things that occurred behind baseball's closed doors, including the frequent boozing of former teammate Mickey Mantle. After the book's release, Bouton was criticized by commissioner Bowie Kuhn and basically blackballed from Major League Baseball.

---

11. Why did I wear number 24 during my collegiate and professional careers?

a. My father wore 24

b. Sam Jones wore 24

c. Willie Mays wore 24

d. It was the only number available in college

GAME 15 Q10 ANSWER c
I had always admired Elgin Baylor, and used to practice controlling my body in the air like he did. While a senior at Miami, I found two preseason basketball magazines—one with a photo of Baylor driving to the basket in mid-air, the other with a photo of me doing the same. Amazingly, our bodies and ball positions were almost identical.

---

11. Who was the first PGA Tour golfer to break 60 for a round?

a. Sam Snead

b. Raymond Floyd

c. Don January

d. Al Geiberger

GAME 35 Q10 ANSWER b
Getting his hundredth point on March 2, 1969, Bruins forward Phil Esposito did not hold the record for long, as less than three weeks later, teammate Bobby Orr also broke the 100-point mark. "Espo" wound up leading the league with 126 total points in the 1968-1969 season, and took home the Hart Trophy as league MVP.

---

11. "Pearl Jam"

a. Mookie Blaylock

b. Mario Elie

c. Mark Aguirre

d. Kenny Smith

GAME 55 Q10 ANSWER b
In his most famous bout, Chuck Wepner, whose nickname referred to his face, which ripped easily, went into the fifteenth round with Muhammad Ali in 1975 before losing by TKO. After watching Wepner take a pummeling during the fight, Sylvester Stallone was inspired to write the screenplay for *Rocky* (1976).

---

11. Which coach of the San Jose Sharks lost a record 71 games in a season?

a. George Kingston

b. Al Sims

c. Jim Wiley

d. Kevin Constantine

GAME 75 Q10 ANSWER b
Quarterbacked by Florida legend Steve Spurrier, the 1976 Tampa Bay Buccaneers are the last team to go winless. After nine years with San Francisco, the 1966 Heisman Trophy winner returned to his home state to run the fledgling Bucs. While his QB rating was better than Terry Bradshaw's, his team failed to produce a single victory.

---

3. Which legendary Yankee Stadium announcer was said to have "the voice of God"?

a. Robert Merrill
b. John Condon
c. Bob Sheppard
d. Mel Allen

GAME 6 Q2 ANSWER b
The lowest point of the Yankees 1990 season came on July 1, when Andy Hawkins managed to pitch a no-hitter and still lose the game 4–0 (defensive errors led to the runs). Purists debate whether this was a true no-hitter since the White Sox didn't have to bat in the bottom of the ninth, meaning that Hawkins pitched only eight full innings.

3. Who won five Grey Cups before passing for over 40,000 yards in the NFL?

a. Doug Flutie
b. Fran Tarkenton
c. Warren Moon
d. Dave Krieg

GAME 26 Q2 ANSWER d
In his nineteen-year career, Ferguson Jenkins won an overall 284 games (including seven seasons in which he won an impressive 20), struck out over 3,000 batters, and tossed an eye-opening 49 shutouts. The NL's 1971 Cy Young Award winner is also on a short list of pitchers to win 100 games in both leagues.

3. Which school won both the NCAA and NIT Championships in the same season?

a. City College of New York
b. Kansas
c. UCLA
d. St. John's

GAME 46 Q2 ANSWER b
While playing with the Maine Black Bears—the 1993 NCAA-winning hockey team—freshman winger Paul Kariya scored an amazing 100 points at age 18. Kariya, who split the next season between Maine and the Canadian National team, has blossomed into one of the NHL's premier scoring threats.

3. Who wrote *It's Not About the Bike: My Journey Back to Life*?

a. Greg LeMond
b. Lance Armstrong
c. Miguel Indurain
d. Bernard Hinault

GAME 66 Q2 ANSWER a
Writer of over thirty-five novels, the British-born Dick Francis was a top rider in the 1950s before becoming a racing writer for English publications. The leap to equine books began in his 1957 autobiographical work, *The Sport of Queens*. His first novel, *Dead Cert*, hit the shelves in 1962.

10. After which player did I attempt to pattern my game?

a. Dolph Schayes
b. Bob Petit
c. Elgin Baylor
d. George Yardley

While at Oregon State, Brent used the underhanded technique for two seasons and shot 85.1 percent from the line his sophomore year—the highest percentage of his collegiate career. He reverted back to the conventional style in his junior year. Brent is a good free throw shooter in the pros, but passed his high collegiate mark only once.

---

10. Who was the first NHL player to score 100 points in a season?

a. Bobby Orr
b. Phil Esposito
c. Bobby Hull
d. Stan Mikita

With a talent almost as big as his ego, outspoken 49ers receiver Terrell Owens snared 20 receptions in a single game against the Bears on December 17, 2000. Grabbing 20 of quarterback Jeff Garcia's 44 completions, Owens broke former Rams wideout Tom Fears' fifty-year record of 18 catches, and added 2 more for good measure.

---

10. "The Bayonne Bleeder"

a. Vito Antuofermo
b. Chuck Wepner
c. Vinny Pazienza
d. Greg Haugen

Given the nickname due to his size (5'7" and 160 pounds), Henri Richard tallied 358 goals and 1,046 points in his twenty years with the Montreal Canadiens. In addition to winning eleven Stanley Cups, Richard played in ten All-Star Games and won the 1974 Masterson Trophy for dedication to the game.

---

10. Which starting quarterback of the 1976 Buccaneers went 0–14?

a. Doug Williams
b. Steve Spurrier
c. Parnell Dickinson
d. Mike Livingston

Even worse than the Flyers getting swept by Detroit in the 1997 Cup Finals, was their losing the 2000 Eastern Conference Finals to the New Jersey Devils after dominating the first games of the series 3 to 1. The stands also saw Eric Lindros play his last game as a Flyer after getting knocked senseless by Scott Stevens in Game 7.

4. Who pitched the final out of the 1996 World Series?

a. Ramiro Mendoza

b. Jimmy Key

c. Jeff Nelson

d. John Wetteland

GAME 6 Q3 ANSWER c
Since April 17, 1951, Bob Sheppard has been as much a part of Yankee history as Mickey Mantle and Joe DiMaggio, and, in fact, was there to announce both of their names in starting lineups! Called "the voice of God" by Reggie Jackson, Sheppard has also been the voice of the NFL's NY Giants since 1956.

---

4. Which member of the LA Lakers championship teams of the early 2000s was born in Canada?

a. Rick Fox

b. Robert Horry

c. Kobe Bryant

d. Ron Harper

GAME 26 Q3 ANSWER c
Before playing for seventeen seasons in the NFL, Warren Moon was a standout in the Canadian Football League, winning consecutive Grey Cups with the Edmonton Eskimos from 1978 to 1982. During the '83 season, he passed for a league-leading 5,648 yards, tossed 31 touchdowns, and won the Schenley Award as the league's MVP.

---

4. Who is the last golfer to win consecutive individual NCAA titles?

a. Ben Crenshaw

b. Tiger Woods

c. Phil Mickelson

d. Justin Leonard

GAME 46 Q3 ANSWER a
In 1950, the City College of New York became the first and only school to accomplish this feat. It is a record that will never be broken, as the tournaments are now run concurrently, with the better teams going to the NCAAs. The squad was coached by hoops pioneer Nat Holman, who compiled 423 career wins.

---

4. Which NHL team was the subject of the 2001 book *Nightmare on 33rd Street*?

a. New York Rangers

b. Philadelphia Flyers

c. Chicago Blackhawks

d. Washington Capitals

GAME 66 Q3 ANSWER b
Chronicling his recovery from testicular cancer, top cyclist Lance Armstrong released the story of his amazing journey from death's doorstep to multiple Tour de France victories. Armstrong details the long road back to his status as a world-class athlete.

---

9. Which of my sons tried my underhanded free throw technique in college?

a. Scooter

b. Jon

c. Brent

d. Drew

During my career, I was fortunate enough to appear on four covers. The first was in 1967 and the last in 1974. Three of the covers featured me as a Warrior. The fourth had me in an ABA Virginia Squires uniform with the headline, "The Reluctant Virginian."

---

9. Who was the first NFL player to catch 20 passes in a game?

a. Tom Fears

b. Jerry Rice

c. Elroy Hirsch

d. Terrell Owens

In 1984, Miami's Dan Marino became the first and only quarterback to pass for over 5,000 yards. It was the same year he reached his only Super Bowl. The holder of almost every NFL passing record, Marino remains the only quarterback to pass for more than 60,000 career yards.

---

9. "The Pocket Rocket"

a. Rick Tocchet

b. Theo Fleury

c. Jean Beliveau

d. Henri Richard

When he started with the Bruins in the 1930s, goalie Frank Brimsek was called "Kid Zero," but moved on to "Mister Zero" after shutting out the opposition in 6 of his first 8 contests. In a career that totaled 42 shutouts, Brimsek picked up several accolades, including the 1939 Calder Trophy, and the '39 and '42 Vezina Trophies.

---

9. Which team blew a lead of 3 games to 1 in the 2000 NHL Eastern Conference Finals?

a. New Jersey Devils

b. Washington Capitals

c. Philadelphia Flyers

d. Buffalo Sabres

Defeating a young Ty Cobb and the Detroit Tigers, the Cubs won their last World Series in 1908. They did manage to win 7 National League pennants since then, but lost all 7 World Series. Despite a nice run in 2003, the Cubbies haven't been to a Fall Classic since 1945.

5. Which teammate battled Don Mattingly for the 1984 batting title?

a. Rickey Henderson

b. Dave Winfield

c. Don Baylor

d. Ken Griffey, Sr.

GAME 6 Q4 ANSWER d
When the final out was recorded in the 1996 World Series, John Wetteland had made history. Not only had he brought the Bronx Bombers their first World Championship in eighteen years, but he had also become the first pitcher to record saves in all four wins of baseball's final stanza, deservedly winning the Series MVP.

5. Who won a Grey Cup and Super Bowl playing for teams in the same city?

a. Robert Bailey

b. Kipp Vickers

c. O.J. Brigance

d. Corey Harris

GAME 26 Q4 ANSWER a
Rick Fox was born and bred in Toronto. After six seasons as a Boston Celtic, the 1992 NBA All-Rookie Team member joined the Lakers in 1997, and won three rings with them. Fox last represented Team Canada at the 1994 World Championship.

5. Which NCAA Women's Soccer Team won 16 of the first 21 possible championships?

a. North Carolina

b. Santa Clara

c. Florida

d. Portland

GAME 46 Q4 ANSWER c
Arizona State's Phil Mickelson took home the NCAA individual crown in 1989 and 1990. Winning again in 1992 made Mickelson only the second three-time winner since the tournament was established in 1939. He joined Texas Longhorn duffer Ben Crenshaw, who won in 1971, split in 1972 with Tom Kite, and took it again in 1973.

5. Which former NBA star released *I May Be Wrong, But I Doubt It*?

a. Kareem Abdul-Jabbar

b. Michael Jordan

c. Bill Laimbeer

d. Charles Barkley

GAME 66 Q4 ANSWER a
Penned by regular beat writer Rick Carpinello, this book chronicles the turbulent 2000-2001 season of New York's "Broadway Blueshirts," focusing on the futile acts of new GM Glen Sather, bewildered coach Ron Low, and aging captain Mark Messier.

8. On how many covers of *Sports Illustrated* have I appeared?

a. Two
b. Three
c. Four
d. Five

Bill Bradley of Princeton was top pick, followed by Fred Hetzel of Davidson. Dave Stallworth of Wichita State was fourth. It was the only season in which the last place teams in each conference flipped a coin, and the winner (NY Knicks) won the first and fourth draft picks, while the loser (San Francisco Warriors) chose second and third.

8. Who was the first NFL quarterback to pass for 5,000 yards in a season?

a. Dan Fouts
b. Dan Marino
c. John Elway
d. Fran Tarkenton

Jumping in the saddle on February 7, 1969, at Florida's Hialeah Racetrack, Diane Crump became the first woman to ride at a major track. A year later in Louisville, Crump became the first woman to ride in the Kentucky Derby. Although history was made, Crump did not fare too well, with her horse finishing fifteenth in a field of seventeen.

8. "Mister Zero"

a. Gerry Cheevers
b. Frank Brimsek
c. Mike Liut
d. Bernie Parent

Before his managerial career, journeyman first baseman Mike Hargrove earned his "Human Rain Delay" nickname because he constantly stepped in and out of the batters' box, took practice swings, and performed other procrastination techniques. He did, however, earn the '74 AL Rookie of the Year Award while playing with the Texas Rangers.

8. What was the last year in which the Chicago Cubs won a World Series?

a. 1906
b. 1908
c. 1910
d. 1912

Enshrined in the Basketball Hall of Fame as both a player and a coach, Lenny Wilkens is the both the winningest and losingest coach in NBA history. He does, however, have company in the 1,000-loss department, as former colleague Bill Fitch dropped over 1,100 games in his twenty-plus years on a basketball sideline.

6. Who was the last individual pitcher to throw a complete-game no-hitter against the Yankees?

a. Hoyt Wilhelm

b. Roger Clemens

c. Mike Flanagan

d. Bob Feller

GAME 6 Q5 ANSWER b
The Yankees final days of the 1984 season ended with a clubhouse war. Veterans aligned themselves with Dave Winfield, while younger players favored Mattingly. With the crown still on the line in the season's final game, Mattingly finished with a .343 average, while Winfield averaged .340.

6. Who was the first Canadian pitcher to throw a no-hitter in the Major Leagues?

a. Dick Fowler

b. Ryan Dempster

c. Ferguson Jenkins

d. Derek Aucoin

GAME 26 Q5 ANSWER c
A backup linebacker with the Baltimore Ravens during the team's 2000 Super Bowl season, O.J. Brigance was also on the Canadian Football League's Baltimore Stallions in 1995—the year the team won the Grey Cup. Brigance also went to the Super Bowl in 2002 with the St. Louis Rams.

6. John McEnroe was an NCAA Champion tennis player at which college?

a. UCLA

b. USC

c. Florida

d. Stanford

GAME 46 Q5 ANSWER a
Coached by Anson Dorrance, the Tar Heels squad of North Carolina has benefited over the years from outstanding players like Mia Hamm, Kristine Lilly, and Cindy Parlow.

6. Which tennis great authored *Days of Grace*?

a. John McEnroe

b. Arthur Ashe

c. Jimmy Connors

d. Rod Laver

GAME 66 Q5 ANSWER d
Never at a loss for words, sports commentator and former rebound machine Charles Barkley decided to put his thoughts to pen in his 2002 release. In it, "Sir Charles" espouses his thoughts on just about everything, including politics, his basketball experiences, and his views on minorities in sports.

7. I was the third pick in the 1965 NBA Draft. Who was the first?

a. Bill Bradley

b. Dave Stallworth

c. Billy Cunningham

d. Fred Hetzel

GAME 15 Q6 ANSWER d
In 1980, I underwent off-season knee surgery, and felt better than I had in years. Unfortunately for me, the NBA voted to reduce team roster spots to only 11. (Until this ruling, the Celtics, Lakers, and Sonics had shown interest in me.) I had to continue playing for the Rockets or retire. That's when I decided to go into broadcasting.

7. Who was the first female jockey to ride in a pari-mutuel race?

a. Julie Krone

b. Diane Crump

c. Chandra Rennie

d. Diane Nelson

GAME 35 Q6 ANSWER c
For years, the 30/30 Club (30 home runs and 30 stolen bases) was an elite group, representing a rare combination of power and speed. Then in 1988, Oakland's Jose Canseco raised the bar, finishing with 42 round trippers and 40 thefts. Canseco has since been joined by Barry Bonds (1996) and Alex Rodriguez (1998).

7. "The Human Rain Delay"

a. Andre Thornton

b. Dave Kingman

c. Gaylord Perry

d. Mike Hargrove

GAME 55 Q6 ANSWER c
Born in Royston, Georgia in 1886, Ty Cobb was named for his state's most popular fruit. "The Peach" hit .366 for his career, scored over 2,200 runs, belted 4,191 hits, but never won a World Series in his twenty-four professional seasons. Known as a nasty human being, Cobb used any angle to gain an advantage over the opposition.

7. Who is the only NBA head coach to win 1,000 games and lose 1,000 games?

a. Gene Shue

b. Bill Fitch

c. Lenny Wilkens

d. Don Nelson

GAME 75 Q6 ANSWER a
Since the Super Bowl era began in 1966, Don Coryell was the only Cardinal coach to post a winning mark during his tenure. Taking St. Louis to consecutive playoff games in 1974 and 1975, "Air Coryell" compiled an overall mark of 42–27–1 during his five years at the helm from 1973 to 1977.

7. Which pitcher won his 300th game at Yankee Stadium in 1985?

a. Phil Niekro

b. Don Sutton

c. Nolan Ryan

d. Tom Seaver

GAME 6 Q6 ANSWER a
The last time the Yankees were no-hit by a single pitcher was September 20, 1958, when Hoyt Wilhelm pitched for the Baltimore Orioles. Wilhelm tossed a 1–0 beauty, beating Don Larsen. Incidentally, it was Wilhelm's first complete Major League game.

7. Before 2002, what was the last year Canada won Olympic gold in ice hockey?

a. 1956

b. 1952

c. 1960

c. 1940

GAME 26 Q6 ANSWER a
Philadelphia Athletic Dick Fowler hurled a no-hitter against the St. Louis Browns in September 1945. Even more impressive is that it was Fowler's first start after serving three years in the Canadian Armed Forces. He also once pitched all 16 innings against St. Louis in a 1942 game that ended in a 1–0 St. Louis defeat.

7. At which university did wrestling coach Dan Gable win fifteen NCAA Wrestling Championships?

a. Oklahoma State

b. Minnesota

c. Iowa

d. Arizona State

GAME 46 Q6 ANSWER d
While attending Stanford, tennis great John McEnroe won NCAA individual and team championships in 1978. Before attending college, the man famous for his on-court tirades, qualified for Wimbledon as an unseeded 18-year old. Shocking the world, Johnny Mac made it all the way to the semifinals before bowing out to Jimmy Connors.

7. Which basketball figure penned *Sacred Hoops: Spiritual Lessons of a Hardwood Warrior*?

a. Bill Walton

b. Hakeem Olajuwon

c. Phil Jackson

d. Larry Bird

GAME 66 Q6 ANSWER b
Although Arthur Ashe's 1994 work looks at his memorable tennis career, it focuses mainly on his losing battle with AIDS. Ashe, who contracted the virus after open-heart surgery in the 1980s, ends the book with an emotional letter to his young daughter, Camera, who would lose her father before publication of the book.

6. For which team did I play my final NBA Game ?

a. Golden State Warriors

b. LA Clippers

c. New Jersey Nets

d. Houston Rockets

GAME 15 Q5 ANSWER b
Although I had been known to launch a few shots in my day, even I was shocked when I looked at the stat sheet after the game. Let me tell you, it isn't easy getting up 48 shots in a 48-minute game . And in case you're wondering, I scored 55 points that night.

---

6. Who was the first baseball player to hit 40 homers and steal 40 bases in a season?

a. Willie Mays

b. Howard Johnson

c. Jose Canseco

d. Bobby Bonds

GAME 35 Q5 ANSWER a
After playing on the 1980 "Miracle on Ice" team, which took home the gold medal at Lake Placid, defenseman Ken Morrow joined the New York Islanders for the final 18 games of the 1979-1980 regular season, when the Isles captured their first cup ever.

---

6. "The Georgia Peach"

a. Chipper Jones

b. John Rocker

c. Ty Cobb

d. Johnny Mize

GAME 55 Q5 ANSWER b
After fanning 744 batters in his first three Major League seasons, NY Mets ace Dwight Gooden was nicknamed "Dr. K." Shortened to "Doc," Gooden would strike out 200 batters in a season only once more after 1986. After beating substance abuse, he had a brief return to the limelight, throwing a no-hitter for the Yankees in 1996.

---

6. Who is the only coach to have a winning career record with the NFL Cardinals since 1966?

a. Don Coryell

b. Vince Tobin

c. Gene Stallings

d. Buddy Ryan

GAME 75 Q5 ANSWER a
With the exception of the 1999 "expansion" Cleveland Browns team, every NFL franchise competed in a playoff between January 1 and December 31, 1999 except the Seahawks. Last making the postseason after the 1988 campaign, the Birds waited until January 8, 2000 for their next tournament contest, a 20–17 loss to the Miami Dolphins.

8. Which player flipped the bird to the Yankee Stadium crowd in 1995?

a. Charlie Hayes
b. Mike Stanley
c. Ruben Sierra
d. Jack McDowell

GAME 6 Q7 ANSWER d
August 4, 1985 was a bittersweet day for Yankee fans. The pregame was dedicated to honoring one of the most beloved Bombers of all time, "The Scooter," Phil Rizzuto. Then Hall of Famer Tom Seaver stole the day as his White Sox beat the Yankees 4–1, giving Tom Teriffic win number 300.

8. What was the last Canadian team of the twentieth century to win the Stanley Cup?

a. Montreal
b. Toronto
c. Edmonton
d. Calgary

GAME 26 Q7 ANSWER b
Moments after clinching the gold in 2002, a wave of euphoria swept the Great White North. The 5–2 victory over the US gave Canada its first gold since the 1952 Games in Oslo, Norway. The Canadian team's chances looked tenuous at the outset as they lost the opener to Sweden 5–1, and then barely beat Germany in the second game.

8. At which school did Isiah Thomas win an NCAA Basketball Championship?

a. Michigan State
b. Louisville
c. Indiana
d. North Carolina

GAME 46 Q7 ANSWER c
During twenty years at the University of Iowa, coaching icon Dan Gable led his wrestlers to fifteen NCAA titles—a record that is not likely to be matched. During his own wrestling days at rival Iowa State, Gable won a pair of NCAA titles in 1968 and 1969. He also took home the gold at the 1972 Olympic Games in Munich.

8. Which famous coach was the subject of *When Pride Still Mattered*?

a. John Wooden
b. Bear Bryant
c. Vince Lombardi
d. Red Auerbach

GAME 66 Q7 ANSWER c
A self-professed Zen Christian, Phil Jackson takes the opportunity in his 1996 work to explain how his philosophy led the Chicago Bulls to focus more on the team aspect of the game than individual accomplishments. Whatever Jackson does to his team, it works, as evidenced by his nine championship rings.

5. Which NBA Finals record do I still hold from a 1967 game against the 76ers?

a. Most free throws made in one quarter

b. Most field goals attempted

c. Most points scored

d. Most free throws attempted

GAME 15 Q4 ANSWER b

In 1980, I ended my career with an NBA record 90-percent accuracy rate from the free throw line. The record held until 1998, when Mark Price retired with a career percentage of 90.4. If I had only refined my underhanded technique earlier in my career, I might still have that record.

5. Who was the first man to win an Olympic gold medal and the Stanley Cup in the same year?

a. Ken Morrow

b. Roger Christian

c. Jack McCartan

d. Bill Dawe

GAME 35 Q4 ANSWER d

When the Los Angeles Raiders fired head coach Mike Shanahan midway through the 1989 season, Art Shell was named his successor, becoming the first black head coach in NFL history. Shell, who had only one losing year during his five seasons with the Raiders, was let go after the 1995 season and didn't receive another coaching offer.

5. "Dr. K"

a. Tom Seaver

b. Dwight Gooden

c. Sam McDowell

d. Carl Hubbell

GAME 55 Q4 ANSWER b

The often-surly but infinitely talented NBA point guard Gary Payton received his nickname, "The Glove," because he plays defense as tight as a glove. Payton is among the annual league leaders in assists, and in 1996, he became the first guard since Michael Jordan to win NBA Defensive Player of the Year.

5. Which NFL franchise did *not* participate in a playoff game during the 1990s?

a. Seattle Seahawks

b. New Orleans Saints

c. Cincinnati Bengals

d. Atlanta Falcons

GAME 75 Q4 ANSWER c

The much-maligned Derek Lowe, who pitched the Red Sox past the Yankees in Game 7 of the 2004 ALCS, also picked up the win in the game that saw Boston end eighty-six years of misery. Lowe's seven scoreless innings paced the Sox, as they cruised past the St. Louis Cardinals 3–0 to win their first title since 1918.

GAME 6

9. From 1996 to 2000, what was the only team to eliminate the Yankees from the post-season?

a. Boston Red Sox
b. Cleveland Indians
c. Baltimore Orioles
d. Seattle Mariners

GAME 6 Q8 ANSWER d
Famous for his split-finger fastball, Jack McDowell showed a booing crowd his gangly middle finger after a poor outing against Chicago. Traded to New York before the 1995 season, McDowell managed to finish his only year in the Bronx with a respectable 15–10 record, and a 3.93 earned run average.

GAME 26

9. Who played college football in Canada and was a first-round NFL draft pick?

a. Tom Nutten
b. Steve Christie
c. Mike Schad
d. Jesse Palmer

GAME 26 Q8 ANSWER a
The Montreal Canadiens took home hockey's Holy Grail in June of 1993—the last time a North-of-the-Border team won the championship. Backed by Patrick Roy, Montreal took out the Barry Melrose-coached LA Kings in 5 games.

GAME 46

9. Who quarterbacked Miami's 1987 NCAA Championship team?

a. Craig Erickson
b. Vinny Testaverde
c. Gino Torretta
d. Steve Walsh

GAME 46 Q8 ANSWER c
Scoring 23 points in the title game for the Indiana Hoosiers, Isiah Thomas was awarded the Final Four MVP and gave coach Bob Knight his first NCAA Championship. Thomas led the Hoosiers to a 63–50 win over a pre-Jordan North Carolina team, and went on to eventually win a pair of NBA championships with the Detroit Pistons.

GAME 66

9. *The Bronx Zoo* was written by which former Yankee?

a. Graig Nettles
b. Sparky Lyle
c. Roy White
d. Brian Doyle

GAME 66 Q8 ANSWER c
Author David Maraniss captured the life and times of Vince Lombardi, including family, religion, and football. The man for whom the Super Bowl Trophy was named led the Packers to five NFL Championships, and finished with a .740 winning percentage. Lombardi succumbed to cancer in June of 1970 at the age of 56.

4. Who broke my career free throw shooting percentage record?

a. Calvin Murphy

b. Mark Price

c. Jeff Hornacek

d. Larry Bird

My father changed me to the "granny" style while I was in high school and my hands were large enough to hold the ball properly. It wasn't something I did with great enthusiasm. (I only tried his way to stop him from bugging me.) I'm glad he was so persistent. Isn't there an old saying that "father knows best"?

---

4. Who was the first black head coach in the NFL?

a. Sherman Lewis

b. Dennis Green

c. Emmitt Thomas

d. Art Shell

As coach of the Oakland Raiders, Jon Gruden defeated the New York Jets 38-24 in a 2002 AFC Wild Card game. Later that year, Gruden became coach of the Tampa Bay Buccaneers, and in 2003, his team knocked off the San Francisco 49ers in an NFC second-round game by a score of 31–6.

---

4. "The Glove"

a. Terrell Brandon

b. Gary Payton

c. Nick Van Exel

d. Darius Miles

Houston's "Phi Slamma Jamma" teams of the early '80s featured future Hall of Famers Hakeem Olajuwon and Clyde Drexler. The Cougars made it to the National Championship Game in 1983 and 1984, losing both times to NC State and Georgetown respectively. Despite being on the losing side, Olajuwon was named Final Four MVP in 1983.

---

4. Who was the winning pitcher for Boston in the decisive Game 4 of the 2004 World Series?

a. Derek Lowe

b. Curt Schilling

c. Pedro Martinez

d. Tim Wakefield

Out of baseball's postseason since the 1981 strike-shortened season (in which they lost the NLCS to the Dodgers in 5 games), the Expos hold the longest playoff drought to date. They were, however, the best team in the game when the 1994 strike ended the season in August. Their final record stood at 74–40 with 48 games remaining.

GAME 6

10. For which team did Joe DiMaggio play before becoming a Yankee?

a. Oakland Oaks
b. Los Angeles Angels
c. San Francisco Seals
d. Seattle Rainiers

GAME 6 Q9 ANSWER b
The Yankees were on quite a run between 1996 and 2000, winning four World Championships and losing only one, when the Cleveland Indians beat them in the 1997 playoffs. New York took a 2-to-1 game lead in the best-of-5 series, but the Indians rallied in the final 2 contests at home, beating the Bombers.

GAME 26

10. Which nation beat Canada for the disputed gold in the 2002 Olympic Pairs Skating event?

a. France
b. Czech Republic
c. Russia
d. Latvia

GAME 26 Q9 ANSWER c
The only player to spend his college years in Canada (Queen's University) and get drafted in the NFL's first round is former offensive lineman Mike Schad. Taken twenty-third overall by the Los Angeles Rams in the 1986 draft, Schad spent eight seasons in the NFL, mostly with the Philadelphia Eagles.

GAME 46

10. Which college basketball coach was dubbed "The Wizard of Westwood"?

a. Joe Lapchick
b. John Wooden
c. Dean Smith
d. Adolph Rupp

GAME 46 Q9 ANSWER d
Jimmy Johnson's only national championship came by defeating Oklahoma and coach Barry Switzer. While the duo would both win Super Bowls with Dallas in the '90s, it was Steve Walsh who ran the offense for Johnson's Hurricanes that day. Walsh was 23–1 during his three seasons at Coral Gables.

GAME 66

10. Which sportswriter authored *Flashing Before My Eyes: 50 Years of Headlines, Deadlines and Punches*?

a. Tony Kornheiser
b. Mike Lupica
c. Dick Schapp
d. Heywood Hale Broun

GAME 66 Q9 ANSWER b
Released in 1979 by Cy Young winner Sparky Lyle, the book encapsulates the ins and outs of the Yankees 1978 World Championship season. It includes a look at some of the more-interesting, sometimes strange personalities of the organization, such as George Steinbrenner, Billy Martin, Reggie Jackson, and Thurmon Munson.

3. From whom did I learn my unorthodox underhanded free throw technique?

a. My father
b. My older brother
c. My college coach
d. My high school coach

GAME 15 Q2 ANSWER c
Much to my dismay, 1975 was also the year *Sport Magazine* decided to switch sponsors from Chevrolet to American Motors. So, instead of a sporty Corvette, which previous winners had received, I drove home as the "proud" owner of a silver 1975 AMC Pacer.

3. Who is the first NFL coach to win playoff games in consecutive years with different teams?

a. Bill Parcells
b. Dan Reeves
c. Jon Gruden
d. Don Shula

GAME 35 Q2 ANSWER a
Several had come close, but in 1938, Don Budge was the first tennis player to complete the nearly-impossible Grand Slam as an amateur. A 1964 Tennis Hall of Fame inductee, Budge remains the only American male to have accomplished the feat. Maureen Connolly, an American woman, completed the Grand Slam in 1953.

3. "Phi Slamma Jamma"

a. Georgetown University Basketball
b. Villanova Basketball
c. St. John's University Basketball
d. University of Houston Basketball

GAME 55 Q2 ANSWER c
ESPN's Chris Berman has dubbed many pro athletes with monikers that go along with their last names, such as Bert "Be Home" Blyleven and Jim "Two Silhouettes on" Deshaies. Andre "Bad Moon" Rison is another example of Berman's wit, as he used the NFL receiver's name as a play on Credence Clearwater Revival's "Bad Moon Rising."

3. Which ML baseball team has not made the playoffs since 1981?

a. Milwaukee Brewers
b. Detroit Tigers
c. Baltimore Orioles
d. Montreal Expos

GAME 75 Q2 ANSWER c
In the 1990s, Stanley Cup droughts were ended by both the Rangers (54 years) and Red Wings (42 years). The Blackhawks, who haven't hoisted the Holy Grail since 1961, are now atop the list. The Maple Leafs aren't far behind, with their last triumph occurring in 1967.

11. Against which team did David Cone pitch his perfect 1999 game?

a. Montreal Expos

b. Minnesota Twins

c. Texas Rangers

d. Philadelphia Phillies

GAME 6 Q10 ANSWER c
While the 56-game hitting streak that Joe DiMaggio enjoyed in 1941 seems untouchable, he accomplished an even more impressive feat eight years earlier. As a rookie for the San Francisco Seals, DiMaggio managed an unheard of 61-game batting run. The Yankees purchased Joe D's contract from the Seals in 1934 for $50,000.

11. Who hit the walk-off home run to clinch the 1993 World Series for Toronto?

a. Dave Winfield

b. Joe Carter

c. Roberto Alomar

d. John Olerud

GAME 26 Q10 ANSWER c
When Russians Yelena Berezhnaya and Anton Sikharulidze scored higher marks than Canadians Jamie Sale and David Pelletier on an obviously substandard performance, eyebrows were raised. After an investigation, a French skating judge was suspended, and the Canadian tandem was awarded honorary gold medals.

11. Where did coaching legend Rod Dedeaux win ten national baseball titles?

a. Arizona State

b. University of Arizona

c. USC

d. Louisiana State

GAME 46 Q10 ANSWER b
John Wooden won an astounding ten NCAA National Championships while coaching some amazing UCLA teams in the '60s and '70s. Beside posting an unfathomable 149–2 home record with the Bruins, Wooden won six NCAA Coach of the Year Awards, and is enshrined in the Naismith Basketball Hall of Fame as both player and coach.

11. Which college hoops team did John Feinstein profile in *A Season on the Brink*?

a. UCLA

b. Georgia Tech

c. Michigan

d. Indiana

GAME 66 Q10 ANSWER c
In this 2001 book, released just before his death at age 67, longtime journalist, excellent storyteller, and friend to many, Dick Schapp recounts a number of the amazing events he witnessed in his half-century of covering sports. The Schapp legacy will live, as son Jeremy continues to ply the family trade as a reporter on ESPN.

2. In which year was I named MVP of the NBA Championship series?

a. 1973

b. 1974

c. 1975

d. 1976

GAME 15 Q1 ANSWER b
Joining me on the Oakland Oaks were Larry Brown and Doug Moe, who had been my teammates the previous season with the New Orleans Buccaneers. The Oaks defeated the Indiana Pacers to capture the 1969 ABA Championship.

---

2. Who was the first man to complete tennis's Grand Slam in one year?

a. Don Budge

b. Rene LaCoste

c. Fred Perry

d. Jack Crawford

GAME 35 Q1 ANSWER c
While Arlene Hiss was the first woman to drive in an Indy-style race in March 1976, Janet Guthrie was the first female to compete in America's most famous auto race. On May 29, 1976, Guthrie made history by finishing twenty-ninth. She competed two more times, her last appearance being a thirty-fourth place finish in 1979.

---

2. "Bad Moon"

a. Chris Calloway

b. J.J. Birden

c. Andre Rison

d. Ike Hilliard

GAME 55 Q1 ANSWER c
Pele was born Edson Arantes de Nascimento. Try putting that one on the back of a uniform shirt!

---

2. Which NHL team has the longest Stanley Cup drought?

a. St. Louis Blues

b. Toronto Maple Leafs

c. Chicago Blackhawks

d. Buffalo Sabres

GAME 75 Q1 ANSWER b
The man who once served as Muhammad Ali's sparring partner might have been the most unpopular coach in the history of the Jets, as he guided the club to a pitiful 4 wins and 28 losses in his two seasons at the helm (1995 and 1996).

---

12. Who was the first non-baseball person to be honored with a plaque in Yankee Stadium's Monument Park?

a. John F. Kennedy
b. Franklin D. Roosevelt
c. Nelson Mandela
d. Pope Paul VI

GAME 6 Q11 ANSWER a
The Bombers have a habit of turning big days into historical ones—a habit evidenced on July 18, 1999. On an afternoon that honored Yogi Berra, immortality was reached when David Cone got shortstop Orlando Cabrera to pop out, becoming the fifteenth pitcher in Major League history to toss perfection.

12. Why was there no Stanley Cup Champion in 1919?

a. Fire
b. Rioting
c. Power failure
d. Influenza

GAME 26 Q11 ANSWER b
The highlight of Canadian baseball history saw Joe Carter wallop a series-clinching homer off Philadelphia's Mitch Williams. Trailing by 1 run in the bottom of the ninth in Game 6, Carter stepped to the plate with 2 men on base and 1 out. With a 2–2 count, Carter smashed the ball into the left-field seats of Toronto's SkyDome.

12. As of 2004, who was the last player to win the Heisman Trophy and National Championship in the same year?

a. Ricky Williams
b. Charles Woodson
c. Danny Wuerffel
d. Charlie Ward

GAME 46 Q11 ANSWER c
Before he began coaching at USC, Rod Dedeaux was an infielder at the school, and had a short Major League run. He found his niche in coaching. In over forty-five years with the Trojans, Dedeaux won twenty-eight conference titles and ten National Championships, including five in a row from 1970 to 1974.

12. Which nineteenth-century writer was dubbed the "Father of Baseball"?

a. Alexander Cartwright
b. Abner Doubleday
c. Henry Chadwick
d. Larry Corcoran

GAME 66 Q11 ANSWER d
This 1989 work summarizes writer John Feinstein's observations of the 1985-1986 Indiana Hoosiers basketball team and its explosive coach, Bob Knight. One of the best-selling sports hardcover books of all-time, *A Season on the Brink* also spawned the 2002 ESPN film of the same name, starring Brian Dennehy as coach Knight.

1. The championship ABA team I played on was:

a. Virginia Squires
b. Oakland Oaks
c. NY Nets
d. Washington Capitols

The answer to this question is on:

page 154, top frame, right side.

---

1. Who was the first woman to compete in the Indianapolis 500?

a. Arlene Hiss
b. Desire Wilson
c. Janet Guthrie
d. Lyn St. James

The answer to this question is on:

page 154, second frame, right side.

---

1. What is the given first name of Brazilian soccer star Pele?

a. Marco
b. Adolfo
c. Edson
d. Ignacio

The answer to this question is on:

page 154, third frame, right side.

---

1. Which NY Jets head coach went 4 and 28 during his two-year tenure?

a. Bruce Coslet
b. Rich Kotite
c. Pete Carroll
d. Lou Holtz

The answer to this question is on:

page 154, bottom frame, right side.

GAME 7

"Name That College"

Famed Jocks and Their Schools

Turn to page 159 for the first question.

After celebrating mass in the stadium in 1965, Pope Paul VI was honored with a plaque in the famed Monument Park area behind the left/center outfield fence. Two other non-baseball homages can be found in that area as well—one for Pope John Paul II (1979) and one for the victims of September 11 (2001).

GAME 27

"Untimely Deaths"

They Left Us Too Soon

Turn to page 159 for the first question.

GAME 26 Q12 ANSWER d
The Montreal Canadiens and Seattle Metropolitans were tied at 2 games apiece when the Department of Health called off the series due to a serious outbreak of influenza. The illness incapacitated most of the Montreal team, including its tough guy "Bad" Joe Hall, who died as a result.

GAME 47

"The Los Angeles Lakers"

From Showtime to Shaqtime

Turn to page 159 for the first question.

GAME 46 Q12 ANSWER b
While it has happened nine times since the Heisman Trophy was initiated in 1935, the last player to achieve this feat was Michigan's defensive back Charles Woodson in 1997. Woodson joins an elite list of players that includes Ricky Williams, Tony Dorsett, John Lujack, and Doak Walker.

GAME 67

"Signal-Caller Central"

Quarterback Facts, Figures, and Trivia

Turn to page 159 for the first question.

GAME 66 Q12 ANSWER c
The inventor of the box score and writer of baseball's first detailed rule book, Henry Chadwick was the first writer to be inducted into Cooperstown in 1938, thirty years after his death. A cricket writer for *The New York Times,* Chadwick also convinced newspapers to start covering America's newest sport.

GAME 15

"All About Me"

How Much Do You Know About Rick Barry?

Turn to page 156 for the first question.

GAME 14 Q12 ANSWER d
By winning the 1993 French Open Double Championship—their only Grand Slam finals appearance—Luke and Murphy Jensen remain the last brother pairing to win a Major. The long-haired duo has won no other Major to date.

GAME 35

"Fabulous Firsts"

Sports Figures Who Accomplished Feats First

Turn to page 156 for the first question.

GAME 34 Q12 ANSWER a
Citing cultural difficulties in small town Wisconsin, Manhattan-bred Jabbar had demanded a move to a major East or West Coast city. So on June 16, 1975, against his will, Milwaukee Bucks general manager Wayne Embry sent his franchise's best player to the Los Angeles Lakers.

GAME 55

"More Nicknames"

Recognize These Great Sports Monikers?

Turn to page 156 for the first question.

GAME 54 Q12 ANSWER b
After beaning him on the head earlier in the season, Yankee pitcher Roger Clemens hurled a piece of jagged lumber at Mike Piazza after the Mets catcher shattered his bat on a pitch in Game 2 of the 2000 World Series. Clemens was fined $50,000 for the incident.

GAME 75

"Lovable Losers"

But They Were Sure Fun to Watch

Turn to page 156 for the first question.

GAME 74 Q12 ANSWER c
One of the most dominating pitchers of the 1980s, Jack Morris took home his first ring with the Detroit Tigers in 1984—the same year he tossed his only career no-hitter. In 1991, he won another ring with the Minnesota Twins, and went on to win two more titles with Toronto in 1992 and 1993.

GAME 7	1. Which school did notable signal caller Bob Griese attend? a. Nebraska b. Purdue c. Ohio State d. Northwestern	The answer to this question is on: **page 161, top frame, right side.**
GAME 27	1. Which NFL team drafted All-American running back Ernie Davis? a. Broncos b. Browns c. Steelers d. Redskins	The answer to this question is on: **page 161, second frame, right side.**
GAME 47	1. Who coached the Lakers to their first NBA Championship in California? a. Joe Mullaney b. Jerry West c. Bill Sharman d. Bill Van Breda Kolff	The answer to this question is on: **page 161, third frame, right side.**
GAME 67	1. Which NFL signal caller holds the twentieth-century record for most passing attempts in a game? a. Vinny Testaverde b. Tony Eason c. Norm Van Brocklin d. Drew Bledsoe	The answer to this question is on: **page 161, bottom frame, right side.**

GAME 14

12. Which was the last brother combo to win a Grand Slam Doubles Championship?

a. John and Patrick McEnroe

b. Laurie and Reggie Doherty

c. Gene and Sandy Mayer

d. Luke and Murphy Jensen

GAME 14 Q11 ANSWER b
The brother of Billie Jean King, pitcher Randy Moffitt played for the San Francisco Giants from 1972 through 1978. A sinkerballer with good control, he was second in the NL with 15 saves in 1974, and sixth in 1976 with 14. Moffitt retired in 1983 with 96 career saves.

GAME 34

12. Which general manager traded away Kareem Abdul-Jabbar?

a. Wayne Embry

b. Dave DeBusschere

c. Jerry Krause

d. Tex Winters

GAME 34 Q11 ANSWER d
Canadiens' fans can thank ex-coach Mario Tremblay for driving away St. Patrick. After Tremblay left Roy in a game to absorb the brunt of a 12–1 beating, the goalie stormed off the ice. Roy was soon traded to Colorado for Martin Rucinsky, Jocelyn Thibault, and Andrei Kovalenko.

GAME 54

12. At which player did Roger Clemens throw a broken bat in 2000?

a. Robin Ventura

b. Mike Piazza

c. Todd Zeile

d. Edgardo Alfonzo

GAME 54 Q11 ANSWER d
Leading the Packers to victory, quarterback Bart Starr took home the MVP Award after both games. Going 16 of 23 for 250 yards, and scoring 2 touchdowns in the first game, Starr was the catalyst of the Pack's 35–10 dismantling of Kansas City. The next year, Green Bay thumped the Raiders 33–14.

GAME 74

12. With which of the following clubs did Jack Morris *not* win a World Series?

a. Toronto Blue Jays

b. Detroit Tigers

c. Cleveland Indians

d. Minnesota Twins

GAME 74 Q11 ANSWER a
The most valuable player of Montreal's cup-winning teams in 1986 and 1993, living legend Patrick Roy took home the trophy again in 2001 with the Colorado Avalanche to become the only player to win the award with two separate clubs.

GAME 7

2. At which school did Barry Bonds play college baseball?

a. Louisiana State

b. Arizona State

c. Texas State

d. Clemson University

GAME 7 Q1 ANSWER b
While his NFL career was amazing, Griese was legendary while plying his trade for Purdue. A two-time All-American, Griese was voted all-time quarterback for the Boilermakers' first 100 years.

GAME 27

2. How did Hall of Famer outfielder Ed Delahanty meet his demise?

a. Fell out of a window

b. Fell off a horse

c. Fell off a bridge

d. Fell asleep at the wheel

GAME 27 Q1 ANSWER d
Soon after Syracuse University's Ernie Davis, the first black player to win the Heisman Trophy (1961), was drafted by the Redskins, he was diagnosed with acute leukemia. Davis passed away at the age of 23.

GAME 47

2. How many NBA Finals did the Lakers lose in LA before winning the 1972 title?

a. Four

b. Five

c. Six

d. Seven

GAME 47 Q1 ANSWER c
Taking over a 48-win squad from Joe Mullaney in the 1971-1972 season, Bill Sharman guided the team to a then-record 69-win season right off the bat. Winner of four rings with the Celtics, Sharman had played both pro baseball and basketball during his first five years out of college.

GAME 67

2. With which team did Steve Young start his NFL career?

a. Kansas City Chiefs

b. San Francisco 49ers

c. Tampa Bay Buccaneers

d. St. Louis Cardinals

GAME 67 Q1 ANSWER d
In the November 13, 1994 game between the Minnesota Vikings and the New England Patriots, Drew Bledsoe lofted 70 passes skyward in a 26–20 overtime victory at Foxboro. He completed 45 passes and tossed 3 touchdowns to rally the Patriots back from a 20–0 halftime deficit.

---

11. Who is tennis great Billie Jean King's athletic sibling?

a. Tommy John

b. Randy Moffitt

c. Don Sutton

d. Steve Carlton

GAME 14 Q10 ANSWER d
Combine 58 goals by Florida's Pavel and 35 by Calgary's Valeri in the 1999-2000 season, and you will have the highest goal total by two brothers in NHL history. It took over thirty years to break the previous record of 88 goals set by Bobby and Dennis Hull in the 1968-1969 season.

11. Which team received three players in a 1995 trade of Patrick Roy?

a. Boston Bruins

b. St. Louis Blues

c. Edmonton Oilers

d. Montreal Canadiens

GAME 34 Q10 ANSWER c
Focusing on the short term, Boston traded future superstar Jeff Bagwell to the Houston Astros for reliever Larry Andersen. Bagwell went on to become one of the premier first basemen, combining power and speed, while Andersen appeared in three games for the Sox in the 1990 postseason, losing one and compiling an ERA of 6.00.

11. Who won the MVP Award in the first two Super Bowls?

a. Ray Nitschke

b. Jim Taylor

c. Max McGee

d. Bart Starr

GAME 54 Q10 ANSWER a
During the seven-year stretch (1970–1976), the Cincinnati Reds won 4 Pennants and 2 World Series, but Bench never hit above .289. He ended his seventeen-year career with a lifetime average of .267.

11. Who is the only NHL player to win the Conn Smythe Award with two different clubs?

a. Patrick Roy

b. Tony Esposito

c. Mike Vernon

d. Glenn Hall

GAME 74 Q10 ANSWER c
With the exception of the 1994 strike year, Justice went to the playoffs with Atlanta (1991-1996), Cleveland (1997-1999), New York (2000-2001) and Oakland (2002). He won a pair of rings with the Braves in 1995 and the Yankees in 2000.

3. Keith Smart led which NCAA basketball team to a championship?

a. Indiana University
b. Kansas State
c. Georgetown
d. Villanova

Long before he hit 73 home runs in a season, Barry Bonds was playing for the Arizona State Sun Devils. In his three seasons in Tempe, Bond managed to compile a .347 average, tie an NCAA record with 7 consecutive hits at the 1984 College World Series, and set the ASU freshman home run record with 11 dingers in 1983.

---

3. Addie Joss played his entire career with which American League team?

a. Detroit Tigers
b. Cleveland Indians
c. Chicago White Sox
d. Philadelphia Athletics

At age 35, Delahanty was put off a train on the International Bridge near Niagara Falls for being drunk and disorderly. He then fell though an open drawbridge and was swept over the falls. Playing most of his turn-of-the-century career with the Phillies, Delahanty's .346 batting average landed him fifth best of all time.

---

3. Which Laker hit twelve 3-point field goals in a game?

a. Derek Harper
b. Magic Johnson
c. Kobe Bryant
d. Nick Van Exel

The Lakers had appeared in seven finals after moving from Minneapolis following the 1959-1960 season. They lost to the Celtics in their first six title bids, taking Boston to seven games in four of those series. After losing to the New York Knicks in 1970, the Lakers waited two years before getting their revenge, and the first California crown.

---

3. Which quarterback did the Indianapolis Colts select first overall in 1990?

a. Jim Harbaugh
b. Casey Weldon
c. Jeff George
d. Andre Ware

After coming out of Brigham Young, the undrafted Steve Young played briefly for the USFL's Los Angeles Express in 1984. One year later, he found himself wearing the orange and white of the Tampa Bay Buccaneers. Young started for the team in 1986, throwing 8 touchdowns and 13 interceptions before moving to San Francisco in 1987.

---

10. Which two players hold the single-season NHL goal-scoring record by brothers?

a. Henri and Maurice Richard

b. Wayne and Brent Gretzky

c. Bobby and Dennis Hull

d. Pavel and Valeri Bure

GAME 14 Q9 ANSWER a
In the 1995 championship game, both O'Bannons contributed to UCLA's 89–78 victory over defending titlist Arkansas. Older brother Ed was named the game's outstanding player, thanks to his 30-point, 17-rebound explosion; while Charles chipped in with 11 points and 9 rebounds.

---

10. For which player did the Red Sox trade Jeff Bagwell in 1990?

a. Matt Young

b. John Marzano

c. Larry Andersen

d. Joe Hesketh

GAME 34 Q9 ANSWER b
In possibly the worst baseball transaction ever made, Red Sox owner Frazee sold Ruth to the Yankees for $125,000. A man deeply involved in the theater, Frazee had a habit of selling off his best players to cover his entertainment ventures. In July 1919, for instance, he sold top pitcher Carl Mays—again to New York.

---

10. In the "Big Red Machine" era, how many times did superstar catcher Johnny Bench hit over .300?

a. 0

b. 1

c. 3

d. 4

GAME 54 Q9 ANSWER b
Fed up with owner Charlie Finley's meddling, Dick Williams resigned after the '73 season. Finley refused to let Williams (still under contract) manage anywhere else unless he received compensation. In 1974, the Angels paid Finley for the right to hire Williams.

---

10. Which baseball player made 11 straight postseason appearances with four different clubs?

a. Bob Turley

b. Don Baylor

c. Dave Justice

d. Jimmy Key

GAME 74 Q9 ANSWER a
After winning three NCAA basketball titles with UCLA in the late '60s, Kareem Abdul-Jabbar led the Milwaukee Bucks to their only NBA championship in 1971, earning Finals MVP honors along the way. As a Laker, Kareem helped the team win five titles, taking home the 1985 award after defeating the defending champion Celtics in 6 games.

---

4. Chris Drury is a hockey legend at which New England school?

a. Boston College
b. Northeastern University
c. Boston University
d. Harvard University

GAME 7 Q3 ANSWER a
Forever known for his sixteen-foot baseline jumper in the 1987 NCAA Championship game, Keith Smart's shot gave Indiana its third NCAA hoops crown. Banging home 12 of the Hoosiers' final 15 points in the 74–73 win over Syracuse, Smart was one of only four Indiana players to get on the score sheet the entire game.

4. How many Olympic medals were won by track and field star Florence Griffith-Joyner?

a. 4
b. 5
c. 6
d. 7

GAME 27 Q3 ANSWER b
Pitching for the Indians at the start of the twentieth century, Joss dominated AL batters for nine straight years. He died suddenly two days after he turned 31 from what is now believed to be kidney disease. He was the only player inducted into the Hall of Fame with less than the required minimum ten years playing time.

4. In which town is the Great Western Forum located?

a. Inglewood
b. Hollywood
c. Compton
d. Burbank

GAME 47 Q3 ANSWER c
On January 7, 2003, in a game against Seattle, Kobe Bryant broke the NBA record for 3-pointers in a game, by going 12 of 18 from beyond the arc. The previous record of 11 in a game was pulled off by Orlando's Dennis Scott in 1996. Kobe also set the mark for consecutive treys by nailing 9 in a row.

4. Which backup quarterback was on five straight Super Bowl teams?

a. Terry Hanratty
b. Gale Gilbert
c. Steve Bono
d. Earl Morrall

GAME 67 Q3 ANSWER c
Indianapolis selected local boy Jeff George out of Illinois, and had lofty aspirations for the surly signal caller to become its franchise quarterback. Unfortunately for the Colts, George was gone by 1994, and spent the next nine seasons bouncing between five teams.

9. Who were the last two brothers to play together on an NCAA basketball championship team?

a. Charles and Ed O'Bannon

b. Grant and Thomas Hill

c. Deno and Gene Melchiorre

d. Isaiah and Jim Thomas

GAME 14 Q8 ANSWER b
Both Martinez brothers managed the feat in 1995, but only one was credited with a no-hitter. On July 14, Ramon threw a true no-hitter. But on June 3, Pedro had a perfect game through nine innings, with a score of 0–0. Then Montreal picked up a run in the tenth, and Martinez was replaced with a relief pitcher.

9. Which executive sold Babe Ruth to the Yankees in 1919?

a. Ban Johnson

b. Harry Frazee

c. Cap Huston

d. Bob Quinn

GAME 34 Q8 ANSWER a
After calling outfielder Frank Robinson "a very old thirty," Cincinnati Reds GM Bill DeWitt shipped the Hall of Famer to Baltimore. Quickly disproving DeWitt's assessment, Robinson won the American League Triple Crown, captured the league's Most Valuable Player Award, and led the O's to a World Series title.

9. Which manager quit after consecutive World Series wins with Oakland in '72 and '73?

a. Alvin Dark

b. Dick Williams

c. Bob Lind

d. Billy Martin

GAME 54 Q8 ANSWER b
After winning a record seven consecutive NCAA Men's Basketball Championships, UCLA's hopes were dashed in the 1974 national semifinals by the NC State Wolfpack, who defeated them by a score of 80–77. Still, UCLA's record of seven straight is an impressive mark in all of sports to attain.

9. Who is the only NBA player to win Finals MVP Awards with two different teams?

a. Kareem Abdul-Jabbar

b. Moses Malone

c. Bill Walton

d. Wilt Chamberlain

GAME 74 Q8 ANSWER b
A tight end for the Dallas Cowboys, "Iron Mike" Ditka earned his first ring in Super Bowl VI. In that 24–3 victory over the Miami Dolphins, he caught a 7-yard touchdown pass from Roger Staubach. In Super Bowl XX, as head coach of the dominant Chicago Bears, Ditka took home another ring when his team crushed New England 46–10.

5. At which university did Tiger Woods play college golf?

a. USC
b. UCLA
c. San Diego State
d. Stanford University

The man known for his clutch NHL play-off goals was famous as a Boston University Terrier before he ever played a pro game. Drury's numerous trophies are topped by the 1998 Hobey Baker Award as the NCAA's top player, and his crowning moment came when his team won the 1995 NCAA Championship.

---

5. In what country was New Jersey Nets All-Star guard Drazen Petrovic born?

a. Croatia
b. Serbia
c. Slovenia
d. Montenegro

"Flojo" won a silver in 1984, and three golds and one silver in 1988. In 1988, she also won the Sullivan Award as the nation's top amateur athlete. Ten years later, she died of an apparent heart seizure at the age of 38.

---

5. Who owned the Lakers prior to Dr. Jerry Buss?

a. Gene Autry
b. George Gund
c. Jack Kent Cooke
d. Wells Fargo Bank

Before moving to the plush Staples Center in 1999, the Lakers made their home for over thirty years in the Great Western Forum, located in Inglewood. Built in the mid-60s at a cost of $16 million, the Roman-style Forum housed both the Lakers and the NHL's Los Angeles Kings from 1967 until the beginning of the 1999-2000 season.

---

5. Which former Ohio State quarterback made his name in the NFL as a punter?

a. Tom Tupa
b. Shane Lechler
c. Brad Maynard
d. Mark Royals

The third-string quarterback during Buffalos' four consecutive Super Bowl losses in the early '90s, Gale Gilbert signed with the Chargers in 1994 and made it to five straight Super Bowls. The only game Gilbert appeared in was his fifth with the Chargers, completing 3 of 6 passes for 30 yards and an interception in Super Bowl XXIX.

---

8. Who were the last two brothers to throw a nine-inning no-hitter in the same season?

a. Bob and Ken Forsch

b. Pedro and Ramon Martinez

c. Mickey and Rick Mahler

d. Christy and Henry Mathewson

GAME 14 Q7 ANSWER c
Horace and Harvey Grant, who attended Clemson University together, have grabbed the most rebounds of any brother combination in NBA history. While Harvey spent most of his career in Washington with the Bullets/Wizards, Horace won four NBA Championships with the Bulls and Lakers.

---

8. For which player did the Baltimore Orioles trade Milt Pappas, Jack Baldschun, and Dick Simpson?

a. Frank Robinson

b. Jim Palmer

c. Brooks Robinson

d. Dave McNally

GAME 34 Q7 ANSWER c
In a move initially disliked by the Green Bay brass, general manager Ron Wolf made one of the most astute trades in NFL history when he obtained quarterback Brett Favre from Atlanta for a 1993 first-round pick. Favre went on to win three NFL MVP Awards, as well as Super Bowl XXXI.

---

8. Which team ended UCLA's hopes of eight straight NCAA hoops titles in 1974?

a. Marquette

b. North Carolina State

c. Kansas

d. Indiana

GAME 54 Q7 ANSWER b
When Wayne Gretzky left for LA in 1988, most Oiler fans thought the championship run was over. Although the team missed a beat in 1989, it took the Stanley Cup in 1990. During the playoffs, goaltender Bill Ranford went 3 1/2 games without giving up a goal, making him an easy choice for the Conn Smythe Trophy.

---

8. Who is the only one to win Super Bowls as a player and a coach for different teams?

a. Tom Flores

b. Mike Ditka

c. Brian Billick

d. Jon Gruden

GAME 74 Q7 ANSWER a
Coming into the NHL with the Canadiens in 1988, gritty forward Mike Keane was able to capture the 1993 Cup with Montreal, the 1996 Cup with Colorado, and then one more in 1999 with the Dallas Stars. Keane joined a short list of people, including Al Arbour and Claude Lemieux, who have won Stanley Cups with three different franchises.

---

6. NBA guard Steve Nash honed his skills at which small West Coast school?

a. Gonzaga

b. Pepperdine

c. St. Mary's

d. Santa Clara

GAME 7 Q5 ANSWER d

Prior to conquering the world, Tiger Woods won ten NCAA golf matches in his three years competing for Stanford University. Woods took home the trophy in the last six college matches in which he competed, the grand finale being the 1996 NCAA Championships held in Chattanooga, Tennessee. Woods turned pro later that year.

---

6. Which statement about Yankee great Thurmon Munson is not true?

a. Rookie of the Year

b. Most Valuable Player

c. Hall of Famer

d. Has a plaque in Yankee Stadium's center field

GAME 27 Q5 ANSWER a

Considered to be the all-time greatest European basketball player, Petrovic died tragically in an automobile accident at the age of 28.

---

6. Who is the only Lakers coach to hold his job more than a full season and have a losing record?

a. John Castellani

b. Magic Johnson

c. Jerry McKinney

d. Randy Pfund

GAME 47 Q5 ANSWER c

Jack Kent Cooke purchased the Lakers in 1965 for $5.2 million from Jerry Short. A year later, he added the expansion LA Kings to his arsenal, and proceeded to build the Great Western Forum. The tycoon, who would later own the NFL's Washington Redskins, sold both teams to Dr. Jerry Buss in 1979 for a then-record $67 million.

---

6. For which Arena Football League team did Kurt Warner play before joining the NFL?

a. Orlando Predators

b. Grand Rapids Rampage

c. Detroit Fury

d. Iowa Barnstormers

GAME 67 Q5 ANSWER a

Appearing mostly as a quarterback during his first five NFL seasons with Arizona and Indianapolis, Tom Tupa threw for over 2,000 in 1991 with the Cardinals. After going to Cleveland in 1994, he switched to mostly punting, and earned a trip to the 1999 Pro Bowl.

---

7. Which brothers hold the NBA all-time sibling rebound record?

a. The Wilkins

b. The Van Ardsdales

c. The Grants

d. The McGuires

GAME 14 Q 6 ANSWER a
With Phil's 318 wins and brother Joe's 221 career victories, the Niekros combine to form the most winning brother team of all time. Second in line are the Perry brothers, led by Gaylord's 314 wins and brother's Jim's 215. The Niekros and Perrys are the only sets of brothers who have each posted 200 big-league victories.

7. Who did the Atlanta Falcons trade for a first-round pick in the 1992 NFL Draft?

a. Deion Sanders

b. Brian Jordan

c. Brett Favre

d. Robert Brooks

GAME 34 Q6 ANSWER b
After the Celtics won just 29 games in the 1979-1980 season, general manager Red Auerbach shipped off the first and thirteenth overall picks to Golden State for a third overall pick and center Robert Parish. Auerbach then drafted Kevin McHale with the third pick, setting up the Celtics to win three future championships.

7. Who won the 1990 Conn Smythe Award after Edmonton won its fifth Stanley Cup in seven seasons?

a. Jari Kurri

b. Bill Ranford

c. Mark Messier

d. Wayne Gretzky

GAME 54 Q6 ANSWER c
By crushing the Denver Broncos 55–10 in Super Bowl XXIV, the 49ers posted the largest margin of victory to date in big-game history, and took their second straight Super Bowl—the fourth in nine seasons. Their run in the '80s saw Joe Montana and Jerry Rice become career leaders in almost every Super Bowl passing and receiving category.

7. With which of the following teams did Mike Keane *not* win a Stanley Cup?

a. Pittsburgh Penguins

b. Montreal Canadiens

c. Dallas Stars

d. Colorado Avalanche

GAME 74 Q6 ANSWER b
Serving mainly as a designated hitter for the 1989 World Champion Oakland A's, Dave "The Cobra" Parker added another ring to the band he earned while playing for the Pittsburgh Pirates in 1979. Parker was more than a nominal member of the Pirates as he contributed 22 homers and 97 RBIs at the age of 38.

7. At which college did Paul Kariya make his name on the ice?

a. Lake Superior State
b. University of Maine
c. Michigan State
d. Colorado State

GAME 7 Q6 ANSWER d
Before being known for wild haircuts and dating Spice Girls, Steve Nash was a clean-cut point guard for the Santa Clara Broncos. He garnered national attention for Santa Clara by being a two-time WCC Player of the Year, and by playing instrumental roles in NCAA tournament upsets over Arizona in 1993 and Maryland in 1996.

7. Undefeated heavyweight champion Rocky Marciano gained his title by defeating:

a. Joe Louis
b. Ezzard Charles
c. "Jersey" Joe Walcott
d. Archie Moore

GAME 27 Q6 ANSWER c
The revered Yankee catcher died in a plane crash while practicing takeoffs and landings in his new airplane. To this day, Munson's clubhouse locker remains empty in silent tribute.

7. How many games did Phil Jackson win in his first year as Lakers coach?

a. 61
b. 63
c. 64
d. 67

GAME 47 Q6 ANSWER d
At the end of the "Showtime" era, Coach Randy Pfund inherited a team in desperate need of rebuilding. He had a 39–43 record in the 1992-1993 season, and began the next campaign with stats of 28–39. Magic Johnson replaced Pfund for the last 15 games, and guided the team to a 5–10 finish.

7. Which NFL quarterback coined the phrase "Hail Mary" to describe a desperation pass?

a. Fran Tarkenton
b. Y.A. Tittle
c. Roger Staubach
d. Johnny Unitas

GAME 67 Q6 ANSWER d
Before joining the Rams in 1998, Kurt Warner was something of an icon in the Arena Football League while playing for his home state Iowa Barnstormers. In 40 games from 1995 to 1997, Warner threw 180 touchdown passes, and after signing with St. Louis, he played briefly for NFL Europe's Amsterdam Admirals in the spring of 1998.

6. Which two pitchers have posted the most wins by a brother tandem?

a. Phil and Joe Niekro
b. Dizzy and Daffy Dean
c. Gaylord and Jim Perry
d. Greg and Mike Maddux

GAME 14 Q5 ANSWER a
In the early years of the NHL All-Star Game, the Stanley Cup winner would play the best of all the other teams. In 1963, Frank Mahovlich of the champion Toronto Maple Leafs took home the MVP. Brother Peter of the Montreal Canadiens grabbed the hardware in 1976, completing the brother double.

6. Who did the Celtics acquire for two first-round draft picks in 1980?

a. Dennis Johnson
b. Robert Parish
c. Larry Bird
d. Bill Walton

GAME 34 Q5 ANSWER a
Sometimes obtaining an all-world goaltender like Dominik Hasek can be as easy as trading a benchwarmer like Stephane Beauregard to the Chicago Blackhawks. Hasek went on to win two Hart Trophies and seven Vezinas for the Buffalo Sabres.

6. Which team did the 49ers beat by 45 points in Super Bowl XXIV?

a. Cincinnati
b. San Diego
c. Denver
d. Miami

GAME 54 Q5 ANSWER c
On a team with more than one set of siblings, brothers Chris and Jason Peter were both lineman on the Huskers back-to-back National Championship teams of the mid-1990s. Both brothers went on to play in the NFL.

6. Slugger Dave Parker won his second World Series ring with which team?

a. Cincinnati
b. Oakland
c. Los Angeles
d. Minnesota

GAME 74 Q5 ANSWER d
Winning the Lombardi Trophy in each of his Super Bowl appearances, defensive end Charles Haley earned three rings while playing with the San Francisco 49ers, and two with the Dallas Cowboys. He was coaxed out of retirement by San Francisco in 1999 to go for ring number six, but the team collapsed after an injury to Steve Young.

8. Rebecca Lobo was a hoops star at which university?

a. Notre Dame
b. San Jose State
c. Connecticut
d. Tennessee State

Hobey Baker Award winner Paul Kariya played for the University of Maine Black Bears. During the 1993 NCAA Championship Game, with his team trailing 4–2, Kariya helped spearhead an impressive comeback, and Maine won its first national title. He was picked by the Mighty Ducks fourth overall in the 1993 NHL Draft.

8. Josh Gibson, the Negro Leagues' greatest home run hitter, played what position?

a. Catcher
b. Third base
c. First base
d. Outfield

In 1952, the "Bronx Bomber" knocked out Walcott in Round 13 of their bout, and defended his title six times before retiring in 1955. He was killed in a plane crash one day short of his 47th birthday.

8. Who copyrighted the term "three-peat" after Los Angeles' second straight title in 1988?

a. Pat Riley
b. Magic Johnson
c. Jerry West
d. Chick Hearn

After taking over the team for the 1999-2000 campaign, Phil Jackson guided the team to a 67-win season. He also helped motivate Shaquille O'Neal to improve his confidence, conditioning, and maturity, and go on to win the league MVP. Most important, he led the Lakers to their first title since 1988.

8. Which Hall of Fame quarterback threw 47 more interceptions than touchdowns?

a. Joe Namath
b. Norm Van Brocklin
c. Richard Todd
d. Sonny Jurgensen

After his desperation last-second throw in a 1975 playoff game against the Vikings, Roger Staubach told reporters he was praying the "Hail Mary" as he heaved the ball that would be caught by Drew Pearson for the game-winning score. The term is now used at the end of almost every football game that requires a miracle throw.

5. Who were the only two brothers to be named MVP of an NHL All-Star Game?

a. Frank and Peter Mahovlich

b. Bobby and Dennis Hull

c. Pavel and Valeri Bure

d. Maurice and Henri Richard

GAME 14 Q4 ANSWER c
On November 26, 2000, the Huard boys became the first brothers in NFL history to start at quarterback for separate teams on the same weekend. Brock led the Seahawks, while Damon got the nod in Miami. Tim and Matt Hasselbeck repeated the feat in 2003. In 1997, Ty and Koy Detmer both played for Philadelphia in the same game—another first.

---

5. Who did the Buffalo Sabres get by trading Stephane Beauregard in the early '90s?

a. Dominik Hasek

b. Mike Modano

c. Ed Belfour

d. Chris Chelios

GAME 34 Q4 ANSWER d
Never getting a legitimate chance to prove himself in Southern California, Pedro Martinez was sent to Montreal by the Dodgers in December 1993. While Martinez went on to become an impressive pitcher, Delino DeShields' best Dodger season came in 1995, when he hit .256 with 8 homers and 39 stolen bases.

---

5. Which brothers played on the defensive line of Nebraska's 1994 and 1995 NCAA Football Championship teams?

a. The Wistroms

b. The Makovickas

c. The Peters

d. The Millers

GAME 54 Q4 ANSWER a
In Game 7 of the 1965 Eastern Finals, the Celtics held a 1-point lead over the Philadelphia 76ers with 5 seconds left. As the Sixers Hal Greer tried to inbound the ball to Chet Walker, Boston's John Havlicek appeared from nowhere to make the steal and send Boston to the finals, where the team took title number seven out of eight in a row.

---

5. Who is the only player to win five Super Bowls?

a. Bill Romanowski

b. D.D. Lewis

c. Marv Fleming

d. Charles Haley

GAME 74 Q4 ANSWER c
Joining Frank Saul as the only player to win consecutive NBA titles with different teams, 3-point specialist Steve Kerr won titles in 1998 with Chicago, and in 1999 with San Antonio. In the 1994-1995 season, Kerr posted the best-ever 3-point percentage, connecting on better than 52 percent of his shots from beyond the arc.

9. Charles Woodson won the Heisman Trophy while playing for which college?

a. UCLA

b. University of Michigan

c. University of Nebraska

d. Florida State

GAME 7 Q8 ANSWER c
Competing for the University of Connecticut Huskies from 1991 to 1995, Rebecca Lobo earned her place as one of the best all-time women's collegiate basketball players. The defining season of Lobo's college career was 1994-1995, when she led the Huskies to a national championship.

---

9. How did American League batting champion George "Snuffy" Stirnweiss die?

a. In an avalanche

b. In a tornado

c. As a shooting victim

d. In a train wreck

GAME 27 Q8 ANSWER a
Often called "The Black Babe Ruth" because of his home run-hitting prowess, Georgia-born Gibson died at age 35 after suffering a stroke. His death occurred in 1947, just as the doors to Major League ball were opening for black players.

---

9. Who dumped a record 25 points on the Lakers in one quarter of the 1988 NBA Finals?

a. Joe Dumars

b. Isiah Thomas

c. Bill Laimbeer

d. James Edwards

GAME 47 Q8 ANSWER a
After the Lakers won their second straight title in 1988, the term "three-peat" began to be spoken by Lakers personnel. Seizing the opportunity, coach Pat Riley tried to have the phrase copyrighted. Unfortunately for Riley, his team lost in the 1989 finals to Detroit, so the Lakers use of the slogan had to wait until 2002.

---

9. Which NFL team selected 2002 MVP Rich Gannon in the 1987 Draft?

a. Kansas City Chiefs

b. New England Patriots

c. Minnesota Vikings

d. Washington Redskins

GAME 67 Q8 ANSWER a
Despite throwing 220 career interceptions and only 173 touchdowns, Broadway Joe Namath is forever enshrined in Canton, mainly because his Jets were the first AFL team to win a Super Bowl, taking down the Colts in 1969. He also completed only 50.1 percent of his passes, and had a mediocre 65.5 quarterback rating in thirteen seasons.

4. Who were the first brothers to start as NFL quarterbacks on the same day?

a. The Hasselbecks

b. The Mannings

c. The Huards

d. The Detmers

GAME 14 Q3 ANSWER c
While the other families featured only two brothers as kickers, the Zendejas family could boast three booting brothers. Joaquin, Luis, and Max Zendejas all kicked in the NFL during the '80s. Meanwhile, cousin Tony Zendejas—the most successful family member—spent eleven seasons in the league, mostly with Houston and LA.

4. Who did the Montreal Expos send to Los Angeles in exchange for Pedro Martinez?

a. Marquis Grissom

b. Mark Grudzielanek

c. Dave Roberts

d. Delino DeShields

GAME 34 Q3 ANSWER b
As hard as it is to believe, the Charlotte Hornets traded rights to first-round draft pick Kobe Bryant for Lakers player Vlade Divac. The Lakers quickly made up for losing Divac by signing free agent center Shaquille O'Neal about a week later.

4. In the 1965 NBA playoffs, John Havlicek stole an inbound pass thrown by which Philadelphia player?

a. Hal Greer

b. Billy Cunningham

c. Wilt Chamberlain

d. Chet Walker

GAME 54 Q3 ANSWER d
Under three managers, the Yankees won 15 AL Championships. In ten of those years, they won the World Series as well. With streaks of 5 straight, 4 straight, and then 5 straight again, the only years the "Bombers" were denied the pennant over that stretch were 1948 (Cleveland), 1954 (Cleveland), and 1959 (Chicago White Sox).

4. Which guard won NBA titles with the Bulls and the Spurs in the 1990s?

a. Mario Elie

b. Sean Elliott

c. Steve Kerr

d. B.J. Armstrong

GAME 74 Q3 ANSWER b
An outstanding defensive back who made it to the Hall of Fame, Herb Adderly won his first two Super Bowls with Green Bay in the '60s, and then became the first to win another with a second team in January of 1972, when he won Super Bowl VI with the Dallas Cowboys.

Answers are in right-hand boxes on page 163.

Answers are in right-hand boxes on page 171.

Answers are in right-hand boxes on page 177.

8. Who was the oldest golfer to win two major championships in the same year?

a. Arnold Palmer
b. Mark O'Meara
c. Payne Stewart
d. Tom Watson

GAME 9 Q7 ANSWER c
By winning the 2003 World Series with the Florida Marlins at the tender age of 72, McKeon surpassed legendary Casey Stengel, who was 68 years old when his Yankees won the series in 1958. McKeon, who was a mid-season replacement for Jeff Torborg, rejuvenated the young squad by playing a loosie-goosie brand of ball.

8. Which owner managed his baseball team for a single game?

a. Ted Turner
b. Bud Selig
c. Jerry Reinsdorf
d. John Moores

GAME 29 Q7 ANSWER b
Cuban founded MicroSolutions in 1983, and built it into a $30-million-a-year company, which he sold to CompuServe in 1990. In addition to owning the Mavericks, which he bought in 2000, Cuban is an active investor in cutting-edge technologies.

8. Which NCAA legend left his school for three years to coach the ABA's Nets?

a. Lefty Driesell
b. Denny Crum
c. Lou Carnesecca
d. Jim Boeheim

GAME 49 Q7 ANSWER b
The 8-game exhibition hockey tournament featured the first 4 games in Canada and the final 4 in the USSR. After 7 games, the series was deadlocked at 3 wins and a tie. Down 2 goals in the third period, Canada rallied to tie, and then sealed the series victory on a Paul Henderson game winner with 34 seconds remaining.

8. Who was the first closer to accumulate 300 career saves?

a. Rich Gossage
b. Bruce Sutter
c. Dan Quisenberry
d. Rollie Fingers

GAME 69 Q7 ANSWER a
Known for his wiry body and wire-rimmed shades, Kent Tekulve appeared in 1,050 games as a reliever from 1974 to 1989, more than any other pitcher without making a start. Spending most of his career with the Pirates, Tekulve twice saved more than 30 games, but was named to only one career All-Star Game in 1980.

5. Which fighter spurned a young Cassius Clay's autograph request?

a. Joe Louis
b. Sugar Ray Robinson
c. Sandy Saddler
d. Rocky Marciano

GAME 12 Q4 ANSWER a
Handing Ali only his second career defeat, Ken Norton broke Ali's jaw in the second round of their nationally televised fight on March 31, 1973 in San Diego. Besides sending Ali for an infamous x-ray after the fight, the 5-to-1 underdog won the bout thanks to a split decision after the twelfth round.

5. In which country was tennis player Marat Safin born?

a. Spain
b. Russia
c. Turkey
d. Brazil

GAME 32 Q4 ANSWER b
In a game that will be forever remembered for then-skipper Grady Little leaving Pedro Martinez in to blow the Red Sox 4–0 lead, it was knuckleballer Tim Wakefield who gave up the monster shot to Boone on the first pitch of the eleventh inning. The Sox got their revenge in the 2004 ALCS.

5. Who was the first number-one overall pick in Cowboys history?

a. Bob Lilly
b. Ed Jones
c. Tony Dorsett
d. Drew Pearson

GAME 52 Q4 ANSWER c
Rejuvenated by their return to prominence, the Cardinals headed into Wild Card Weekend—their first post-season appearance in sixteen years. Although the Cowboys were 7-point favorites, Jake Plummer proved clutch as Arizona burnt the Cowboys 20–7 for the franchise's first playoff victory since 1947.

5. Which country won tennis's 1974 Davis Cup by default?

a. Soviet Union
b. United States
c. India
d. South Africa

GAME 72 Q4 ANSWER a
With 4,657 personal fouls over his twenty-year career, Kareem Abdul-Jabbar holds a slight edge over fellow legends Hakeem Olajuwon, Robert Parish, and Charles Barkley, who have all busted the 4,000 foul mark. Jabbar was tossed from only 48 contests, which pales in comparison to Parish's 86 ejections and Olajuwon's 80 early exits.

9. Who was the oldest boxer to hold a heavyweight title?

a. Max Schmelling
b. Larry Holmes
c. John L. Sullivan
d. George Foreman

GAME 9 Q8 ANSWER b
In 1998, at age 41, Mark O'Meara won his first major championship, breaking an 0-for-56 dry spell in majors by taking home the green jacket at Augusta. As if that wasn't enough, O'Meara then proceeded to defeat Brian Watts in a four-hole playoff at Royal Birkdale, adding the British Open's Claret Jug to his collection.

9. Which pro team owner's brother was once fired from his team for stealing money?

a. Wayne Weaver
b. Pat Bowlen
c. Pat Croce
d. Mike Ilitch

GAME 29 Q8 ANSWER a
With his team mired in a 16-game losing streak, Atlanta Braves owner Ted Turner decided to manage the team himself. So on May 11, 1977, with Turner at the helm, Atlanta dropping a 2–1 decision to Pittsburgh, extending the losing streak to 17. Turner was barred by the league from managing again.

9. Which city hosted the first Super Bowl played on artificial turf?

a. Miami
b. Houston
c. New Orleans
d. Los Angeles

GAME 49 Q8 ANSWER c
After coaching the St. John's Redmen for six years, Lou Carnesecca pursued a professional opportunity with the New York Nets. With them, he compiled a 114–138 record, but managed to lead the team to the league finals in 1972. A year later, he returned to St. John's, where he stayed until retiring in 1992.

9. Who is the all-time Major League saves leader?

a. Jeff Reardon
b. Lee Smith
c. John Franco
d. Bruce Sutter

GAME 69 Q8 ANSWER d
Known for his distinctive handlebar mustache, Rollie Fingers broke the career-save barrier in 1982. A three-time World Series champ with Oakland in the 1970s, Fingers earned the AL's Most Valuable Player and Cy Young Awards in 1981, after posting 28 saves in the strike-shortened season. He received a ticket to Cooperstown in 1992.

4. Which boxer broke Ali's jaw during their 1973 fight?

a. Ken Norton
b. Buster Mathis
c. George Foreman
d. Chuck Wepner

Before his February 26, 1964 fight against Liston, Clay duped everyone into believing he was crazy. In fact, at the weigh-in, the doctor declared him "emotionally unbalanced and scared to death." But after nearly quitting due to an injured eye, Clay battled his way to a seventh-round TKO, when Liston failed to come out for the round.

4. Which pitcher served up Aaron Boone's ALCS winning homer in 2003?

a. John Burkett
b. Tim Wakefield
c. Mike Timlin
d. Ramiro Mendoza

In 1959, Floyd Patterson lost the heavyweight title he had held for over three years when Ingemar Johansson of Sweden knocked him out in Round 3. About a year later, Patterson became the first fighter to regain the championship by disposing of Johansson in 5 rounds. When they fought again in '61, Patterson beat Johansson in 6 rounds.

4. Which underdog defeated the Cowboys at home in the 1998 NFL playoffs?

a. Atlanta Flacons
b. Washington Redskins
c. Arizona Cardinals
d. Philadelphia Eagles

The only time the NFL's title game MVP was given to two players was Super Bowl XII, a Cowboys win over the Broncos 27–10. The award celebrated the Cowboys' outstanding defensive players White and Martin, whose constant pressure on Denver quarterback Craig Morton allowed him to complete only 4 passes and throw 4 interceptions.

4. Who is the NBA's all-time leader in personal fouls?

a. Kareem Abdul-Jabbar
b. Robert Parish
c. Karl Malone
d. Charles Barkley

Drafted first overall by Baltimore in the 1983 NFL Draft, Elway refused to sign with the Colts, forcing Baltimore to deal his rights to Denver for Mark Herrmann, Chris Hinton, and a 1984 first-round pick. Also proficient in baseball, Elway was drafted by the Yankees in 1981, and batted .319 for their Oneonta farm club in 1982.

10. Who is the oldest male athlete to win an Olympic medal?

a. Slava Fetisov

b. Anders Haugen

c. Oscar Swahn

d. Kurt Helbig

George Foreman originally captured the title by beating Joe Frazier in 1973. Foreman retired in 1977, only to make a comeback ten years later. The high point of his second wind came in 1994, when he beat Michael Moorer to win the WBA and IBF heavyweight crowns at age 45.

---

10. Which owner forced legendary coach Don Shula to resign?

a. Red McCombs

b. H. Wayne Huizenga

c. Alex Spanos

d. Tom Benson

After several petty thefts were reported in the Philadelphia 76ers locker room, GM Billy King ordered surveillance cameras installed. When part-owner Pat Croce viewed the tape and saw his brother John (the strength and conditioning coach), taking money from a player's pants, he had no choice but to fire him.

---

10. In 1975, who became only the second Major Leaguer to belt 7 hits in one game?

a. Rennie Stennett

b. Bill Madlock

c. Ralph Garr

d. Lee May

The January 1971 Super Bowl V at the Orange Bowl in Miami featured the first edition of the big game to be played on an artificial surface. After losing to the Jets two years earlier, the Colts took care of the Dallas Cowboys 16–13 on a last minute field goal by Baltimore's Jim O'Brien.

---

10. Who was the first pitcher to win 20 games and record 50 saves in separate seasons?

a. Hoyt Wilhelm

b. John Smoltz

c. Mike Marshall

d. Dennis Eckersley

During his dominant seventeen-year run, right-hander Lee Smith earned 428 saves, putting him at the head of the pack. A seven-time All-Star, Smith, who retired in 1997, was the league's top stopper on four separate occasions, and has a lengthy lead over second-place holder John Franco, who is the all-time leader in saves by a lefty.

GAME 12

3. Whom did Cassius Clay defeat to win his first heavyweight title?

a. Floyd Patterson

b. Jimmy Ellis

c. Ingemar Johansson

d. Sonny Liston

GAME 12 Q2 ANSWER c
Legend has it that after winning the gold at the 1960 Summer Games, Ali—who was still Cassius Clay—returned to his native Louisville, Kentucky, where he was denied service in a whites-only restaurant and then chased by a militant white motorcycle gang. Disgusted, Clay flung his medal into the Ohio River.

GAME 32

3. Who was the first heavyweight boxer to regain the championship?

a. Tommy Burns

b. Primo Carnera

c. Jack Johnson

d. Jack Dempsey

GAME 32 Q2 ANSWER b
For nearly 100 years, the mint julep has been the traditional drink served at Churchill Downs. During the two days in which the Kentucky Derby and the Kentucky Oaks are run, nearly 100,000 mint juleps are served there. The simple cocktail is made with sugar, water, mint sprigs, and bourbon.

GAME 52

3. Which player shared the Super Bowl XII MVP Award with Randy White?

a. Tony Dorsett

b. Roger Staubach

c. Drew Pearson

d. Harvey Martin

GAME 52 Q2 ANSWER c
From 1956 to 1981, "America's Team" put together an incredible string of opening day wins that was shattered by the Pittsburgh Steelers in the Monday Night opener of the 1982 season. The Chuck Noll-coached Cowboys lost in a 36–28 decision.

GAME 72

3. Which NFL team originally drafted Hall of Fame quarterback John Elway?

a. Cleveland Browns

b. Atlanta Falcons

c. Baltimore Colts

d. Seattle Seahawks

GAME 72 Q2 ANSWER b
Jack Ramsay was hired as coach of the Trailblazers in 1976, and led the Oregon team to championship in his first season. Ramsay, who also coached the 76ers and Buffalo Braves, stayed in Portland until 1986, before moving to Indiana, where he coached one season before retiring.

11. Who was the oldest baseball player to join the 3,000-hit club?

a. Dave Winfield
b. Cal Ripken, Jr.
c. Honus Wagner
d. Cap Anson

GAME 9 Q10 ANSWER c
Already 60 when he received his first gold medal in the 1908 Winter Games, Swedish shooter Oscar Swahn took home the silver in the Running Deer, Double Shot event at the 1920 Winter Games in Antwerp, Belgium. What was Swahn's age? A sprite 72 years young.

---

11. Who duped the NHL into believing he had enough money to purchase a franchise?

a. John Spano
b. Steven Gluckstern
c. John Rigas
d. Edward Milstein

GAME 29 Q10 ANSWER b
After the 1995 season, Miami Dolphins owner H. Wayne Huizenga reportedly gave 66-year-old Don Shula an ultimatum—resign with dignity or be fired. Not the best way to treat a Miami icon, but Huizenga did replace Shula with Jimmy Johnson, a man who had previously replaced legendary Cowboys' coach Tom Landry in 1989.

---

11. Who is the youngest female tennis player to win the US Open?

a. Chris Evert
b. Wendy Turnbull
c. Tracy Austin
d. Maureen Connelly

GAME 49 Q10 ANSWER a
On September 16, 1975, Pittsburgh second baseman Rennie Stennett collected 7 hits in a 22–0 drubbing against the Chicago Cubs. (Wilbert Robinson was first to accomplish the feat in 1892). Stennett hit .286 for the year, and had his best season two years later, when he finished second in the NL batting race with a .336 average.

---

11. Who is the only closer to save at least 48 season games with two different clubs?

a. Jeff Shaw
b. Randy Myers
c. Rod Beck
d. Ugueth Urbina

GAME 69 Q10 ANSWER d
Long before he saved 51 games with the Oakland A's in 1992, Dennis Eckersley was a capable starter. "Eck" won 20 games with the Boston Red Sox in 1978, and was on the AL All-Star Team as a starting pitcher in 1977 and 1982. In 1987, he reinvented himself as a closer.

---

2. Into which river did Ali allegedly throw his Olympic gold medal?

a. Colorado
b. Mississippi
c. Ohio
d. Sacramento

GAME 12 Q1 ANSWER d
In the early 1960s, Cassius Clay was introduced to the Muslim religion and became friends with leader Malcolm X. At that point, Clay dropped his "slave name" and became Cassius X. After a fallout with Malcolm X, Clay aligned himself with Nation of Islam leader Elijah Mohammed and was given the name Muhammad Ali.

2. What is the traditional beverage associated with the Kentucky Derby?

a. Southern Comfort
b. Mint Julep
c. Sloe Gin Fizz
d. Jack Daniels

GAME 32 Q1 ANSWER d
Tied after four rounds, the 1989 British Open concluded with a three-man play-off involving Calcavecchia, Grady, and Norman. American Mark Calcavecchia was the winner of the Open's first aggregate multi-hole playoff, when his score of 15 beat Grady and Norman's tally of 18 for the four additional holes.

2. Which team ended the Cowboys' streak of 17 consecutive opening day victories?

a. New York Giants
b. San Francisco 49ers
c. Pittsburgh Steelers
d. Washington Redskins

GAME 52 Q1 ANSWER d
"The Tuna" won the big game with the 1986 and 1990 New York Giants, and then tasted defeat with the 1996 Patriots. Parcells came very close to taking a third team, as the 1998 New York Jets had a lead over Denver in that season's AFC Championship Game.

2. Which coach led the Portland Trailblazers to their first NBA Championship in 1977?

a. Mike Shuler
b. Jack Ramsay
c. Gene Shue
d. Al Attles

GAME 72 Q1 ANSWER a
Coming up with the St. Louis Cardinals in 1985, Vince Coleman stole an amazing 110 bases as a rookie and earned NL Rookie of the Year honors. "Vincent Van Go" followed that up with 107 swipes in his sophomore season and another 109 thefts in 1987, leading the league in each of his first three seasons.

12. Who is the oldest player in NBA history to score 50 points in a game?

a. Michael Jordan

b. Earl Monroe

c. Kareem Abdul-Jabbar

d. Karl Malone

GAME 9 Q11 ANSWER d
Go all the way back to the nineteenth century, and you'll find that Cap Anson pulled the trick at the age of 45, when he slapped a single off St. Louis pitcher Bill Hart on August 3, 1897 in Chicago's West Side Grounds. Anson was also the first one to reach the magical 3,000-hit mark.

12. Which expansion team owner guided his/her team to a World Series win in just four years?

a. Paul Allen

b. Jerry Colangelo

c. Joan Payson

d. Paul Godfrey

GAME 29 Q11 ANSWER a
When John Spano offered $160 million to buy the Islanders in 1996, the NHL approved him, but after several bank cover-ups, forgeries, and lies, it was revealed that Spano had barely $100,000. Ultimately arrested on fraud charges, Spano embarrassed the Islanders and the NHL.

12. Which baseballer struck out a record 189 times during the 1970 season?

a. Gorman Thomas

b. Bobby Bonds

c. Dave Kingman

d. George Scott

GAME 49 Q11 ANSWER c
At 16 years old, Tracy Austin defeated Chris Evert Lloyd in the 1979 US Open Final. She won the Open again in 1981, but her career derailed shortly after due to chronic neck and back problems. Austin also holds the distinction of being the only individual ever inducted into the Tennis Hall of Fame before the age of 30.

12. Which closer set a record with 84 straight saves?

a. Tom Gordon

b. Mariano Rivera

c. Trevor Hoffman

d. Eric Gagne

GAME 69 Q11 ANSWER c
Although several have come close, only the well-traveled Rod Beck can make this claim. The portly reliever with the long hair and Fu Manchu mustache closed out 48 contests with the Giants in 1993 and then nailed down 51 with the Cubs in 1998.

GAME 12

1. When joining the Nation of Islam, what was Cassius Clay's first new name?

a. Elijah X
b. Muhammad Clay
c. Muhammad Elijah
d. Cassius X

The answer to this question is on:

page 232, top frame, right side.

GAME 32

1. Which golfer won the three-man British Open playoff in 1989?

a. Greg Norman
b. Wayne Grady
c. Nick Faldo
d. Mark Calcavecchia

The answer to this question is on:

page 232, second frame, right side.

GAME 52

1. Who is the only Cowboy coach to take two separate franchises to the Super Bowl?

a. Jimmy Johnson
b. Barry Switzer
c. Tom Landry
d. Bill Parcells

The answer to this question is on:

page 232, third frame, right side.

GAME 72

1. Who is the only baseball player to steal 100 bases in each of his first three seasons?

a. Vince Coleman
b. Lou Brock
c. Ty Cobb
d. Rickey Henderson

The answer to this question is on:

page 232, bottom frame, right side.

GAME 10

"Wonderful Women"

Trivia Tidbits on Historical Female Athletes

Turn to page 237
for the first question.

Turn to page 237
for the first question.

When he threw down 51 against the Charlotte Hornets on December 29, 2001, 38-year-old Michael Jordan became the oldest player in NBA history to score 50 in a game. Two nights later, Jordan scored 45 points against the Eastern Conference-leading New Jersey Nets, once scoring 22 consecutive points for the Washington Wizards.

GAME 30

"Mascots"

Mascots Are as Much a Part of Their Team as the Players

Turn to page 237
for the first question.

Turn to page 237
for the first question.

In 2001, the Arizona Diamondbacks, under the management of owner Jerry Colangelo, were World Champions. Colangelo also owned the NBA's Phoenix Suns and the WNBA's Phoenix Mercury.

GAME 50

"Expansion Teams"

Notable Feats in Their Infancy

Turn to page 237
for the first question.

Turn to page 237
for the first question.

Giants outfielder Bobby Bonds set a standard that has yet to be achieved. Milwaukee infielder Jose Hernandez came pretty close in 2002, as he pulled within one of the all-time mark, and then proceeded to sit out most of the final week of the season. Hernandez struck out 185 times in 2000 as well.

GAME 70

"Centers' Club"

Let's Hear It for Basketball's Big Men

Turn to page 237
for the first question.

Turn to page 237
for the first question.

With an incredible 84 straight saves from August 28, 2002 to July 5, 2004, goggled-hurler Eric Gagne demolished Tom "Flash" Gordon's previously held record of 54 straight saves. Gagne did blow a save for the NL in the 2003 All-Star Game, but that one didn't count.

GAME 12

"Muhammad Ali"

**All About the Man
Who Proclaimed
"I Must Be the Greatest"**

*Turn to page 234
for the first question.*

*Turn to page 234
for the first question.*

GAME 11 Q12 ANSWER d
On October 18, 1977 at Yankee Stadium, Reggie Jackson became the second player in history to hit 3 home runs in a single World Series game. After drawing a second inning walk in Game 6, Jackson hit bombs against three different pitchers, driving them all out of the park on the first pitch.

GAME 32

GRAB BAG

*Turn to page 234
for the first question.*

*Turn to page 234
for the first question.*

GAME 31 Q12 ANSWER b
With a National League seven-year winning streak on the line, Pete Rose charged prone American League catcher Ray Fosse full bore while running home in the twelfth inning. The NL won the game on Rose's run, but Fosse suffered a fractured shoulder in what was basically a meaningless exhibition game.

GAME 52

"The Dallas Cowboys"

**The Cowboys Will Always Be
Known as "America's Team"**

*Turn to page 234
for the first question.*

*Turn to page 234
for the first question.*

GAME 51 Q12 ANSWER b
Although Major League Baseball declared spitballs illegal in 1920, a grandfather clause allowed established spitballers to continue throwing them until they retired. Burleigh Grimes was the last of them. During his nineteen-season career, he played in four World Series, had five 20-win seasons, and was the NL complete games leader for four years.

GAME 72

GRAB BAG

*Turn to page 234
for the first question.*

*Turn to page 234
for the first question.*

GAME 71 Q12 ANSWER d
Arnold Palmer dropped the 1962 Open to Jack Nicklaus, the 1963 title to Julius Boros, and the 1966 Open to Billy Casper. Palmer did, however, manage to secure six major victories during his competitive days, including four Masters triumphs.

GAME 10

1. Who scored the winning goal for the US in the 1999 Women's World Cup?

a. Julie Foudy
b. Carla Overbeck
c. Brandi Chastain
d. Mia Hamm

The answer to this question is on:

page 239, top frame, right side.

GAME 30

1. Which university's mascot goes by the name "BeVo"?

a. New Mexico
b. South Carolina
c. Nebraska
d. Texas

The answer to this question is on:

page 239, second frame, right side.

GAME 50

1. Which NFL team won a record 7 games in its first season?

a. Jacksonville Jaguars
b. New Orleans Saints
c. Carolina Panthers
d. Atlanta Falcons

The answer to this question is on:

page 239, third frame, right side.

GAME 70

1. Who is the tallest player ever to compete in the NBA?

a. Shawn Bradley
b. Manute Bol
c. Gheorghe Muresan
d. Yao Ming

The answer to this question is on:

page 239, bottom frame, right side.

237

12. Who is the only player besides Babe Ruth to hit 3 home runs in a World Series game?

a. Mickey Mantle

b. Ralph Kiner

c. Jose Canseco

d. Reggie Jackson

With his New York Rangers down 3–2 in the Eastern Conference Finals, captain Mark Messier "guaranteed victory" heading into Game 6. At the start of the third period, New Jersey had a 2–1 lead, and it looked as if Messier's guarantee might fall by the wayside. Then he scored 3 straight goals, and the Rangers won the game.

---

12. Which catcher was badly injured by Pete Rose at the 1970 All-Star Game?

a. Bill Freehan

b. Ray Fosse

c. Joe Azcue

d. Dick Dietz

Charged by a stalker, whose sole motivation was to keep her from taking the number-one ranking from Steffi Graf, Monica Seles took a blade to the back during a break in a 1993 match in Germany. After sitting out for over two years, Seles returned to tennis, but she was never the same great player she once was.

---

12. Who was the last pitcher to legally use a spitball?

a. Eppa Rixey

b. Burleigh Grimes

c. Grover Cleveland Alexander

d. Babe Ruth

The man who won the 1971 US Open and 1972 Wimbledon Championships achieved more notice in the sporting goods store than on the court, as Stan Smith Adidas have become one of the best-selling sneakers ever. The shoes debuted in the mid-1960s under original endorser Robert Haillet; but in 1971, Smith became the endorser.

---

12. Who is the only golfer to lose three US Open playoffs?

a. Tom Watson

b. Ben Crenshaw

c. Greg Norman

d. Arnold Palmer

The golf world went into a state of shock upon hearing that a plane carrying popular golfer Payne Stewart had crashed in South Dakota. Known for his traditional knickers and hat, Stewart had been on top of his game that year, taking home his second US Open Championship in June.

---

2. Kate Hnida made NCAA history by appearing in a football game for which school?

a. North Texas
b. New Mexico
c. Cincinnati
d. Utah

GAME 10 Q1 ANSWER c
On July 10, 1999, after the US had played 120 scoreless minutes against China, the Women's World Cup Final came down to penalty shots. After scoring the deciding goal, which gave the United States a 5–4 win, Brandi Chastain ripped off her jersey and fell to her knees, covered only by a black sports bra.

---

2. "Iceburgh" is the mascot of which NHL team?

a. The Penguins
b. The Blues
c. The Sharks
d. The Canucks

GAME 30 Q1 ANSWER d
Keeping with the University of Texas' team nickname of Longhorns, the school's mascot, named BeVo, is a live long-horned steer. BeVo made its first appearance in Austin for the 21–7 defeat of rival Texas A&M in 1916. To date, thirteen different BeVos have been christened as the school mascot.

---

2. Which baseball team lost 120 games in its first season?

a. New York Mets
b. Milwaukee Brewers
c. Houston Colt .45s
d. Los Angeles Angels

GAME 50 Q1 ANSWER c
Debuting in 1995, the Carolina Panthers produced an expansion-best record of 7 wins and 9 losses. Coached by Dom Capers (who would coach the expansion Houston Texans in 2002), the team quickly acquired seasoned veterans. In its second year, the Panthers finished with a record of 12–4 and made it to the NFC Championship Game.

---

2. Which former center was given the nickname "Chocolate Thunder"?

a. Moses Malone
b. Darryl Dawkins
c. Pervis Ellison
d. Tree Rollins

GAME 70 Q1 ANSWER c
Topping out at 7'7", Romanian import Gheorghe Muresan stands as the tallest player ever to hit the NBA hardwood. Muresan's best season came in 1995-1996 when he averaged 14.5 points per game and almost 10 rebounds per contest. Film buffs will fondly remember Muresan's appearance on the silver screen in *My Giant* (1998).

---

11. Who delivered on his "guaranteed victory" in the 1994 NHL playoffs?

a. Wayne Gretzky
b. Wendel Clark
c. Mark Messier
d. Scott Stevens

GAME 11 Q10 ANSWER d
Playing for the Michigan Wolverines, Rumeal Robinson—a 65-percent free-throw shooter—stepped up to the line for a pair of foul shots with Michigan down 79–78. Robinson coolly hit them both like a pro to give the Wolverines their first NCAA title.

11. Which female tennis player was stabbed by a stalker?

a. Jana Novotna
b. Monica Seles
c. Tracy Austin
d. Zina Garrison

GAME 31 Q10 ANSWER a
Brooklyn outfielder "Pistol Pete" Reiser smashed into (unpadded) outfield walls while chasing flies a number of times! His worst injury came in 1947 after crashing hard into the wall at Ebbets Field. A priest was called to administer last rites. Athough briefly sidelined, Reiser soon returned to the field.

11. Which former tennis player endorses Adidas sneakers?

a. Virginia Wade
b. Tony Roche
c. Robert Haillet
d. Stan Smith

GAME 51 Q10 ANSWER b
Bears quarterback Jim McMahon led the '85 team to a Super Bowl win, but often butted heads with Commissioner Pete Rozelle. Known for his message-bearing headbands on game day, McMahon was fined $5,000 for wearing one with the Adidas logo during the '85 playoffs. The next week, Mac responded with a headband that said "Rozelle."

11. Which popular golfer died tragically in a 1999 plane crash?

a. David Frost
b. Payne Stewart
c. Hal Sutton
d. Bob Tway

GAME 71 Q10 ANSWER b
After joining the tour in late August 1996, Woods' first outing in the Greater Milwaukee Open concluded in an un-Tigerlike tie for 60th place. But in October, Woods entered the final round of the Las Vegas Invitational 4 strokes off the lead. He finished in a tie with Davis Love III, whom he beat on the first play-off hole.

GAME 10

3. Who is the only woman to win six consecutive Wimbledon singles titles?

a. Martina Navratilova

b. Helen Wills Moody

c. Venus Williams

d. Suzanne Lenglen

GAME 30

3. Which team boasts "Youppi" as its mascot?

a. Buffalo Sabres

b. New England Patriots

c. Toronto Raptors

d. Montreal Expos

GAME 50

3. Which NHL club was the quickest expansion team to reach the Stanley Cup Finals?

a. Minnesota North Stars

b. Florida Panthers

c. Los Angeles Kings

d. Philadelphia Flyers

GAME 70

3. Who is the NBA career leader in blocked shots?

a. Patrick Ewing

b. Kareem Abdul-Jabbar

c. Sam Perkins

d. Hakeem Olajuwon

GAME 10 Q2 ANSWER b
When New Mexico's Kate Hnida stepped up to attempt an extra point in the 2002 Las Vegas Bowl, she became the first woman to appear in a Division I-A college football game. Unfortunately, the low kick was blocked by Bruins linebacker Brandon Chillar.

GAME 30 Q2 ANSWER a
The correct answer lies in the name Ice-*burgh*. The lovable mascot resides in the Igloo, home of the Pitts*burgh* Penguins. And naturally, Iceburgh is a, well, a penguin.

GAME 50 Q2 ANSWER a
Posting a 40–120 record in their 1962-1963 initial season, the New York Mets hold the record for most losses by a first-year expansion team. Coached by Casey Stengel, the team featured a pair of hurlers who each lost 20 games (Roger Craig 10–24, and Al Jackson 8–20) and a pitching staff with an ERA of 5.04.

GAME 70 Q2 ANSWER b
Given the moniker due to his ability to rattle the rim, Dawkins was the first player to regularly shatter NBA backboards with his monstrous dunks. A force in the middle, Dawkins holds the New Jersey Nets record for blocked shots in a game with 13 in a 1983 contest against the 76ers.

10. Whose two overtime free throws gave Michigan the 1989 NCAA Championship?

a. Glen Rice

b. Loy Vaught

c. Terry Mills

d. Rumeal Robinson

In a November 1989 game against the Saints, Rams wide-out Flipper Anderson caught 15 passes for an unbelievable 336 total yards receiving. As if breaking the record wasn't enough, Anderson also caught a huge pass from Jim Everett in overtime to set up the game's winning field goal.

---

10. Which ball player was given last rites after crashing into the center field wall?

a. Pete Reiser

b. Lenny Dykstra

c. Crash Davis

d. Jim Edmonds

In 2000, while playing for the Maple Leafs, Calder Trophy winner Byran Berard suffered one of the worst eye injuries in NHL history. After taking a stick to the face from Ottawa's Marian Hossa, Berard came within millimeters of losing the eye. Seven surgeries later, Berard miraculously returned to the NHL as a NY Ranger.

---

10. Which NFL quarterback got into a tiff with the commissioner over his headbands?

a. Tommy Kramer

b. Jim McMahon

c. Joe Namath

d. Don Majikowski

Yankee manager Billy Martin ordered the bat measured to see if it exceeded the 18 inches of pine tar. It did. Brett was called out, and then all hell broke loose. The game was protested, and ultimately, the run was considered valid. The game was completed three weeks later with Kansas City winning 5–4.

---

10. Tiger Woods claimed his first PGA Tour victory in which 1996 event?

a. Bell Canadian Open

b. Las Vegas Invitational

c. Walt Disney World Oldsmobile Classic

d. Western Open

Entering the final round of the event, the US team was 4 points behind the Europeans. By the end of the day, the Americans had staged the biggest comeback in the history of the event. After Justin Leonard's amazing putt on the seventeenth hole, a wild celebration ensued, which was criticized by commentators as "unprofessional."

GAME 10

4. Who was the first woman to play in a men's pro basketball league?

a. Sheryl Swoopes

b. Nancy Lieberman

c. Jennifer Azzi

d. Teresa Weatherspoon

GAME 10 Q3 ANSWER a

In the middle of a stretch in which she won nine out of a possible thirteen Wimbledon singles championships, Martina Navratilova captured six straight crowns from 1982 through 1987. During the thirteen-championship span, Navratilova failed to win only in 1980, 1981, 1988, and 1989.

GAME 30

4. What does the University of New Mexico call its teams?

a. Coyotes

b. Lobos

c. Wolfpack

d. Dogs

GAME 30 Q3 ANSWER d

A cross between an overgrown Muppet and Bigfoot, Youppi has been the Expo's mascot since 1979. Described as a "youthful prankster possessing good humor, an impish grin, and an abundance of energy," Youppi has been the highlight of Expos baseball to a great many fans (unlike the team, which has been a perennial cellar dweller).

GAME 50

4. Which NBA team joined the league as an expansion team in 1966?

a. Buffalo Braves

b. Chicago Bulls

c. New Orleans Jazz

d. San Diego Rockets

GAME 50 Q3 ANSWER b

Three years after joining the NHL in the 1993-1994 season, the Florida Panthers made it to the finals against the Colorado Avalanche. A key to the team's sudden rise was the hiring of Coach Doug MacLean in 1995. Although MacLean took the team from futility to respectability in just one year, he was fired in the 1997-1998 season.

GAME 70

4. Which big man holds the record for most games played in NBA history?

a. Buck Williams

b. Elvin Hayes

c. Robert Parish

d. Kevin Willis

GAME 70 Q3 ANSWER d

Since the 1973-1974 season in which blocked shot statistics were recorded for the first time, long-time Houston Rockets star Hakeem Olajuwon has compiled the most rejections, recording 3,830 blocks during his eighteen-year NBA career.

Answers are in right-hand boxes on page 245.   243

9. Which NFL player accumulated 336 receiving yards in one game?

a. Jerry Rice

b. Flipper Anderson

c. Kyle Rote

d. Stephone Paige

GAME 11 Q8 ANSWER d
By striking out 20 Houston Astros on May 6, 1998, Kerry Wood became the first rookie and second player to strike out 20 batters in a game. A month into his first big-league season, the 20-year-old matched fellow Texan Roger Clemens' remarkable feat on his way to winning the 1998 National League Rookie of the Year Award.

9. With which NHL team was Bryan Berard when he suffered a devastating eye injury?

a. New York Islanders

b. Boston Bruins

c. New York Rangers

d. Toronto Maple Leafs

GAME 31 Q8 ANSWER c
During a 1967 game between the Red Sox and Angels, Boston outfielder Tony Conigliaro was beaned in the face by Hamilton, causing permanent damage to his left eye. Conigliaro made an amazing comeback in 1969, hitting 20 homers; a year later, he hit an astounding 36. But within two seasons, the mighty slugger's career was over.

9. Which manager disputed George Brett's ninth inning go-ahead run during the "Pine Tar Game"?

a. Billy Martin

b. Bob Lemon

c. Gene Michael

d. Yogi Berra

GAME 51 Q8 ANSWER b
Feared hockey tough guy Rob Ray used to throw off his jersey before a brawl to avoid getting decked while having it pulled over his head. Tired of seeing bare-chested Ray skate to the penalty box after a scrum, the NHL enacted the unofficial "Rob Ray Jersey Rule"—a game misconduct penalty for wearing a jersey that is not tied down.

9. Who sank a 45-foot putt to clinch the 1999 Ryder Cup for the United States?

a. Phil Mickelson

b. Tom Lehman

c. Mark O'Meara

d. Justin Leonard

GAME 71 Q8 ANSWER a
Longtime PGA Tour personality Mike "Fluff" Cowan teamed up with the 20-year-old Woods when he first joined the tour. Before Tiger, the bushy mustached Cowan put in almost twenty years as the caddy for popular duffer Peter Jacobsen.

5. Who defeated Bobby Riggs in the "Battle of the Sexes"?

a. Chris Evert
b. Margaret Court
c. Billie Jean King
d. Virginia Wade

In addition to leading Old Dominion to back-to-back AIAW National Championships in 1979 and 1980, Nancy Lieberman became the youngest basketball player to medal in the Olympics, earning the silver in 1976. In 1986, she joined the USBL's Springfield Fame, becoming the first female to play in a men's pro league.

---

5. What is the name of the Chicago Bulls original mascot?

a. Barry
b. Bonny
c. Benny
d. Bully

Beginning in 1917, the school's student body began its search for a mascot, as the name "Varsities" just wasn't cutting it. In 1920, the manager of the football team suggested "Lobos" the Spanish word for wolves, and a tradition was born.

---

5. Who was the Tampa Bay Devil Rays first manager?

a. Hal McRae
b. Frank Howard
c. Rene Lachemann
d. Larry Rothschild

In 1996, when the NBA expanded to ten teams in two divisions, the Chicago Bulls joined. The team then proceeded to set the NBA standard for expansion victories with 33 wins. By their fifth season, the Bulls went on a four-year streak of winning over 50 games under coach Dick Motta.

---

5. Who is the only man to win Defensive Player of the Year with three different clubs?

a. Wilt Chamberlain
b. Dikembe Mutombo
c. Bill Walton
d. Wes Unseld

Robert Parish stands atop the NBA career games-played list. "The Chief" played twenty-one seasons and won four championships with the Celtics and Bulls, in addition to being among the career rebound leaders, ripping down almost 15,000 boards. At age 40, Parrish was still productive, averaging 13 points per game.

8. Who is the only rookie to strike out 20 batters in a game?

a. Roger Clemens

b. Randy Johnson

c. Bob Feller

d. Kerry Wood

GAME 11 Q7 ANSWER c
After throwing twelve perfect innings against the Braves on May 26, 1959, Pittsburgh's Harvey Haddix came out for the bottom of the thirteenth. After an error and an intentional walk to Hank Aaron, Joe Adcock drilled a homer. Haddix lost the game, but was charged with only 1 run due to a mental error by Adcock—he passed Aaron while circling the bases.

8. Which pitcher hit Red Sox slugger Tony Conigliaro in the face?

a. Dick Raditz

b. Ryne Duren

c. Jack Hamilton

d. Sam McDowell

GAME 31 Q7 ANSWER a
During the last turn of the final lap of the 2001 Daytona 500, the man known as "The Intimidator" was involved in a fatal crash. The accident took away NASCAR's version of Michael Jordan. Initially, the cause of Earnhardt's death was blamed on a faulty seatbelt—a theory that was later disproved.

8. Which NHL enforcer had a penalty created in his honor?

a. Enrico Ciccone

b. Rob Ray

c. Mick Vukota

d. Gino Odjick

GAME 51 Q7 ANSWER b
Billy "White Shoes" Johnson wore light-colored cleats because "they made him run faster." Drafted in the late 1970s against the wishes of Houston coach Sid Gillman, who said he didn't want a "midget" on his club, the 5'9" Johnson had his best year in 1975, when he returned 4 kicks for scores.

8. Who served as caddy for Tiger Woods from 1996 to 1999?

a. Mike Cowan

b. Carl Jackson

c. Steve Williams

d. Ronald Whitfield

GAME 71 Q7 ANSWER b
Winning three Masters in four years (1963, 1965, 1966) established Jack Nicklaus as one of the game's greatest. As the "Golden Bear" continued his legend into the next decade, he earned two more green jackets in 1972 and 1975. In 1986 at age 46, he won the Masters once again for a total of eighteen wins in major tournaments.

GAME 10

6. Who was the first female jockey to win a Triple Crown race?

a. Diane Nelson
b. Andrea Seefeldt
c. Donna Barton
d. Julie Krone

GAME 10 Q5 ANSWER c
Bobby Riggs got blown out of the water by Billie Jean King, losing in straight sets 6–4, 6–3, 6–3 in the 1973 made-for-television "Battle of the Sexes." King took home a prize of $100,000, and Riggs admitted that his much-younger challenger was "just too good."

GAME 30

6. Which NFL team is known for its Dawg Pound?

a. Pittsburgh Steelers
b. Cleveland Browns
c. Baltimore Ravens
d. Oakland Raiders

GAME 30 Q5 ANSWER c
First appearing at Bulls games in the late 1960s, Benny the Bull has been as much a team figure over the years as Michael Jordan (except he can't shoot as well). The furry red bull was joined during the 1995-1996 season by another bovine mascot named "Da Bull."

GAME 50

6. Who did the Tampa Bay Buccaneers defeat to end their 26-game losing streak in 1977?

a. New Orleans Saints
b. New York Jets
c. Buffalo Bills
d. Detroit Lions

GAME 50 Q5 ANSWER d
Hired for the inaugural 1998 season, former Detroit pitcher Larry Rothschild didn't fare too well in his Major League managerial debut. Never winning more than 69 games in his three full seasons on the job, Rothschild was relieved of his duties early in the 2001 campaign after a 4–10 start.

GAME 70

6. Who was the first center to win the NBA Finals MVP trophy?

a. Wilt Chamberlain
b. Kareem Abdul-Jabbar
c. Wes Unseld
d. Willis Reed

GAME 70 Q5 ANSWER b
If you knew that this award was established in 1983, then the answer is simple. Dikembe Mutombo, who made his name at Georgetown University, has won the trophy with Denver, Atlanta, and Philadelphia. Since entering the NBA in 1991, he has steadily been atop the leader board in rebounds and blocked shots.

Answers are in right-hand boxes on page 249.

GAME 11

7. Who pitched a twelve-inning perfect game, only to lose on a hit in the thirteenth?

a. Bob Feller

b. Nolan Ryan

c. Harvey Haddix

d. Allie Reynolds

GAME 11 Q6 ANSWER a
Holding a slim lead heading into the final event, the vault, the Women's Team looked to its best vaulter to secure the gold medal. On her initial jump, Kerri Strug twisted her ankle and received no score. Needing a 7.2 for the win, Strug managed to post a score of 7.3 and then collapsed in agony.

GAME 31

7. NASCAR legend Dale Earnhardt, Sr. was killed at:

a. Daytona International Speedway

b. Texas Motor Speedway

c. Indianapolis Motor Speedway

d. Pocono Raceway

GAME 31 Q6 ANSWER b
While celebrating the Detroit Red Wings 1997 Stanley Cup with friends, star defenseman Vladimir Konstantinov sustained severe head and spinal injuries after a limousine accident. After winning the Cup again in 1998, the Red Wings wheeled a still-recovering Konstantinov onto the ice to pose for pictures with the trophy.

GAME 51

7. Which former NFL player was known for his white cleats?

a. Ken Houston

b. Billy Johnson

c. John Riggins

d. Joe Morris

GAME 51 Q6 ANSWER a
With players seeming to get taller every year, eventually we can expect someone who can slam-dunk a ball into the 10-foot-high rim without leaving his feet. While there has long been talk of raising the rim, the height has been standard since the Basketball Association of America introduced its rules and regulations in 1946.

GAME 71

7. Who is the only golfer to win the Masters in three different decades?

a. Arnold Palmer

b. Jack Nicklaus

c. Bobby Jones

d. Jimmy Demaret

GAME 71 Q6 ANSWER c
The golfer who was the first player to win three out of four Majors in one year is actually named William Hogan. The four-time PGA Player of the Year is also on an esteemed short list of golfers (Woods, Nicklaus, Player, and Sarazen) who have captured all four major tournaments during their careers.

7. Who took home the gold in the first Olympic women's ice hockey competition?

a. Canada
b. United States
c. Russia
d. Finland

GAME 10 Q6 ANSWER d
Winning the 1993 Belmont Stakes aboard Scotty Schulhofer-trained Colonial Affair, Julie Krone became the first woman rider to win a Triple Crown event. Krone, who was inspired to become a jockey by watching Steve Cauthen's Triple Crown run in 1977, was the only female to even compete in the Belmont Stakes up to that point.

7. Who is the man behind the San Diego State "Chicken"?

a. Ted Giannoulas
b. Nikos Tselios
c. Harry Agganis
d. Gus Triandos

GAME 30 Q6 ANSWER b
Chomps the Lab, CB the Bull Mastiff, Trapper the Weimaraner, and TD the German Shepherd are all ferocious inhabitants of Cleveland's famous Dawg Pound. "Bad to the Bone" is one of their signature songs, and their favorite foods include Dawg bones, Baltimore Raven wings, and Bengal Tigers with stadium mustard.

7. Which NHL player has been on three of the four expansion teams since 1998?

a. Tony Hrkac
b. Scott Walker
c. Andrew Brunette
d. Darby Hendrickson

GAME 50 Q6 ANSWER a
During the next-to-last week of the season, the Bucs defeated the New Orleans Saints (another perennial cellar dweller) 33–14 to receive their first taste of victory. Two years later, Tampa Bay would go on a Cinderella playoff run to the 1979 NFC Championship Game, which they lost to the Los Angeles Rams, 9–0.

7. Who was the only center to grab 40 boards in three separate NBA playoff games?

a. Wilt Chamberlain
b. Bill Russell
c. George Johnson
d. Caldwell Jones

GAME 70 Q6 ANSWER d
Knicks center Willis Reed grabbed the trophy in 1970 after his Knicks won their first championship. Named to the NBA's 50 Greatest Players list, Reed also took home the league MVP Award in 1970, and captured his second Finals MVP three years later when New York won its second NBA title.

6. Which gymnast gave the US Women's Team a gold medal in 1996 despite being in severe pain?

a. Kerri Strug

b. Dominique Dawes

c. Amy Chow

d. Shannon Miller

GAME 11 Q5 ANSWER b
Less than a full year into his professional career, 21-year-old Tiger Woods dazzled the world by crushing the field in the 1997 Masters by 12 strokes. With middle-round scores of 66 and 65, Woods not only broke the tournament scoring record, but also enjoyed the largest margin of victory in any major championship.

---

6. Which NHL player was severely injured after winning the 1997 Stanley Cup?

a. Slava Fetisov

b. Vladimir Konstantinov

c. Mikhail Tatarinov

d. Vladimir Krutov

GAME 31 Q5 ANSWER d
Chapman came to bat for the Indians during an August 1920 game against the Yankees. Carl Mays lost control of a pitch and hit Chapman on the left side of the head (batting helmets were not required at that time). Chapman died a few hours later. Cleveland dedicated the season to Chapman, and won its first World Series that year.

---

6. How far off the floor is a regulation NBA rim?

a. 10 feet

b. 10.5 feet

c. 11 feet

d. 11.5 feet

GAME 51 Q5 ANSWER d
Tired of troublesome trips to the bunkers, legendary golfer Gene Sarazen invented the revolutionary club in the early 1930s, and debuted it at the 1932 British Open, which he won. Fearing that his new piece of equipment would be banned, Sarazen kept the wedge under wraps until he pulled it out on the Prince's Course in England.

---

6. What is golf legend Ben Hogan's real first name?

a. Richard

b. Robert

c. William

d. James

GAME 71 Q5 ANSWER a
The flamboyant Swede is a popular PGA fixture, and the son of popular Swedish comedian Bo Parnevik. Winner of several PGA and European events, Jesper is often dressed in colors such as hot pink and bright yellow.

GAME 10

8. Who was the first female pitcher to start a men's minor-league baseball game?

a. Lisa Fernandez

b. Joyce Compton

c. Jennie Finch

d. Ila Borders

GAME 10 Q7 ANSWER b
Led by Captain Cami Granato, the United States defeated favored Canada 3–1 to win the first-ever gold medal in the women's ice hockey event at the 1998 Winter Olympics. Sandra Whyte set up a pair of power play goals, and then clinched the gold for America by scoring an empty netter with 8 seconds left.

GAME 30

8. Which team introduced the first NHL mascot?

a. Detroit Red Wings

b. St. Louis Blues

c. Boston Bruins

d. Calgary Flames

GAME 30 Q7 ANSWER a
On the campus of San Diego State University in 1974, Ted Giannoulas first became the San Diego Chicken. Originally intended to be a seasonal mascot at the San Diego Zoo, Teddy G. parlayed the Chicken into a world-renowned celebrity. The mascot has performed throughout the country and before several presidents.

GAME 50

8. Who coached the Miami Heat for its first NBA season?

a. Ron Rothstein

b. Kevin Loughery

c. Alvin Gentry

d. Garfield Heard

GAME 50 Q7 ANSWER c
If Minnesota Wild's winger Andrew Brunette gets traded to Columbus soon, he will have completed the expansion sweep, as he has also played with the Nashville Predators (1998-1999) and the Atlanta Thrashers (1999-2001).

GAME 70

8. Who was the first center to win the NBA All-Star Game MVP?

a. George Mikan

b. Vern Mikkelsen

c. Paul Arizin

d. Ed Macauley

GAME 70 Q7 ANSWER b
While Wilt Chamberlain holds the NBA playoff record with 41 rebounds in a game, only Celtics great Bill Russell ripped down 40 boards on three separate occasions—in 1958, 1960, and 1962—leading Boston to the finals in each. Russell is also the career playoff rebound leader, with 4,104 rebounds in thirteen NBA seasons.

5. Who blitzed the field to win the 1997 Masters by 12 strokes?

a. Jose Maria Olazabal

b. Tiger Woods

c. Vijay Singh

d. Nick Faldo

GAME 11 Q4 ANSWER d
Down 3 points with less than 6 seconds to play in Game 3 of the 1999 Eastern Conference Finals, the Knicks called upon Larry Johnson to hoist a baseline 3-point attempt, only to be fouled by Indiana's Antonio Davis. Johnson calmly stepped to the line and sank the free throw, giving the Knicks a huge win.

5. Who was the only ML ball player to die from an injury sustained on the field?

a. Ira Flagstead

b. Lyle Bigbee

c. Irish Meusel

d. Ray Chapman

GAME 31 Q4 ANSWER b
One of the worst "turn your head" injuries came during a 1985 *Monday Night Football* Giants-Redskins game. Lawrence Taylor blew past the Washington line, and snapped Joe Theismann's leg like a wishbone. So horrified was LT, that once he realized what had happened, he began frantically summoning the trainers onto the field.

5. Which golfer has been credited with inventing the sand wedge?

a. Byron Nelson

b. Ben Hogan

c. Bobby Jones

d. Gene Sarazen

GAME 51 Q4 ANSWER c
Early boxing matches were actually bare-knuckled brawls. In 1867, the "Queensbury Rules of Boxing" were drawn up, calling for shorter rounds and the wearing of gloves. American boxing legend John L. Sullivan began the new trend. He held the heavyweight title for ten years until "Gentleman" Jim Corbett dethroned him in 1892.

5. Which European golfer is known for his retro attire and flipped-bill cap?

a. Jesper Parnevik

b. Sergio Garcia

c. Nick Faldo

d. Ian Baker-Finch

GAME 71 Q4 ANSWER b
The French golfer who competes mostly on the European Tour will be forever remembered for the triple bogey that forced him into a three-man playoff with Justin Leonard and Paul Lawrie. The Scottish Lawrie, who was 10 strokes behind as the day began, triumphed in the four-hole playoff.

9. Who was the first American female to win three gold medals in one Olympics?

a. Florence Griffith-Joyner
b. Wilma Rudolph
c. Jackie Joyner-Kersee
d. Mary Lou Retton

GAME 10 Q8 ANSWER d
Pitching for the independent Northern League's Duluth-Superior Dukes, Ila Borders made her first pro start on July 9, 1998, giving up 3 runs on 5 hits in five innings. Borders wound up as the night's losing pitcher, but became the first woman to win a men's minor-league baseball game on July 24, 1998.

9. Which was the first NFL team to have cheerleaders?

a. Washington Redskins
b. Dallas Cowboys
c. Oakland Raiders
d. Chicago Cardinals

GAME 30 Q8 ANSWER d
"Harvey the Hound" debuted at Calgary Flames' home games in 1984. Harvey was the idea of Grant Kelba, who had been the "Ralph the Dog" mascot for the CFL's Calgary Stampeders. Harvey's success caused many NHL teams to follow suit.

9. Which city received an NBA expansion franchise in 2004?

a. Oklahoma City
b. Charlotte
c. Tampa
d. San Diego

GAME 50 Q8 ANSWER a
Piloting the Heat for its first three seasons, former Pistons coach Ron Rothstein didn't leave Miami management much choice but to fire him after the 1990-1991 season. After registering a record of 57–179, Rothstein was replaced by veteran coach Kevin Loughery, who guided the team to its first two playoff appearances in 1992 and 1994.

9. Which center is the US all-time Olympic leader in points, blocked shots, and rebounds?

a. Patrick Ewing
b. David Robinson
c. Bill Russell
d. Mark Eaton

GAME 70 Q8 ANSWER d
The 6'8" Celtics center was named MVP of the league's first All-Star Game in 1951 at the Boston Garden. Macauley was traded to the St. Louis Hawks in 1956 for Bill Russell. His only pro championship came with the Hawks in 1958. At 32, Macauley was the youngest man ever inducted into the Basketball Hall of Fame.

4. Which NBA hoops star converted a 4-point play to beat Indiana in the 1999 playoffs?

a. Allen Iverson
b. Tracy McGrady
c. Alonzo Mourning
d. Larry Johnson

GAME 11 Q3 ANSWER c
After going hitless in the first game of a doubleheader against Cincinnati on September 7, 1993, Mark Whiten went wild in the second game, becoming the second man to have 12 RBIs in a single game (the first was "Sunny Jim" Bottomley in the 1920s). Going 4-for-5 with 4 home runs, Whiten also tied Nate Colbert's record of 13 RBIs for a doubleheader.

4. Which defensive player ended Joe Theismann's career in 1985?

a. Mike Singletary
b. Lawrence Taylor
c. Mark Gastineau
d. Greg Townsend

GAME 31 Q3 ANSWER c
During a 1989 regular season game between the Sabres and Blues, St. Louis forward Steve Tuttle was upended in the goal crease, which caused his skate to slice the jugular vein of Buffalo goalie Clint Malarchuk. Miraculously, the netminder survived the freak injury, and was back playing within a month.

4. Who was the first boxing champion to wear gloves?

a. Jim Corbett
b. Bob Fitzsimmons
c. John L. Sullivan
d. James J. Jeffries

GAME 51 Q3 ANSWER a
In the late 1990s, the NFL introduced the K-Ball for special teams plays. The K-Ball has the same dimensions as a regulation football, but is used only for kicking and punting. This prevents home teams from "breaking" in the regulation ball by scuffing it up.

4. Which golfer blew a 3-stroke lead on the final hole of 1999 British Open?

a. Paul Lawrie
b. Jean Van de Velde
c. Justin Leonard
d. Jose Maria Olazabal

GAME 71 Q3 ANSWER d
Although the PGA doesn't allow players to use golf carts during matches, Casey Martin requested the use of one due to a degenerative leg condition. The Tour denied the request, alleging that using the cart would give him an unfair edge. The conflict resulted in a lawsuit with Martin on the winning end.

10. Who was the first woman to appear in an NHL game?

a. Hayley Wickenheiser
b. Manon Rheaume
c. Danielle Goyette
d. Danielle Dube

GAME 10 Q9 ANSWER b
Dubbed "the fastest woman in the world" at the 1960 Summer Olympics, Wilma Rudolph became the first American woman to snare three gold medals in one Olympics. She took the top prize in the 100- and 200-meter races, and served as anchor for the 4x100-meter relay. A true inspiration, Rudolph had overcome polio as a child.

10. Which California school has adopted "Sammy the Slug" as its mascot?

a. San Jose
b. Santa Clara
c. Santa Cruz
d. Santa Barbara

GAME 30 Q9 ANSWER a
In 1962, the Washington Redskinettes took the field to entertain for the very first time. Not to be confused with the "Hogettes"—heavy men who dress like homely women and wear pig snouts—the Redskinettes are actually females. In addition to cheering at games, they have traveled overseas to entertain US troops.

10. Who did the Houston Texans select with their very first pick in the 2002 NFL Expansion Draft?

a. Aaron Glenn
b. Tony Boselli
c. Jamie Sharper
d. Gary Walker

GAME 50 Q9 ANSWER b
In January 2003, the NBA approved Robert Johnson, founder of the BET Network, to own and operate a team in Charlotte, beginning in 2004. The Charlotte Bobcats are the thirtieth NBA franchise.

10. Which center was the first player to record a quadruple-double in NBA history?

a. Hakeem Olajuwon
b. Wes Unseld
c. Mark Eaton
d. Nate Thurmond

GAME 70 Q9 ANSWER b
The only man to play basketball for the US in three separate Olympics, David Robinson is the nation's all-time leader in points (270), blocked shots (34), and rebounds (124). "The Admiral" competed in the 1988 Seoul Games, scored a gold medal in Barcelona with the 1992 "Dream Team," and earned another gold in Atlanta in 1996.

GAME 11

3. Who was the last player to have 12 RBIs in one game?

a. Bob Horner
b. Ivan Rodriguez
c. Mark Whiten
d. Hack Wilson

GAME 11 Q2 ANSWER a
While playing against the Cleveland Browns in 2003, Ravens running back Jamal Lewis shattered Corey Dillon's previously held record of 276 yards. Lewis had touchdown runs of 82 and 63 yards during the game, and would have easily busted the 300-yard mark had a first-half penalty not nullified an additional 60-yard dash.

GAME 31

3. Which NHL goalie almost bled to death during a 1989 game?

a. Bob Froese
b. Vincent Riendeau
c. Clint Malarchuk
d. Roberto Romano

GAME 31 Q2 ANSWER b
During a 1991 game between the Lions and Rams, Mike Utley was involved in a seemingly routine play in which he suffered a spinal cord injury that left him paralyzed. When wheeled off the field, the courageous Utley gave the "thumbs-up" sign. In spite of his injury, Utley participates in extreme sports like skydiving and kayaking.

GAME 51

3. Which sport uses a K-Ball for certain plays?

a. Football
b. Golf
c. Soccer
d. Lacrosse

GAME 51 Q2 ANSWER b
To prevent possible injury to the horses, polo players can use only their right hands to swing the mallet. It may be difficult to picture, but if right- *and* left-handed players came at the ball from opposite directions, the horses would collide head on.

GAME 71

3. Which golfer won a 1998 lawsuit that allowed him to use a cart on tour?

a. Notah Begay
b. Hank Keuhne
c. Rich Beem
d. Casey Martin

GAME 71 Q2 ANSWER b
Curtis Strange won the back-to-back events in 1988 and 1989, the latter proving to be his last victory on the PGA Tour. In 2002, he captained the unsuccessful US Ryder Cup team. Strange is also the first PGA player to break the million-dollar mark in earnings, which he achieved in 1988.

11. Who was the first LPGA golfer to shoot a round under 60?

a. Meg Mallon

b. Juli Inkster

c. Annika Sorenstam

d. Se Ri Pak

GAME 10 Q10 ANSWER b
Playing one period in an exhibition game for the Tampa Bay Lightning in September 1992, goaltender Manon Rheaume became the first woman ever to appear in an NHL contest. Stopping 7 of the 9 shots she faced against St. Louis, Rheaume gave up goals only to veterans Jeff Brown and Brendan Shanahan.

11. "Carlton" the bear is the official mascot of which NHL team?

a. Montreal

b. Toronto

c. Edmonton

d. Ottawa

GAME 30 Q10 ANSWER c
Found in abundance on the Santa Cruz campus, the bright yellow banana slug has been adopted as the school mascot. The choice, which the students felt represented many positive elements of the campus, such as contemplation, flexibility, and nonagressiveness, was awarded Best Mascot in *Reader's Digest* "America's 100 Best." Yuck!

11. Which expansion club became the first wild card team to win a World Series?

a. Colorado Rockies

b. Arizona Diamondbacks

c. Florida Marlins

d. Toronto Blue Jays

GAME 50 Q10 ANSWER b
Offensive lineman Tony Boselli was selected by the expansion Jacksonville Jaguars in the first round of the 1995 NFL Draft. Just seven years later, he became the first pick of the Houston Texans. Although Boselli was projected to be a major "impact" player in the league, he missed the entire 2002 season due to a shoulder injury.

11. Who was the first Chinese player to compete in the NBA?

a. Yao Ming

b. Menk Bateer

c. Hsu Chih Chao

d. Wang Zhizhi

GAME 70 Q10 ANSWER d
On opening night of the 1974-1975 season, Nate Thurmond leaped into the record books by posting the first quadruple-double in NBA history. He notched 22 points, 14 boards, 13 assists, and 12 blocks in his Chicago debut against the Atlanta Hawks. In recent years, Thurmond can be found operating his San Francisco restaurant—Big Nate's Barbeque.

GAME 11

2. Who once rushed 295 yards in an NFL game?

a. Jamal Lewis
b. O.J. Simpson
c. Corey Dillon
d. Shaun Alexander

GAME 11 Q1 ANSWER c
After Sittler was appointed captain of the Toronto Maple Leafs in 1975, his game truly improved, and he became the first Leaf to score 100 points in a season. But the defining night of his career came on February 7, 1976, when he put 6 goals in the net and assisted on 4 others for a record 10-point evening.

GAME 31

2. Which Detroit Lions offensive lineman was paralyzed after a 1991 hit?

a. John Clay
b. Mike Utley
c. James Fitzpatrick
d. David Williams

GAME 31 Q1 ANSWER a
After Foolish Pleasure's '75 Derby win, a match race was set with Ruffian—a ten-time undefeated filly who had equaled or broken the record in every race she ran. During the neck-and-neck match race, Ruffian pulled ahead, but sustained a leg injury. Tragically, she continued to run, causing irreparable damage, and she had to be euthanized.

GAME 51

2. What is the only sport that requires all participants to play right handed?

a. Fencing
b. Polo
c. Hurling
d. Lacrosse

GAME 51 Q1 ANSWER a
During a 1959 contest against the Rangers, Canadiens goalie Jacques Plante took an Andy Bathgate shot to the face, and left the game a bloody mess. Plante returned with a face shield, which he then wore continuously. In 1930, Montreal goalie Clint Benedict was the first ever to wear a mask, donning it briefly after a facial injury.

GAME 71

2. Which golfer won back-to-back US Opens in the 1980s?

a. Larry Nelson
b. Curtis Strange
c. Andy North
d. Scott Simpson

GAME 71 Q1 ANSWER c
Golf history was made on March 28, 1999, as the Duvals both won PGA sanctioned events within minutes of each other. Father Bob won first, taking the Emerald Coast Classic on the Senior PGA tour, while a mere 400 miles away, son David captured The Players Championship at Sawgrass.

12. Who was the first black tennis player to win at Wimbledon?

a. Venus Williams

b. Zina Garrison

c. Althea Gibson

d. Serena Williams

GAME 10 Q11 ANSWER c
Shooting an unbelievable round of 59 in the March 2001 Standard Register Ping, Annika Sorenstam became the first woman golfer to break 60. Sorenstam started the round by making 8 birdies in a row, and finished with 13 total. She has said that her ultimate goal is to shoot a 54.

---

12. Which baseball stadium began the "Sausage Race" tradition?

a. County Stadium

b. Comiskey Park

c. Wrigley Field

d. Tiger Stadium

GAME 30 Q11 ANSWER b
Debuting with Toronto in 1995, the 270-pound, 6'5" polar bear, whose name is taken from the Maple Leaf Gardens' former address (60 Carlton Street), is the "coolest" mascot in the NHL. He lists his favorite food as arena pretzels and favorite singing group as, of course, "Bear" Naked Ladies.

---

12. Which NHL expansion team lost 70 games in its initial season?

a. Washington Capitals

b. Ottawa Senators

c. San Jose Sharks

d. Pittsburgh Penguins

GAME 50 Q11 ANSWER c
Winning the Fall Classic in just their fifth year of existence, the 1997 World Champion Florida Marlins also briefly held the record as the quickest expansion team to win a World Series. That standard, however, was eclipsed in 2002 by the Arizona Diamondbacks, who won the Series in just four years time.

---

12. In which African country was 7'2" defensive superstar Dikembe Mutombo born?

a. Sudan

b. Senegal

c. Nigeria

d. Democratic Republic of the Congo

GAME 70 Q11 ANSWER d
On April 5, 2001, 7'1" Wang Zhizhi scored 6 points and 3 rebounds for the Dallas Mavericks. Prior to the 2002-2003 campaign, he signed as a free agent with the Los Angeles Clippers.

GAME 11

1. Which NHL player scored 10 points in one game?

a. Mario Lemieux
b. Phil Esposito
c. Darryl Sittler
d. Wayne Gretzky

The answer to this question is on:

page 258, top frame, right side.

GAME 31

1. In a match race with which Kentucky Derby winner did champion filly Ruffian break her leg?

a. Foolish Pleasure
b. War Admiral
c. Alydar
d. Genuine Risk

The answer to this question is on:

page 258, second frame, right side.

GAME 51

1. Who was the first NHL goaltender to wear a mask on a regular basis?

a. Jacques Plante
b. Bill Durnan
c. Roy Worters
d. Terry Sawchuk

The answer to this question is on:

page 258, third frame, right side.

GAME 71

1. Which father-and-son tandem both won PGA Tour events on the same day?

a. The Millers
b. The Stadlers
c. The Duvals
d. The Irwins

The answer to this question is on:

page 258, bottom frame, right side.

260

GAME 11

"Memorable Performances"

Single Game Performances that Took Your Breath Away

See page 260 for the first question.

GAME 10 Q12 ANSWER c
The year 1957 was a historic one in tennis, as Althea Gibson became the first black athlete to capture the Wimbledon women's singles title. She followed that by winning the US Open later that year, and repeated the same feat in 1958. A true pioneer, Gibson also won the 1956 French Open.

GAME 31

"Tragic Injuries"

Remember These Catastrophic Sports Injuries?

See page 260 for the first question.

GAME 30 Q12 ANSWER a
County Stadium in Milwaukee hosted the first Sausage Race in the early 1990s, and it has become a tradition during the seventh-inning stretch ever since. Four mascots dressed as American, German, Polish, and Italian sausages conduct a running race down the left-field line to a thunderous ovation from the fans.

GAME 51

"Tools of the Trade"

When Equipment Steals the Headlines

See page 260 for the first question.

GAME 50 Q12 ANSWER b
Playing 84 games in 1992-1993, the Ottawa Senators produced a 10–70–4 record. Interestingly, they weren't even the team with the most losses that season (the second-year San Jose Sharks dropped a humiliating 71 games). To be fair, the 1974-1975 Washington Capitals were just as dreadful, losing 67 contests in an 80-game schedule.

GAME 71

"PGA Personalities"

Can You Identify These Notable Duffers?

See page 260 for the first question.

GAME 70 Q12 ANSWER d
Born in the country formerly known as Zaire, Mutombo attended Georgetown University on a USAID scholarship. After joining the school basketball team, he redirected his pre-med major and graduated with degrees in Linguistics and Diplomacy. He is a four-time NBA Defensive Player of the Year and ranks first in NBA rebounds per game.

RICK BARRY

A Basketball Life

by Mike Kennedy

Rick Barry may be a trivia buff, but there is nothing remotely trivial about his basketball career. Back when pro hoops was making its first inroads into popular culture, Rick was the poster boy for everything good, bad and confusing about the modern game. As a second-year pro, he lifted a forlorn franchise to the NBA stratosphere and pried the scoring title from the iron grip of history's most dominant player. Next he was cast in the role of villain, as he shattered the team sports status quo and joined the upstart ABA. Since then Rick has been on a long, strange journey that continues today.

263

Richard Francis Dennis Barry, III, was born on March 28, 1944, in Elizabeth, New Jersey. His father, Richard Barry, Jr., played basketball for local semipro clubs and also coached at the St. Peter and Paul parochial school. Rick and his older brother, Dennis, learned the game from their dad, who hammered the fundamentals into them from an early age. The teaching continued at the dinner table, much to Mrs. Barry's chagrin. She had only a passing interest in the sport.

Rick's sports hero was Willie Mays, which is why he wore number 24. In fact, baseball was his first love. He was a hard-throwing right-hander who distinguished himself as a pitcher and power hitter. Rick earned All-State honors on the diamond in high school, but by his senior year it was clear his future was on the hardwood.

Rick's first basketball coach was his father. Exceptionally strict and demanding, Richard thought nothing of pulling his son from a game for making a single mistake. Conditioned to playing error-free ball—and used to competing with Dennis's friends—Rick made a team of junior high school players as a fifth grader.

When Rick was ready for high school, the Barry's moved a few towns west to Roselle Park. A versatile athlete, Rick developed into a star for the Panthers. Although he had the ball-handling skills and court vision of a guard, he played forward for the basketball team. Voted All-State twice, Rick grew to more than six feet tall as a teenager, and though he looked skinny in his uniform, he dominated opponents with a physical style of play. Rick could nail jumpers from anywhere on the floor, but he was at his best when taking the ball hard to the hole. This approach resulted in countless bumps and bruises, not to mention regular trips to the foul line, where he took his dad's advice and adopted what would become his signature underhanded style.

Years later, as a pro, Rick added a few improvements and became one of history's great free-throw shooters.

In the fall of 1961, Rick headed to the University of Miami, where he could escape New Jersey's cold winters. The Hurricane program did not offer much in the way of tradition, but Coach Bruce Hale—an NBA star in the 1950s—had installed a pro-style offense and recruited some good players. In 1960, Miami ambushed several top teams and rose to number 10 in the rankings. Hale believed adding a mobile forward like Rick to the squad would make the Hurricanes a championship contender. Rick, meanwhile, understood that Hale could help him reach his full potential.

After a season on the freshman squad, Rick moved right into the starting lineup and blossomed into Miami's best player, averaging almost 20 points and 15 rebounds a game as a sophomore. Miami was all that he expected, with one exception: The school didn't have a field house or gym. The Hurricanes played their home games at the Miami Beach Convention Hall (or the auditorium next door). Practices were held at the campus armory, which the team shared with the U.S. Army. But no one, including Rick, ever complained.

As a coach, Hale was ahead of his time. He always treated his players like sons, inviting them for cookouts at his home, letting them swim in his pool, and running with them in scrimmages. Rick, who thrived in Hale's up-tempo system, eventually became his son-in-law, marrying the coach's daughter, Pamela, in 1965.

In his final two seasons at Miami, Rick established himself as one of the nation's premier players. He raised his scoring average over 10 points from his sophomore campaign to his junior campaign, and then led the country at 37.4 points per game as a senior. During that time, Miami was one of the most exciting teams in the country. With guards like Bernie "Boom Boom" Butts, Junior Gee, Rick Jones, John Dampier, and the underrated forward Wayne Beckner complementing Rick's superb all-around skills, the Hurricanes often ran opponents out of the building. Rick averaged 29.8 points and 16.5 rebounds during his seventy-seven game varsity career, and Miami was regarded as one of the most dangerous teams in the country.

After Rick graduated in 1965, he hoped to play for the Knicks. Some wondered whether he could handle the pounding of the pro game, but the San Francisco Warriors had no doubts. They owned the second and third slots in the draft, but the Knicks—who were granted a territorial pick—had a clear shot at Rick. Instead, New York took Princeton's Bill Bradley. The Warriors chose Fred Hetzel of Davidson and Rick.

Rick joined a Warrior club searching for its identity after trading Wilt Chamberlain to the Philadelphia 76ers. The team's record in 1964-65 had been 17–63, by far the league's worst mark. Working with point guard Guy Rodgers, Rick injected new life into the club. Nicknamed the "Miami Greyhound," he surpassed Elgin Baylor's rookie record for points with 2,059, finished second in the league in free-throw percentage (.862) and tenth in rebounding (10.6 rpg), and was named Rookie of the Year and All-NBA First Team.

Rick was even better his second season. Playing for new coach Bill Sharman, he topped the NBA at just over 35 points a game, breaking Chamberlain's seven-year stranglehold on the scoring title. After taking home honors as the All-Star Game MVP, where he scored 38 points (third highest total ever), Rick was voted All-NBA First Team for the second year in a row. His fine play—plus the emergence of center Nate Thurmond as a true star—boosted the Warriors to 44 wins and a division title.

After sweeping the Lakers and beating the Hawks in six games, San Francisco met Chamberlain and the 76ers in the NBA Finals. In a high-scoring series, the Warriors lost in six games. The series was closer than it looked, turning on a handful of possessions. Rick was the primary reason. He set a new championship series mark with a 40.8 scoring average (which stood until Michael Jordan erased his name from the record books in 1993), including one game in which he hit for 55.

That summer, Rick was courted by the fledgling American Basketball Association, which was placing a team in the Bay Area. The Oakland Oaks had hired Rick's father-in-law to run the club, and were dangling a $75,000 contract and a share of ownership in exchange for switching leagues. Rick informed the Warriors and their owner, Franklin Mieuli, of the Oaks' interest and invited them to give him their best offer. Anything close would have kept him in a Warrior uniform, but when the team low-balled him, he became the first major NBA star to join the ABA. Rick didn't even want to leave the Warriors, and the feeling was mutual. A heartbroken Mieuli hung jersey number 24 in his office and vowed to get his star back some day.

There was a price to pay for leaving the NBA. The sporting press skewered Rick and branded him as a turncoat. The Warriors contested Rick's contract in court, and a judge ruled that he was bound to the team for the 1967-68 season. Either he played for San Francisco or no one at all. Rick stuck to his guns and spent the year doing TV work for a local station. Without its star, Oakland stumbled to a 22–56 record, the worst in the league.

Rick started the 1968-69 season on fire. He led the Oaks to 15 wins in their first 17 games. Sixteen straight victories after that gave Oakland an insurmountable lead in the West and the team cruised to the division title despite a knee injury that ended Rick's season. He led the league in scoring and was named MVP anyway, but had to watch the playoffs from the sidelines. The Oaks—who boasted a starting five that included Doug Moe, Larry Brown and Gary Bradds—still captured the ABA championship.

The Oaks were purchased by Washington lawyer Earl Foreman, who moved them to D.C. Rick was happy on the West Coast and hatched a plan with Mieuli to stay there, signing a five-year deal worth $1 million to rejoin the Warriors. When the Oaks had made their original deal with Rick, he was told he would be released if the team left the Bay Area. But with nothing in writing, he was compelled to remain in the ABA while the Warriors took the matter to court. He played the 1969-70 season in Washington for the renamed Capitols, averaging 27.7 points.

When Foreman uprooted the team again and moved it to Virginia, Rick decided enough was enough. He offered to buy his way out of the contract; but when that didn't work, he launched a media campaign to make himself the most despised man in the state. The ABA, fearful its biggest drawing card would be run out of Virginia and find his way back to the NBA, brokered a trade to the New York Nets.

Playing under Coach Lou Carnesecca, Rick transformed the Nets into a championship contender. Point guard Bill Melchionni blossomed into the league's top assist man, John Roche electrified fans with his fancy dribbling and outside shooting, and St. John's star Billy Paultz became one of the league's best centers. In the 1972 playoffs, the Nets upset the powerhouse Kentucky Colonels, and then edged the Squires in seven games to reach the finals—where they lost to an excellent Indian Pacers club in six games. In two years with the Nets, Rick extended the range and accuracy of his jumper, his assist totals rose, and he further developed his defensive game.

After the 1971-72 campaign, a California judge ruled that Rick had to honor the contract he had signed with the Warriors three years earlier, so it was back to San Francisco, where the team was now known as Golden State. In his third year back in a Warrior uniform, Rick had a season for the ages, with a team that not one expert picked to make the playoffs. Leading a re-vamped squad that featured talented role players Clifford Ray, George Johnson, Charles Johnson and Butch Beard, along with rookie standouts Keith Wilkes and Phil Smith, Rick pumped in 30 a night for coach (and former teammate) Al Attles as Golden State fashioned a 48–34 record during the 1974-75 campaign. The Warriors checked their egos at the door, playing like a team in every sense of the word. Teammates responded to Rick's intense leadership, and he developed friendships that lasted a lifetime.

The Warriors battled their way past the Bulls in the Western Conference Finals to earn a berth in the championship series against the juggernaut Washington Bullets. The experts said Golden State would get swept in four games, but bolstered by timely shooting, stingy defense and fantastic team play, the Warriors swept Elvin Hayes & Company in what ranks among the greatest upsets in team sports history. Rick was the glue in the series, and took home MVP honors.

The following season, Rick was named First Team All-NBA for the third consecutive time, and the Warriors appeared poised to defend their championship. But a bitter playoff loss to the Suns ended their dream of back-to-back titles. Golden State fell short of a title twice more, and Rick decided to test the free agent waters in 1978. He signed with the talent-laden Houston Rockets, where he hoped to win another championship with Moses Malone, Rudy Tomjanovich, John Lucas, Mike Newlin and Calvin Murphy.

Unfortunately, the Rockets gave John Lucas to the Warriors as compensation for losing Rick. That move miscast Rick in the Houston system, where he was often called upon to play a position that would one day come to be known as "point forward." He often handled the ball thirty feet from the basket, which diminished his ability to score and rebound. Rick did set a personal high for assists in 1978-79 with 502, and he captured two more free-throw titles—including an NBA record of 94.7 percent—but the Rockets failed to make noise in the postseason during his two years with the club.

Rick's deal with Houston expired in the spring of 1980. Though he had plenty left in the tank, on paper his skills appeared greatly diminished. He waited for an offer from another team, but no GM was willing to look beyond the stats, and the league, in an effort to save money, cut the rosters to only eleven players. So, when a TV job came along, Rick decided to call it a career.

Bill Sharman, the shooting guard on the great Boston Celtic teams of the 1950s—and the coach of champions in three different pro basketball leagues—once called Rick "the most productive offensive forward ever to play the game." Over ten NBA seasons, Rick averaged 23.2 points, 6.5 rebounds and 5.1 assists, while shooting an even 90 percent from the charity stripe.

In the high-flying ABA, only Connie Hawkins and Julius Erving matched his all-around production. In both leagues, Rick elevated his game during the playoffs and functioned as a second coach on the floor. Elected to the Naismith Memorial Basketball Hall of Fame in 1987, he was named to the NBA's Fiftieth Anniversary team a decade later.

A quick thinker and expert analyst during his playing

days, Rick was a natural as a basketball commentator. Network execs liked that he said what was on his mind, even though his outspoken nature stirred things up from time to time. Basketball insiders knew Rick was sitting on a rich store of basketball knowledge and respected him as a teacher. To them, he seemed destined for an NBA coaching job. However, the call never came. Eventually Rick decided to apply his skills in the business world—where he would have the freedom to watch his four basketball-playing sons (Scooter, Jon, Brent and Drew) pursue their own hoop dreams.

Today, Rick Barry devotes himself to numerous business interests, including Barry-Van-Arriola, LLC, a company that markets the e-Volution Marketplace e-procurement platform. He continues to share his opinions with sports fans through his daily talk show on San Francisco's KNBR radio and in a weekly column for the *San Francisco Examiner*. Rick and his wife, Lynn, have a ten-year-old son, Canyon, who is showing signs of being a gifted athlete. Perhaps there will be yet another Barry in the NBA, which, of course, would make for yet another great trivia question some day.

Biography courtesy of JockBio.com

Visit www.JockBio.com and Get A Life!
Access free comprehensive athlete biographies,
including an exclusive Q&A with Rick Barry.

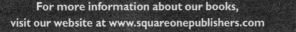